INNOVATION AND AUTOMAT

To Henri and Paul, who between them made a work place in which humans were valued above all other factors.

Innovation and Automation

PAUL SATCHELL
Director
Sattress

Routledge
Taylor & Francis Group

LONDON AND NEW YORK

First published 1998 by Ashgate Publishing

Reissued 2018 by Routledge
2 Park Square, Milton Park, Abingdon, Oxon, OX14 4RN
711 Third Avenue, New York, NY 10017, USA

Routledge is an imprint of the Taylor & Francis Group, an informa business

Publisher's Note
The publisher has gone to great lengths to ensure the quality of this reprint but points out that some imperfections in the original copies may be apparent.

Disclaimer
The publisher has made every effort to trace copyright holders and welcomes correspondence from those they have been unable to contact.

A Library of Congress record exists under LC control number: 97045521

ISBN 13: 978-1-138-32637-8 (hbk)
ISBN 13: 978-1-138-32639-2 (pbk)
ISBN 13: 978-0-429-44988-8 (ebk)

Contents

Figures

Examples

Preface and acknowledgments

Innovation is an increasingly important factor in organisational competitiveness, but the concepts and processes underlying innovation remain in a state of flux. Automation surrounds us, helps us, controls us and protects us, but concepts and processes that have provided benefit are also ill defined. Automation and innovation often occur simultaneously but not often independently. Some of the interactions between innovation and automation have been beneficial, some have impaired both processes, while others have caused catastrophes. We have failed to appreciate the consequences of these interactions.

Understanding how innovation and automation coexist and how they can be mutually optimised is the purpose of this book. While both have impinged upon my research and industry activities in a number of ways, a fuller understanding of their interactions has come about because a number of individuals have acted as sounding boards. Those who have suffered most include John Shaw, John Boyle and Ling Yoong. Sharing with the 'Boulders Group', Chris Russell, Brian Thomas, Doug Shaw, Geoff Eagleson and John Lysaght has helped, as have the reflections of Kim Paul, David Cox, Graham Beaumont and Janne Graham. At work, many have tossed in ideas and observations, particularly Alison, Ruth, Bernie, Peter and my fellow directors. Lastly, my family, Anne, Amy and Olivia have provided much critical and even some uncritical support, vital factors in producing the following.

Paul Satchell,
Sattress Pty. Limited, August 1997.

1 Introduction

Innovation is an important factor in organisational competitiveness. Competitiveness also depends upon automation. Innovation and automation have been pursued simultaneously but often independently, the assumption being that their differences exclude them from affecting one another. Increasingly, interactions and interdependencies are appearing between innovation and automation, though their compatibility has been little considered. Current approaches to blending innovation and automation are failing to comprehend the consequences for humans or machines.

Central to this book is the proposition that organisational success will depend upon optimisation of the interaction between the organisation's ability to innovate and the manner in which organisational functions are automated. It is possible that evidence for or against this proposition will be difficult to obtain, because of our primitive understanding of the behavioural and attitudinal changes induced by and required for useful automation and innovation. However, our inability to measure these changes does not mean that the trade-off between innovation and automation should be ignored. Indeed, the converse is true. Innovation and automation are interlinked in ways, assumed to be beneficial. Often they are not, and frequently have been mutually harmful. The need for both has occasionally produced interactions which have been unexpected and disastrous, as evidenced by some commercial aircraft accidents, industry incidents and other untoward events in medical care systems. This is reason enough to consider innovation and automation and their interactions in some detail. There are many other interactions which have not produced disasters, but which have resulted in unforeseen consequences sufficient to question current approaches. At present, both innovation and automation are topical, although most fail to appreciate their potential for affecting each other. A proven approach for pursuing them simultaneously does not exist.

This book develops a framework for understanding the interactions between innovation and automation. It starts by considering each as distinct entities. Innovation is considered first, its importance, and its current place in organisations. Our understanding of innovation has not been helped by confusion about its contribution to organisational competitiveness and by the variety of explanatory schemes. In addition to reviewing these schemes, the process underlying innovation is considered at the level of human creativity, as this is the key element.

Unfortunately, our understanding of creativity has been too much gleaned from studies of creative individuals. This conceptual framework has recently been modified by viewing creativity in an environmental context. Thus, for each individual there is an interactive environmental effect, composed of the individual's reaction to the environment and often the environment's reaction to the individual. This requires little modification for those who are not 'creatives'. The environmental view is particularly apt, because creativity in organisations is not the creativity of a particular individual in isolation, but reflects a mixing of the creativity of many people in social networks, faced with challenges specific to their work place. Understanding the organisational context for creativity is vital and can be described in relation to prevailing behavioural rituals. Rituals vary in their capacity to act as a starting point for creativity with many factors in organisations contributing to rituals that dampen creativity, and hence innovation.

Having considered innovation, creativity and ritual in organisations, the book next addresses current approaches to the process of automation. Despite automation having a myriad of beneficial effects, it has frequently proved disappointing, even impinging harmfully on creativity. Harmful effects are contained within the current technology-centred approach and its propensity to control without providing feedback. It is associated with a variety of complex behavioural responses which alter motivation and involvement. A key behavioural response involves humans being distanced or peripheralised from their surroundings, with damaging effects on the capacity of individuals to continuously engage with changes in their environment. Thus, there have been general unwanted effects from automation which have been unexpected, costly and have reduced usefulness. As well, there have been specific effects on an individual's capacity to deploy their creativity, because of automation's capacity to disrupt interaction with the environment. To a large degree, these consequences reflect the underlying value that the technology-centred approach has ascribed to humans, which manifests as humans and machines being seen as comparable. A new approach called human-centred automation has tried to break free from viewing human-machine sharing in terms of comparability, but has struggled with achieving what many have desired for a long time, namely true complementarity. Current approaches to automation are at best neutral in their effect on the capacity of individuals to be innovative, but more often than not have been harmful.

In illustrating the benefits and harm that come from the interaction of automation and innovation, this book uses many examples. A number come from the aviation industry because of automation's seminal role in this work environment. Examples from other industries are also used, selection depending more on opportunity than on an impartial sampling technique. Aviation is a particularly useful industry for understanding the interactions and interdependencies between innovation and automation, in that it provides a picture of what will happen to other industries well in advance of their current practice. Despite innovative behaviour being rightfully frowned upon on modern highly automated flightdecks, the flighdeck is a work place where humans and machines will always share tasks, because the human will always be required to provide creativity. Creativity is in much greater demand in other industries including health systems, but automation is less thinkingly being used than in aviation. Most industries have not come to terms with the unwanted interactions and interdependencies between automation and innovation and the failure of these two vital processes to lie compatibly with one another. Nor is it apparent that the means for enhancing the benefits and reducing the harm of these interactions is at hand.

In the last section, this book develops a framework for bringing about a more useful coexistence between innovation and automation. A further development of the human-centred approach to automation is proposed where complementarity in sharing tasks between humans and machines is a feature, but where the process of sharing between humans and machines is made similar to the process of sharing that occurs between humans. There is nothing specific for promoting creativity in this approach to automation, for it is the basis for addressing all attempts to have machines assist humans with cognitive, rather than physical activities. It is from this base that it is possible to tailor approaches to automation and innovation where the key asset that must be nurtured is creativity. Features of this tailoring are illustrated by a series of examples which draw on present and mooted developments, and involve people and technology in organisational contexts. Without this blended approach, there is little chance of organisations and individuals realising their innovative potential in the presence of, and hopefully because of, advancing automation.

2 Humans and machines I

This chapter provides some examples of humans and machines sharing tasks. In each example, the reader should consider how well tasks are shared. This means how well the machine and the human share a common purpose, how much trust there is, and how easy it is for the human to provide uniquely human contributions. In each, the reader should also try to appreciate the balance between creative and routine involvement, and the balance between human and machine control. The examples in this chapter describe sharing between humans and machines which have beneficial outcomes, though the creative potential of humans may not be fully tapped, and the benefits from automation may not be fully realised. Sharing which produces undesired outcomes is considered later (Chapter 8).

2.1 Flexible control automation

Human-machine sharing occurs in the control rooms of refinery complexes. The following example illustrates sharing in a refinery on the outskirts of a capital city[1]. The sharing is noteworthy on a number of grounds, particularly the flexible use of automated systems, and the ease with which improvement, and even innovative contributions, can be made.

Example 1. Dark screens, alarms and patterns
The operator scanned the panels of the Aunovat Systems 8500 control panel. The control room had been added to the refinery about seven years ago and was considered to be halfway though its operational life. The refinery had been built well beyond the city limits about thirty years ago, but the rapid spread of the city had surrounded the refinery with light industry and dense housing estates. The refinery produced nearly half of the city's petroleum. The issues of safety, profitability, and the community's need for fuel, dominated decisions related to control room operating procedures.

The Aunovat System 8500 was the central control unit for the whole refinery, almost all refinery processes being interconnected to control units, servo modules and display systems, all housed within a concrete bunker. At the hand over from the previous shift in the mid afternoon, refinery systems had been performing satisfactorily. The control panel reflected this happy state, eleven of the fourteen visual display units being blank, the three remaining screens showing flow charts and control systems which were under manual supervision. The 8500 series had 92 alarms, consisting of buzzers, bells, horns and voice tapes. Eighty of these remained armed, protecting those processes not visible to the operators.

There was an alarm and one of the screens automatically lit up. The operator cancelled the alarm. The visual display unit showed the key components of a heating system which altered the viscosity of the crude oil before entering a catalytic cracking unit. The operator used his keyboard to bring up the heating unit's prior performance, noting that the operations team had decided that it should be allowed to run near the lower control limit and that alarm triggering had occurred intermittently during the last shift. He carried out the standard operating procedure of logging the problem and resetting the alarm via his keyboard. The screen went blank. Within ten minutes the lower control limit was exceeded again. This time the operator left the screen lit and disabled the alarm, electing to track the performance of the heating unit. Over the next four hours there were six more alarms in other systems, which resulted in two more screens remaining lit and their alarms disabled.

When the ninth alarm sounded and manual control was called for again, the operator and his companion chose to change the entire operating mode. By displaying essential systems on all the screens, the system could be run in a very different way. These experienced operators were able to tell the state of health of the complete refinery using pattern recognition applied to all fourteen screens. This mode was preferred by most of the operators and their supervisors, because of the multiplicity of alarms, their similarity, and their concern about control states when the overall system was being operated in two modes simultaneously.

Automation of the controlling processes in the refinery could have relegated control room personnel to the roles of passive watchers, alarm monitors and fault fixers (*Example 8*). Humans could have been peripheralised (Chapter 9). However, the role change to system monitor had not significantly distanced operators from sharing the controlling role (7.3.1), even with the alarm systems operating. Their willingness to be flexible and make improvements had not been thwarted, and the move to and from various levels of automation remained under human control (10.1). It is unlikely that the approach to human-machine sharing adopted in this control room had a precise return for the owners in terms of their allocation of resource to personnel and process. Allowing human and machine to be flexibly involved was more likely the outcome of a philosophy[2] encompassing values about people, machines, and safety for employees and local communities.

2.2 Useful automation and information provision

Work places have a significant, though often unrealised potential, to facilitate the creativity of individuals. Knowledge is a critical factor in creativity, the delivery of appropriate and timely information being vital and very much influenced by machines. The opportunity for people to choose the information that they want, rather than have it chosen for them, can produce useful change. The following example from a telecommunications organisation illustrates these points[3].

Example 2. Troublesome control boxes

On his way out from the repair depot, John looked at the print out of troublesome telephone control boxes in his area. Control box #41 had had another insulation fault, the second in as many weeks. He presumed that the weather was a factor as this was the time of the year when electrical storms were relatively frequent. He was not sure whether he had repaired control box #41 more or less than last year, but he knew that it, box #38 and box #44 were regular sources of trouble. In the last four years, the fault identification capability of the network had been extensively automated, fault site and type being identified to repair teams like his by the start of each working day. Despite this efficiency, he was disgruntled by having to return to the same control boxes.

That evening in the pub, John muttered to his two team members how hacked off he was at repeating work. One of them reminded him that he could now do something about it. A recent company directive had outlined yet another programmatic change, this one shifting the authority for decision making to those in the field.

Next morning at the meeting of the four local area repair teams, John brought up the topic of recurrent control box visits, the new organisational directive and the use of spare, monthly budgeted hours. He suggested that they should put the hours into preventive maintenance. The area leader pointed out that there were sixty control boxes in their coastal area and their thirty spare hours would not even scratch the surface of the maintenance problem, even if they knew which faults were best tackled with a preventative approach.

John brooded over this all day. In the pub that evening, he was just about to get the third round of drinks when he realised that he knew a way to obtain value from the thirty spare hours. Next morning while out in his truck, he contacted a friend in information services and, as a favour, asked for a record of all the faults in boxes in his area for as long back as the system had been running. When he arrived back at the depot that evening, there was a cardboard box half full with a computer readout which contained the faults for the last twelve months. A note explained that records where not kept longer.

He took the readout to the pub and the three of them logged the control box number, the fault and the date for the preceding 365 days. Box #38 appeared to be the major culprit peaking at 45 faults per month, mostly being input lead problems, followed by Box #41 (41 faults) and then Box #44 (35 faults), both with insulation problems. All agreed that in the previous year, the pattern had been similar, but not identical. The three of them discussed what they would do to a control box to prevent insulation breakdown. They agreed that input lead problems required a very much larger investment in time.

7

At the 7.30 am morning meeting John's group described their calculations to the area leader. The area leader muttered some word, which sounded like pareto, and told the group to stay back while he organised for his supervisor to visit from the central office. By lunchtime, it had been decided that the thirty spare hours budgeted for that month were to be spent in carrying out preventative maintenance on Box #41. In addition, John and his team were to be responsible for monitoring all the faults in all the area boxes for the next four months.

Within three months, it had become obvious that Box #41 had virtually stopped producing faults while the other relatively faulty installations had continued to do so, albeit at a reduced rate because of seasonal factors. Very quickly the automated fault information system was restructured. The whole system was converted from an error logging system with a daily cycle to one where the same information was used to identify error processes. John and his two coworkers were offered 600 hours of preventative maintenance, as well as flexible rosters to tell other teams of their experience.

The power of information systems to dampen improvement initiatives is illustrated in this example. Automation of information provision has often been disappointing, either due to limitations in the range of information, how it has been supplied, or how amenable information provision systems have been to being tailored to the needs of individuals (*Example 17*). The example also illustrates the potential of such systems, because of the primary position that knowledge has in fuelling creativity (5.6). Task sharing technology which has the flexibility (7.3.2) to allow users to tailor their access to information has particular potential. The place of the extraordinary individual is noteworthy, the constraints of the existing automated systems having been unacceptable to one person, but acceptable to most.

2.3 Automation and dynamic training

Machines assist training. In many circumstances, it is uncertain how much technology improves training processes, despite the seemingly indispensable nature of many machines. Education and training for non-specific knowledge or competencies can be met by machine-human combinations, though probably much less than is touted by enthusiasts[4]. When training is required for specific skills and knowledge, automation can be useful in a multitude of ways, from detecting need, to defining specific training issues, to facilitating innovatory education and training approaches. The aviation industry has been at the forefront of these developments, as illustrated in the following example[5].

Example 3. Autumn flaring[6]
Jack pulled gently back on the control yoke and felt the aircraft start to flare. Landing a very large passenger aircraft in the late afternoon on a calm autumn day was one of the pleasures of flying. Even after thirty years on the flightdeck, the majestic finale of a flight gave Jack pleasure, particularly with the airport so softly

lit by the grey-pink, setting sun. Jack became aware of the co-pilot tensing as the flare continued longer than expected, but the distant rumble of the undercarriage quickly dissipated any concern and landing procedures swamped any reflection. His daughter's birthday dominated his thinking on his drive home, displacing the review process that he routinely conducted with himself about his day's flying.

Two weeks later, while logging in for mail and messages in the crew room, Jack noticed a training alert for all senior check captains like himself. Mystified, Jack interrogated the training system. He was not aware that he or any other senior pilots were due for training, evaluation, trial of a new standard operating procedure, or training related to management of a notified incident or accident. The timetable for the training module showed that the session was a developmental one called 'autumn flaring'. Jack momentarily felt irritated by the need for the training department to name their modules, as if they were ice creams or lipsticks. His irritation was quickly replaced by a niggling uncertainty, as he indistinctly remembered something that was unsatisfactory about his flying on his daughter's birthday.

A week later Jack sat with eleven others in a small auditorium in the training building, curious to see what the quick access recorders had thrown up[7]. The usual format of these training alert sessions was to display data first. The pilots enjoyed the non-punitive and constructive nature of these sessions. All quickly realised that there was a trend in measurements coming from the data related to landing. The sensors on the undercarriage mechanism which detected how quickly the undercarriage was compressed at landing were providing the trending data. They showed that the speed at which aircraft had been descending vertically had been increasing over the last two months. While still within the specification of the aircraft, the data was unmistakably signalling a change in human-machine performance. Not all landings were affected, but almost all pilots, including Jack, had made a landing which contributed significantly to the trend line. One of the pilots in the front row suddenly started waving his hands excitedly. Everyone enjoyed this 'hunt' for the issue, and eagerly followed his observation of a possible association between the time of landing and the higher than usual descent rates.

The facilitator stood up from the front row, nodded assent, and displayed the time of day for the twenty highest descent rate landings for the last four months as well as the time of sunset. All problem landings had occurred during autumn, in the hour before sunset, never after, and only on days when the sun was visible. Other associations like the sector flown, other aircraft types, and the length of duty, were not present. The facilitator showed a video of a series of simulator landings where, in the simulated environment of a local sunset, pilots were starting the flare manoeuvre too high, and suffering higher than usual descent rates. Jack grinned ruefully, as the simulated scenes were exactly that of the afternoon of his daughter's birthday.

The purpose of the session was now clear. It was to devise a simulator training scenario that would help them, and all the other line pilots flying this type of aircraft, improve their judgement of height when starting the flare manoeuvre. The issue to be overcome was the difficulty in perceiving height in such a large aircraft when landing with a setting sun. By the time the senior check captains had devised the simulator scenario, Jack knew that his daughter's birthday would now not be solely associated with that gentle, pink-grey afternoon three weeks ago. The birthday would now be also linked to a very long development session in the training department simulator.

Flightdeck personnel are highly motivated and given the above circumstances are innovative. Despite flightdecks and simulators not being designed (7.3.3) for aiding and abetting human creativity, they are capable of being part of an interactive environment where improvement can occur. In the above example, the reduction in time pressure (5.5), the relative absence of procedural rituals (11.4), and the non-punitive, propitious environment (6.4) in the training department all facilitated creativity. The capacity to be innovative on the flightdeck in normal operations is considerably less (*Example 15*).

2.4 Adaptable technology for leaders

Many current leaders have a broad range of competencies and are aware of the importance of improvement, innovation and taking advantage of new technology. Unfortunately, they and their immediate office staff often struggle to reap benefits from automation, particularly with respect to their business environment. Leaders are often distanced from knowing about the customer interface by a multitude of processes, systems and organisational rituals. A novel approach to this issue follows[8].

Example 4. Customer feedback for a CEO
Belinda returned to her task of cross checking her CEO's diary with those of his direct reports. She wanted to ensure that the unexpected opportunity for her CEO to talk with the Head of the Department of Industry Development would have as few disruptive effects as possible. As she sent the last E-mail from the electronic diary system she noted that there had been another three inputs into the customer contact system in the last hour. It gave her endless satisfaction to see that a system that she had created could run as sweetly as a sewing machine. She reflected for a moment on the last few months happenings.
In her mid-30's Belinda had always been different. Two years ago, her curiosity and her determination to do a programming and database course had been treated with humour, tolerance and some head-shaking from her peers. Some had said that she would not be able to manage the training course requirements, having just been appointed to be the executive assistant for the CEO. Her CEO had been most supportive. He was particularly understanding with the temporary staff when she needed to study and do her exams.
As her course progressed she had realised that what she had learned was opening up a myriad of opportunities, but it was not clear in what area she should try and apply her evolving skills. This decision was made for her by an unfortunate

incident. *A customer complaint from one of the terminals in the reception hall had not been acknowledged for nearly two days by the customer service centre. A response, which eventually proved to be incorrect, had not been sent for another five days. The repercussions of this incident had involved the staff of the CEO's office extensively, because of the intrusion of local and national television reporters.*

Belinda had realised during this incident that it would be very easy for her to improve on the timeliness and usefulness of critical, customer-related information for her CEO. During her lunch breaks, she tracked the type of information coming through the customer contact terminals in the reception hall and other customer contact areas. Her CEO had noticed her saving many of these incidents for her prototype, but made no comment. About two months later she had finished creating her software package which had a variety of selection tools capable of streaming complaints for different actions. She was uncertain of the next step, as some of her colleagues suggested that she needed to talk to the manager of office services, while she felt that some sort of trial was required.

Again circumstances intervened. About ten weeks after the original incident, Belinda was seeking more test items of customer information, when she noticed that one of them was from the same customer responsible for the incident that had focussed her interest. The content of the contact information was such that if her CEO made direct contact with the customer, there would be particular advantages for redressing some of the doubt and growing demotivation that had crept into the customer contact group. She realised that she would have to act immediately and talking to office managers or preparing a proposition for the improvement team were no longer options. With her heart thudding and her mouth dry she knocked on her CEO's door. He was busy answering his E-mail, and only half turned towards her as she tried to speak, his hands still typing as he glanced at her. He stopped, for Belinda was normally very articulate, and seeing her pale and struggling to find words was quite out of character. The mention of the customer name began to produce a similar pallor in his face, but as soon as he began to comprehend what Belinda had been doing, he had ushered her out of his office and pulled up a spare chair beside her terminal. Within ten minutes he had put off his next two appointments and by half way through the afternoon, they had together mapped a triage process for customer contact information for his office. This would run in parallel with other customer contact systems and required Belinda become a member of the customer contact team.

Belinda ceased her ruminations and returned to the task in hand, clearing one of the current customer contact items herself by selecting and sending an immediate response. One of the other two required a vote from the customer contact group. This she put into the repository for electronic group voting, while the last item Belinda added into the relevant section of the organisation's daily news bulletin.

A motivated individual given resources, time and encouragement may be innovatory. The capacity to manipulate technology and to think of technology as a partner (7.3, 7.4, 12.2) is also important in bringing about improvement. The technology in this example is not designed to be altered by users (10.5, 11.1, 11.2) and only a few have the ability to tailor it to their tasks. The environment provided by an organisation (6.3, 6.6, 11.3, 11.4), and the judgement and value sets used by leaders are also vital factors.

2.5 Summary

Humans and machines share tasks in many situations. Outwardly only some of these tasks require that humans be innovatory. For reasons to be detailed (Chapter 3 & 4), the need to be innovatory is no longer the exception in the workplace, but workplaces do not encourage innovatory behaviour (Chapter 6). In particular, workplaces are littered with technology which has not been designed to accommodate, or better, facilitate innovation. In the examples, humans have been creative to varying degrees, but it is not clear that the technology that has surrounded them had been fashioned to facilitate this. Later examples (Chapter 8) will illustrate that much technology in many work situations is not even neutral in its impact on human creativity, but actually impairs it.

2.6 Approach for using this book

This book can be used in a number of ways. Chapters are written such that they can be used individually. For those who want to look at the context for considering creativity and automation, Chapters 2 through to 4 are appropriate. For those who are interested in creativity and creativity in organisations, Chapters 5 and 6 should be read. Current approaches to automation, positive and negative features of these approaches, current consequences, and others' thoughts on human-machine sharing are covered in Chapter 7 to 11. The evolution of an automation philosophy starts in Chapter 12 and Chapter 13 shows how it will be applied. While most chapters can stand alone, the chapters containing the useful (Chapter 2) and detrimental (Chapter 8) examples of human-machine sharing are exceptions. These are provided to illustrate, but it is possible to use the book starting from the examples. Finally, some may read the book from one end to the other, for this approach prepares readers for the propositions that are contained in the last section. As readers are likely to seek material related to their own interests, the index provides means for looking at aviation, health, corporate and general industry areas.

Notes

1   Identifying features have been removed. The alternative use of the control system is accurate, but shift events are fictitious.
2   This organisation did not have on openly stated automation philosophy. Others have observed computer screens being used in different ways. See DeKeyser (1988), pp. 17 and the observation *'The computer screens were used more than before, but more to coordinate staff than to control the process'*. Also see the improvisation in a nuclear power plant control room, pp. 181-182, (Reason, 1990).
3   Identifying features have been removed. The major elements of this example are accurate.

4   Many of the modern information technologies are now being used generally, including, television, the CD ROM, video recorder, intranet, extranet and internet, and with variable levels of interactivity. All of this automation has occurred without evidence of benefit compared with existing approaches.

5   People and events are fictitious, but the use of Quick Access Recorders (see below) to provide rapid feedback into training, and the steps involved are accurate. Judging the height of some of the current large aircraft in the final phase of descent has been an issue and specific procedures have been developed for initiating the flare by some airlines.

6   The flare is the manoeuvre carried out just before landing such that the main wheels of an aircraft rather than the nose wheel make initial contact with the ground. The aircraft rotates from a slight nose-down attitude to a slight nose-up attitude.

7   The Quick Access Recorder is a device fitted in modern aircraft. It records information throughout the flight from sensors in the aircraft, from the flight management system and from the engine management system. At the end of each flight the record is downloaded and analysed by an automated analysis system. There are many issues surrounding this analysis, some airlines having the analysis done in a locked room, supervised by pilots from the pilot's union. Under some circumstances, aggregated information is provided to the training department and this example focussed on one of these occasions. See Phelan (1996) and 7.2.2.

8   Identifying features have been removed. The executive assistant, her skilling and the system she created are all accurate, though the events that triggered it are fictitious.

Part A
Competitiveness, Innovation and Creativity

3 Innovation and competitiveness

Governments now view innovation as an essential factor in their survival, for they believe that it is fundamental in enhancing their national competitiveness. They see innovation programs as a way of achieving economic growth sufficient to minimise unemployment, provide essential services and ensure societal stability. These outcomes of economic growth are assumed to produce grateful electorates, although this assumption may be challenged if there are unwanted consequences of growth. Some have questioned whether the concept of competitiveness is appropriate[1], and whether it makes any sense in national terms. There is doubt about competitiveness having meaning when limited to the economic arena, particularly in being able to bring more new products to market faster. The rapid throughput of new products has been linked to innovation drivers which produce new technologies in response to specific needs, with military needs being uppermost. The needs of education, health, arts, sport, safety and the environment have not been given the same priority. Now and in the future, these needs, coupled with the decline of arms production and burgeoning populations, may see national competitiveness linked to innovations in regulation and environmental management[2]. These innovations may have more sustained benefits than the detritus of war technicians.

Currently, innovation also appears vital to organisations, although its relative importance has not been determined. In times past, innovation was not seen as a distinct issue for it was covered by the rolling surf of management fashion that recurrently washed through organisations. At present, innovation is mistakenly seen as having programmatic properties, like the fashions of total quality management and business process re-engineering, and belief has driven organisational involvement. It has been difficult to provide a straight forward means of estimating innovation's contribution, as simple measures have not been accurate and accurate measures have not been simple. Each organisational area has unique properties, demanding different approaches which compound measurement difficulties. In addition, many systems and processes in organisations are more tuned to corralling and muting innovation than taking advantage of it.

In this chapter, innovation is defined and its importance for national competitiveness considered. Two assumptions related to the importance of innovation in organisations will be discussed separately. The first is that technological innovation in products and services provides competitive advantage. The second is that innovations in non-technological areas, some of which are factors for technological innovation, also provide competitive advantages. The next chapter reviews the topic of innovation, its issues, its processes, and selects a model.

3.1 Definitions

There are many definitions of innovation. It is necessary to consider a definition in the broadest context because innovation interactions are a key element in this book. Thus a dictionary[3] definition of 'innovation' is

> The alteration of what is established, the bringing in of something new or renewal.

For many this definition[4] is too close to the concept of invention (4.5.3). A definition with a more applied flavour[5] is

> Innovation is something that is new or improved done by an enterprise to create significantly added value either directly for the enterprise or indirectly for its customer.

In some circumstances, innovation only has a technology focus, technology describing how production takes place. Other aspects of innovation like management techniques, organisational structures, new sources of supply and novel marketing approaches are complementary features. A technology focussed definition[6] is

> Technological innovation is the employment of new, usually more efficient methods of production which very often achieve qualitative improvements in the goods and services provided.

This book examines the interaction of two complex processes, innovation and automation, particularly with respect to their human involvement. An approach to innovation which focussed on one facet is unwise, particularly as others have suggested that innovation is best viewed as a continuous, complex and often unpredictable process (OECD, 1992)[7]. A wider view of organisational innovation is

> Innovation is a process which continuously brings something new, or renews, the creation, production and delivery of products and services, the management of the skills, morale and roles of the work force, leadership, the characterisation of the needs of and relationships with consumers and suppliers, and the role for the organisation in the community.

However, the above definition and others fail to mention a key entity which is the idea. The idea is implicit, but its absence can result in the issues of idea generation and manipulation being bypassed. Thus, the following is an alternative, and is the definition used in this book.

> Innovation is the conversion of an idea into an outcome, or the actualisation of a concept. Innovation involves continuous rearrangement of the internal and external environment of an enterprise and/or the idea such that the idea becomes tangible, useable and useful. This embodiment of an idea should link directly to future financial return.

3.2 Innovation and theories of competitiveness

The competitiveness of a nation's organisations appears to be a key factor in the well-being of its society. There are many recognised determinants of competitiveness. While the desire and ability to innovate has been frequently promoted as a factor, its importance has been difficult to establish. This difficulty reflects the absence of theory which gives innovation a primary position in the analysis of market structure. In this section the place of innovation in existing schemes of competition is reviewed.

3.2.1 Innovation in classical and neo-classical schemes of competition

Both Adam Smith and Karl Marx recognised the central importance of technological innovation for economic progress[8]. In the classical theory of competition, technical advance has a role because some individuals, in their desire to maximise personal benefit, have been willing to invest in technical change[9]. However, technical advance has not been included as a distinct factor in the schemes used to describe economic progress. Most considerations of the dynamic properties of capitalism have technology as an externality, as a process which does not change and which need not be examined in detail (Freeman, 1974; Teece, 1992).

In the theory of comparative advantage, nations gain factor based comparative advantage in industries that make intensive use of those key production factors with which they are well endowed. These include land, labour, natural resources, and capital. Innovation is not seen to be a competitive factor. The assumptions underlying the theories of comparative advantage, particularly the undifferentiated nature of products and the similarity of technologies, are unrealistic in many industries. The stationary nature of traditional economic analysis is at odds with the dynamic and fluid nature of most markets[10].

The neo-classical theory of competition has no fixed factors of production. In the forms of monopolistic and oligopolistic competition, the competitive state is set by price, quality of the product, labelling, advertising, and sales promotion. Innovation, real or perceived, has a place. Expansion of demand can increase short-run profits, but again technologies are taken as given from outside the market.

Innovation also remains an externality in newer schemes of competition. These use many non-quantity policy variables including price, entry and uncertainty[11]. Entry barriers can consist of economies of scale, absolute cost advantages for well established organisations, product differentiation and legal barriers from patent and design copyright laws. Innovation activities are involved, but they still remain an externality. Similarly there are many temporal facets of innovation which do not fit well with the time-frames of most competitive schemes[12]. Other factors related to voice[13], legal, and political factors affect the competitive consequences of innovation.

3.2.2 Innovation and the 'Austrian' school

Innovation has a quite different role for those from the so called 'Austrian' school of economists. In their view, the individual is the focus, and equilibrium states, quantification, constancy in maximising utility, and completeness of information transfer are all myths. Technology is no longer an externality but a key element in why a market is never in equilibrium. Innovation is a dominant feature.

In the neo-classical view, supernormal profits, that is profits above the opportunity cost of capital, are a functionless surplus. 'Austrians' see profits as an essential lure that attracts the creative and results in the creation of products, while this motivation to discover something new is taken for granted in the neo-classical view. This motivation is a force which perpetually shapes markets and keeps them fluid as long as there is no interference. The 'Austrians' preoccupation with the individual has tended to preclude measurement of economic behaviour, thus obstructing systematic approaches to understanding the place of innovation.

Present views on the competitive process have been influenced by Schumpeter's criticisms of economic analysis and of the values attributed to capitalism. Capitalism is described as a form or method of economic change which can never be stationary[14]. The evolutionary character applies not only to changes in monetary systems, demographics, society and the environment but is also a fundamental internal property that keeps 'the capitalist engine in motion'. It is the creation of new products and services, new methods of production, new markets and new forms of industrial organisation which bar stationary analysis or any tendency to a stationary state. Dynamism is a key feature.

Schumpeter's view on competition is not anti-analytic but is analytically very demanding. There is no place for examination in a real or analytically assumed lull using a dissection of quantity or price. Rather analysis must incorporate the consequence of the destruction of existing systems by the new technology, commodity, the new source of supply, or the new organisation. The competition that needs analysis is that which 'strikes not at the margins of profits and the outputs of existing organisations but at their foundations and their very lives'[15]. Schumpeter proposed that the form of competition that is really relevant is that which embodies innovation.

3.2.3 Innovation in the neo-Schumpeterian or evolutionary view

Wisely, and consistent with his views on the continuous destruction of existing systems, Schumpeter suggested that his work was only to be seen as a set of ideas which would need revision as new evidence became available. The last twenty years has seen a number of significant observations on innovation and competitiveness which have diverged usefully from neo-classical and the original Schumpeterian thinking. These have not been collected into a specific theory.

This evolution in the relationship between innovation and competitiveness is well illustrated by the example of how individuals make decisions. The neo-classical view has agents enjoying equal access to reliable information, and thus being capable of rational calculations about the rate of return on future investment. Schumpeter, in focussing on individual decision-making in the face of uncertainty, initially proposed two types of agent, exceptional individuals who cope with uncertainty by their superior willpower and personal gifts, and a group who are more imitators of the heroic pioneers. More recent work questions whether the decision-making required for successful innovation has much to do with either the extreme rationality-optimisation view, or with the thinking of the exceptional individual. Decision-making by organisations is frequently not optimised by accurate information or rational expectations. Only retrospective analysis tends to be couched in such frameworks[16].

Freeman (1994) has collected other strands of neo-Schumpeterian research which challenge the neo-classical and Schumpeterian views on individual decision making. Thus, others have proposed that decision-making via an evolutionary process is part of the competition mechanism. This has become an unsustainable concept[17], particularly as biologists see the evolutionary process as only having a modifying effect, which is often insignificant in the face of major environmental change (Brown, 1995). In addition, technological systems can end up in states which are suboptimal from a competitive point of view. Prior thinking, the paths of previous decision making, and other causes of irreversibility all promote compromise in a competitive stance[18]. These sub-optimal positions flaw most schemes which seek to explain innovation related decision-making and its effects on competition. Many other aspects of neo-Schumpeterian research are of great interest, but statistical methods that allow easy aggregation of studies and ranking of competitive effects are not well developed (OECD, 1992; Freeman, 1994).

3.2.4 Innovation and the theory of national advantage

The limited usefulness of existing competitive schemes (3.2.1, 3.2.2) has lead to the evolution of theories where investment and innovation have central roles. The theory of national advantage (Porter, 1990) recognises a more appropriate competitive 'climate' in some countries due to better labour and capital situations, but also allows for modifying factors such as useful differences in technology, in methods of competing and in factor quality. This drive for innovation is fuelled by investment in research and development, learning, modern facilities and training.

Innovation in the theory of national advantage has a number of attributes. There is a national component facilitated by sustained investment in research, physical capital and human resources. There is also an organisational component, organisations being competitive because of the innovative ways quality of determinants is changed, productivity is improved, and determinants are mixed. Innovation is mainly incremental rather than radical, depending upon an accumulation of small insights rather than major technological breakthroughs[19]. The scope of useful innovation is broad, ranging from research and development to organisational learning. Differences in innovative ability are attributed to an organisation's strategic view, the possession of appropriate resources and skills, and the drive for change.

The drive for innovation is attributed mainly to factors external to the organisation. These factors include the degree of competition, the presence of domestic rivalry, the ease with which new competitors arise, the presence of significant natural disadvantage, and the perceived need for a quality focus. A number of studies empirically and theoretically support the proposition that competition is

21

associated with greater rates of innovation (Arrow, 1962; Scherer, 1980). The degree of competition is likely to be positively related to the amount of innovation, in that organisations with unrivalled positions have not been noted for their innovative activity, while organisations which have to compete vigorously, innovate vigorously. Some have proposed that it is possible to over innovate in highly competitive situations (Kamien and Schwartz, 1982).

Domestic rivalry is seen as a major innovative force. The presence of multiple organisations competing in the one industry appears to be related to useful innovation. Possible factors include excessive local visibility with respect to relative performance and the need to expand with exports when there are economies of scale to be had. Low labour costs or low debt financing charges do not advantage one local organisation compared with another, forcing organisations to innovate aggressively via proprietary technologies, specific supplier relationships and catering for the needs of relatively sophisticated local buyers. The ease with which new competitors arise is a feature of internationally successful industries. New businesses often revolve around the key innovations as they occur in an industry, with existing organisations having to innovate markedly to maintain a presence. The unhampered initiation of businesses is an important environmental feature for obtaining value from innovation. Similarly, disadvantage in natural factors of production appears to be a significant stimulus to innovation, leading to new production methods, new materials and new types of logistics. In Japan, external shocks such as the Nixon shock, where import surcharges were imposed, the oil shocks and the yen shock have triggered waves of innovation[20]. The success of Italian firms has been attributed to their pragmatism and improvisation, because of capacity to cope with the complex regulatory tangle of the Italian bureaucracy[21].

3.2.5 Summary

Innovation is assuming a more prominent place as schemes of competition evolve. The standard analysis of competitive equilibrium excludes most of the factors which drive innovation. Other more qualitative views of competition give innovation a prominent place, but analytic difficulties focus them on the nature of innovation rather than its relative effect on competitiveness. The theory of national advantage gives innovation a significant place in altering national and organisational competitiveness. Even though it does not describe the process of innovation, nor its measurement, it does not exclude it. Instead, it gauges innovation's effects on competitiveness by focussing on the driving factors of the innovation process. It is safe to conclude that innovation is a prominent but unquantifiable factor in competitiveness.

3.3 Technological innovation and competitiveness

At present there is no fully satisfactory scheme which details the simultaneous interactions between innovation-dependent decisions of organisations, industry-level outcomes, and economic growth rates[22]. Even the most current views on innovation have trouble ranking the importance of technological innovation in products and services at the organisation level. This section collects together some evidence for the effects of technological innovation on organisational competitiveness.

Kennedy and Thirwall (1973) established that technical progress was the prime factor for the growth of output and the single most important determinant of the growth of living standards[23]. They and others have suggested that a preoccupation with aggregate production function models has tended to obscure the effects of technical innovation. At the organisation and industry level, there are many innovatory approaches to technological development of products and services which enhance competitiveness. These include higher quality products, more niche products, greater responsiveness to customer needs, fast time to market, breakthrough technology, supplier partnerships, teamwork for product development and others[24]. The relative competitiveness of these approaches is unknown, their popularity in part depending upon perception (Fig.3.1).

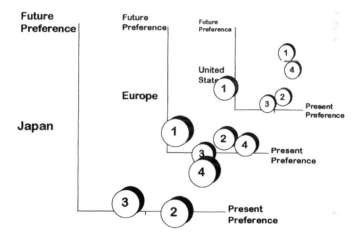

Figure 3.1 **Different technological innovation practices in Japan, Europe and the United States ranked by present and future preferences. Only four practices are shown; 1=simultaneous engineering, 2=total quality management, 3=quality function deployment, 4=design for manufacturability[25]**

Market share and growth in market share are relatively indifferent to capabilities such as quality, management of the supply chain and knowledge of the customer, but are sensitive to the speed of new product development, order to delivery cycle time and being able to anticipate market change. Innovation in these areas probably bears directly on competitiveness. The minimal effect of quality, management of the supply chain, and knowledge of the customer, brings into question many of the methodologies that are currently being touted.

Innovation and automation

The speed of new product development and innovation capability have been identified as the most powerful influences on competitiveness, and they are significantly affected by staff ratios. Here, the balance between design engineers and those providing input, context and support for new product development appears to be critical. Other factors which have been observed to alter competitiveness in new product development include simultaneous engineering and early prototyping. These are features of some innovation processes and will be considered in the next chapter (4.6.2).

The important place of technological innovation in achieving competitiveness is unchallengeable. However, it is no longer sufficient to rely on product innovation, for it is becoming evident that innovation in other areas like processes and people is necessary for organisations to be truly competitive.

3.4 Knowledge, competencies, innovation and competitiveness

The quality of the labour force, its knowledge and competencies, as well as the capacity of organisations to derive benefit from the learning of labour are a key input for organisational innovation. Not surprisingly, measurements of the effect of these factors on idea production and utilisation has been indirect and imprecise.

3.4.1 National investment in knowledge

More than three quarters of the average annual productivity advance from 1909 to 1949 has been attributed to improved production practices and equipment, mixed with increased quality of the labour force (Solow, 1957). Similarly, a fifth of the rise in output per worker between 1929 and 1969 has been attributed to improved work force eduction, while nearly a half has been attributed to the advance of scientific and technological knowledge. Studies on national innovation systems[26] suggest that countries which sustain competitive, innovative organisations have been able to provide them with a flow of people with knowledge and skills directed to industry needs (3.5). Estimates of the effect of advances in knowledge are no longer purely theoretical or retrospective. New approaches to understanding economic growth (Romer, 1990) have made it possible to examine the effect of investment in knowledge. By adding factors such as human capital, measured by years of education, and ideas, measured by patents, to the production function or by treating investment (investment in economic knowledge) as being equivalent to technological progress, macroeconomic growth rates, which are overall estimates of competitiveness, have become meaningful[27].

3.4.2 Organisational knowledge

At the level of the organisation, knowledge accumulation is not a passive, diffuse phenomenon. Freeman (1994) has suggested that the process of knowledge accumulation is interactive and that the competitiveness of an organisation is affected as much by the flows of information and knowledge as the flows of materials, components and intermediaries[28]. Knowledge accumulation by organisations for those innovations that produce competitiveness has not only been organisation-specific but has also involved the external world of science (3.4.3). This knowledge has come from both the direct results of academic research and from indirect sources like young recruits with their new skills and techniques.

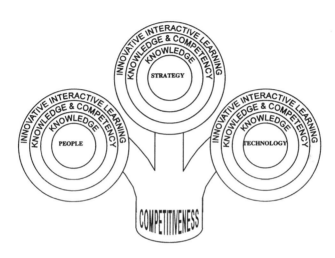

Figure 3.2 **Organisational competitiveness requires merging strategy, people and technology. How much each contributes depends upon how well knowledge is engaged. Few organisations currently have sufficient knowledge in the three areas, let alone competencies and the capacity for interactive learning.**

While the competitiveness induced by harnessing the information flows from the research world, from customers, and from suppliers is very industry specific, those organisations that are adept at continuous interactive learning by whatever means appear to benefit significantly[29]. Improvements in knowledge and competencies can enhance innovatory behaviour (5.6). It is likely that innovation in interactive learning processes and the development of human capital (Paye, 1995) is already a key factor in competitiveness (Fig.3.2).

3.4.3 Research and development and organisational knowledge

Strategic research and development[30], a key input into the innovation process has been accepted as a factor in competitiveness. However, research and development cannot be neatly parcelled[31], for the intention of much research is not closely aligned to its outcome. Some of the most significant pieces of research linked innovation arise incidentally, even while undertaking production. Similarly, much new technology has a knowledge component[32], both embodied and disembodied, which is difficult to assess as a factor in competitiveness (3.6). Some organisations derive benefit from their research and development which is not from specific innovations in product, service, or management, but is related to the learning that has occurred. Thus, the Australian mining industry does not appear to benefit directly from its own research and development, but increases in its research and development improve its ability to make use of external research and development[33]. In the United States, research and development is associated with comparative advantage, but it is not systematically able to predict industrial competitiveness, suggesting that research and development is a necessary but not a sufficient condition for competitiveness. The interrelationships between research and development and innovation are considered in more detail later (4.6.2).

Some features of organisational research and development have been compared for their effect on competitiveness. Research and development which is directly influenced by sales and marketing information as well as customer reactions is a feature of fast product developers and appears to be a source of greater competitiveness[34]. In contrast, when research and development groups determine their own priorities, organisations become less well placed. The determination of research and development priorities by chief executive officers and boards of directors is also detrimental to competitiveness.

3.4.4 Summary

Knowledge is a factor in innovation and although its relative effect on organisational competitveness is currently impossible to measure, there is little doubt as to its importance. There are many facets of knowledge that have not been mentioned, nor has there been consideration of the individual's need for knowledge and their capacity to supply it. Competitveness at the individual, organisational and national level is related to the level of 'knowledge richness' and this bounty is best realised by the innovation process.

3.5 National innovation systems

Nations are very interested in their 'innovation systems' for a variety of reasons. A country's national innovation system[35] comprises the network of public and private institutions that fund and perform research and development, the incentive systems which translate the results of research and development into commercial innovations, and the supporting institutions which capitalise on opportunities and effect the diffusion of new technologies (Mowery and Oxley, 1995).

There is a belief that industries characterised by high research and development intensity are essential for national well-being, despite much economic value occurring downstream of these industries. Countries which want to sustain strong downstream industries argue that they should not allow outsiders to control key upstream technologies, yet they ignore the necessity of risk sharing and equity pooling that 'high-tech' industries need and obtain by trans-national agreements. Despite doubts about national innovation systems[36], some countries are so committed to the concept that these innovation systems have become sources of bitterness and division.

Defence and aerospace industries suffer from accusations of market distortion because of government subsidies for their innovatory activities. While the American state has a commitment to maintaining and recreating the self-regulating 'free' market, there have been multiple instances where there is significant interference via deep and highly bureaucratic regulation on the grounds of 'national security' (Hollingsworth and Streeck, 1994). Unfortunately, sound argument is unlikely to stop government interference, despite doubts about worth, and evidence which suggests that organisations left alone together produce much more viable and competitive industries.

There is no doubt that some countries have benefited from national innovation systems (Mowery and Oxley, 1995). Those that have best exploited foreign technologies have adopted public policies which have strengthened their ability to absorb technology with significant investment in scientific and technical training. The investment in the scientific and production labour force, coupled with trade and economic policies that enforce competition among domestic organisations, and do not discriminate against exports of finished goods or against imports of capital goods, have altered competitiveness at a national level. The argument for a national innovation system centres on optimising the organisation and management of resources vital for technical change (Horwitz, 1979). A country weak in resources, but with a strong innovation system, may become more competitive than one relatively rich in resources, but where the resources are squandered by poor processes targeted at inappropriate objectives[37]. Optimisation of such a complex structure as a national innovation system may be more possible in a developing country, rather than one where entrenched institutional power presents an unleapable hurdle.

3.6 Competitiveness from other factors related to innovation

Other factors, like the new commodity, the new technology, the new source of supply and the new type of organisation can take over from quantity and price as the competitive variables. Schumpeter viewed these variables as sites for innovation (Schumpeter, 1950). The term 'extended rivalry' also describes a broader form of competition which encompasses a number of non-quantity variables including entry, the threat of substitution, bargaining power of buyers, bargaining power of suppliers, and rivalry amongst current competitors (Porter, 1990). A few variables are considered briefly below.

3.6.1 Barriers to entry

One of the transforming effects of innovation is the creation of a barrier to entry to other organisations by the introduction of successful major innovation. There are a number of reasons for this barrier to entry, many of them unrelated to patents, secrecy

27

and similar devices. These are considered in the next chapter (4.6.4). This barrier, even though relatively transient, can alter competitiveness and market position significantly. The benefits from creating a barrier to entry from successful innovation vary enormously from example to example.

3.6.2 Minimum efficient scale of production

Another transforming effect from innovation is the effect it has on the optimal scale of production in an industry. If technological advance results in larger plant size, there is a tendency for industry to become more concentrated as the minimum efficient plant size increases. Conversely some new technology has lead to decreases in the minimum efficient scale of production with marked effects on competitiveness and industry concentration.

3.6.3 Existing knowledge related to technology

Economic theory has often taken the position that if organisations have similar levels of technology, or upgrade their technology simultaneously, the ability to exploit the technology is identical across organisations. In reality, the existing knowledge and learning processes in play when new technology is implemented are likely to differ significantly between organisations, such that these existing differences are a significant source of competitiveness. Heterogeneity between organisations related to knowledge associated with technology is a major competitive factor[38]. For example, in contrast with many other vehicle construction plants, Toyota's plant at Kyushu has technology which has been constrained to be simple, compact, flexible and moveable, thus allowing continuous improvement without massive machinery redesign[39]. This indicates that some organisations are investing in the continual optimisation of knowledge related to human involvement with technology (Hopper and Joseph, 1995). How conducive technology is to people learning about the technology, and being able to use it in novel and competitive ways, should be part of the discipline of human factors[40]. This is rarely if ever considered in analyses of competitiveness.

3.6.4 Leadership

Leaders can use innovation in a number of ways to alter competitiveness. Different leadership types are predisposed to innovation to different degrees. There is significant variation in the depth of leaders' understanding of innovation processes[41]. Some organisations are willing to experiment with leadership itself in order to obtain competitive advantage. If it is assumed that information technology adoption is a marker of technological innovativeness, chief executive officers who have a positive attitude to the adoption of information technology and who possess information technology knowledge, are positive factors in businesses being technologically innovative.

3.7 Competitiveness, innovation, management and structure

Organisational structure is not a key factor in innovation dependent competitiveness. In a survey of many companies[42], particular structural types occurred as frequently in slower, less competitive organisations as they did in faster, more successful organisations. This applied to those that were team focused, were a formal matrix organisation, or described themselves as functional organisations. It was suggested that competitive success from innovation depends less on the organisational form and more on how effectively the form is utilised or continuously examined.

Similarly, many different management approaches can provide competitiveness, as long as they are re-interpreted or tailored to the needs of the organisation. There is evidence that the programmatic approach to any of the management philosophies is detrimental[43] and that a flexible translation of any of the approaches provides competitive advantage (Huse and Beer, 1971; Beer, Eisenstat and Spector, 1990). It is often not realised how much leading organisations shape management approaches.

Even quality management is being re-interpreted and tailored. Examination of the reasons why those Japanese companies which have won the Demming prize introduced total quality control (TQC) has shown a distinct shift in the post-war years (Kano and Koura, 1991). Thus, that group of motivations which were more of a quality consciousness type dominated in the 50's and 60's. Since then the reason for adopting TQC has been dominated by crisis consciousness related to liberalization of trade, oil crisis, changes in value of the yen and industry specific issues. In the 80's a small but increasing proportion of Demming prize winners has adopted the TQC management philosophy because of a desire to adapt to new markets and new technology as well as the achievement of new business. This approach to quality has been labelled a vision type and even this has been tailored by the most competitive companies. Despite these shifts, quality as a factor in market share and growth in market share has not been established (3.3). The relationship between innovation and continuous improvement, one of the key building blocks of current approaches to quality, are complex and are considered later (4.4).

In summary, the type of management approach does not appear that important as a factor for innovation and competitveness. Disciples of different approaches who use them 'off-the-shelf' struggle to demonstrate effectiveness. Successful organisations exhibit flexibility in the way they use management approaches.

3.8 Summary

Although innovation alters competitiveness, this is still not easy to appreciate. Value sets and judgment sets cloud assessment. The relative importance of innovation cannot be determined with any current scheme of competition, and there is little likelihood that a single model will ever be sufficient. Despite this uncertainty, there is no doubt that innovations, the innovation process, and innovatory behaviour are key factors in the competitiveness of organisations

The first assumption considered in this chapter was that technological innovation produces organisational competitiveness. While technological innovation does appear to have a key place, the variation in approaches of successful organisations suggests that technology management 'art', rather than 'science', is still important. There are many other aspects of technological innovation related to knowledge and competencies which can dramatically alter individuals and their capacity to be innovative. Knowledge appears to be a general factor underlying innovation's capacity to provide advantage and many attempts to obtain advantage from technology require a pursuit of technologically relevant knowledge.

The second assumption, that competitveness depends upon non-technological innovation, is much more problematic. Hence, innovation with people, processes, structure and leadership makes sense, although it is not easy to find good evidence for these types of non-technological innovations making much difference to competitiveness. There is the suspicion that much that is touted in these areas makes very little difference.

Notes

1   See Krugman (1994).
2   It has been suggested that the regulation of the environment, health and education may be the driver for innovation which will appear as the military driver declines. Governments feel that intervention is required in actively promoting innovation. Hence many have statements, programs and directives supporting country wide innovation. See Nelson (1993, last chapter), Paye (1995),. Also note that it is not clear that the military driver is more than transiently in decline. The driver to kill humans is particularly long-lived and has many times undergone periods of mild quiescence. This is well illustrated in the development of the warship. See Parkes (1970).
3   The Shorter Oxford English Dictionary.
4   See Point 1. Defining Innovation pp. 1-2, Australian Graduate School of Engineering Innovation (1995).
5   See pp. 3, Business Council of Australia: Managing the Innovative Enterprise.
6   See pp. 59, Industry Commission (1995).
7   See pp. 24, OECD (1992).
8   See quotations on pp. 14 and comments on pp. 16 of Freeman (1974).
9   Classical theory states that the desire to compete is not altruistically driven but reflects self-interest in large part, the desire to maximise personal benefit having a secondary effect of overall maximisation of social wealth. See pp. 4, Kamien and Schwartz (1982).
10 See pp. 81-82, Schumpeter (1950).
11 See Burke et al. (1991), and Odagiri (1992).
12 See pp. 8-11, Odagiri (1992).
13 See pp. 11-15, ibid.
14 See pp. 82, Schumpeter (1950).
15 See pp. 84-85, ibid.
16 See pp. 466-468, Freeman (1994).
17 See pp. 467, ibid.
18 See pp. 468, ibid.
19 See pp. 45, Porter (1990).
20 See pp. 400, ibid.
21 See pp. 439, ibid
22 See pp. 128, Industry Commission (1995).
23 See pp. 166, Kennedy and Thirwall (1973).
24 See pp. 1, Executive summary, Boston Consulting Group (1991).
25 Data for Figure 3.1 comes from pp. 20, Boston Consulting Group (1992).
26 National innovation system is a concept developed by Freeman to analyse postwar Japanese economic policy and growth. See Nelson (1993) and pp. 68 of Mowery and Oxley (1995). A definition is:

The national institutions, their incentive structures and their competencies, that determine the rate and direction of technological learning.
See also pp. 69, Industry Commission (1995).

27   See 'Economic growth' in *The Economist*, Jan 4, 1992.
28   See pp. 468, Freeman (1994).
29   See 'Technical learning from external sources' pp. 469-471, Freeman (1994).
30   See Box A1.1 pp. 60, Industry Commission (1995).
31   See Ambiguities and deficiencies, pp. 61-62, ibid.
32   See Diffusion, pp. 62-64, ibid.
33   Appendix QB.34, Vol.3, Industry Commission (1995).
34   See pp. 7-8, Executive summary, The Boston Consulting Group (1991).
35   See A1.4, pp. 69-77 of Industry Commission (1995).
36   See pp. 505-523, Nelson (1993).
37   See pp. 69, Industry Commission (1995).
38   See A4..2 Competitiveness, pp. 128-129, Industry Commission (1995).
39   Personal communication from John Egan of Toyota (Australia).
40   Some pieces of military technology have proved very versatile and competitive in military and economic terms. The competitiveness is partly embodied in the ability of humans to use the technology in different and novel ways not envisaged during their design (jump-jet use and ground positioning satellite systems).
41   Personal observation across Australian industry.
42   See pp. 32-33, Boston Consulting Group (1992).
43   See pp. 159, Beer et al, (1990).

4 Innovation issues and processes

Humans are able to create new ways of doing things. This is a formidable attribute and a key capability of the human brain. Both humans and primates can convert ideas into useful activities[1], but the latter are relatively limited. Other simpler forms, like bacteria and viruses, are also able to create new ways of doing things, but newness depends upon them changing their genetic code, a ponderous and constrained process[2]. The human cerebrum's ability to rapidly generate ideas and readily use them has so far provided an extraordinary competitive advantage[3].

Innovation, that is the conversion of ideas into beneficial activities (3.1), is currently fashionable. Fashion can be detrimental, for innovation is a concept that is easy to blur and distort. In part, this has been due to the need of some to provide their own words, while others have attempted to channel thinking to their views. Thus, terms such as exnovation, longwaves, stucturation, Balkanization and agentic are novel, but cannot be found in dictionaries[4]. The creation of subtypes of innovation has failed to win sustained support[5]. While some have over-dissected innovation, others have veered too much towards the opposite direction, either using the word but ignored the process[6], or deliberately mixing the terms invention, innovation and creativity[7]. The following consideration of innovation seeks to be clear and uncomplicated, without losing innovation's essential elements.

While innovation's place as a fundamental factor in competitiveness is not likely to be challenged (Chapter 3), individuals and organisations need to be more clear about innovation and the innovation process. Clarity is also essential for understanding the propositions in this book related to automation-innovation interactions. This chapter considers some key issues, some key distinctions, and some uncertainties, before outlining various processes.

4.1 Beyond definitions

When people in organisations are asked what innovation is, answers vary and diverge significantly from 'expert' opinion[8]. This variation leads to misunderstandings between individuals and groups within organisations. If organisations that consider themselves 'innovative' have an incorrect view, then the broader community will have an even poorer appreciation of the nature of innovation[9]. This can make an organisation's resourcing decisions related to innovation incomprehensible, particularly when the investment in innovation is factored into an organisation's pricing of current goods and services[10].

4.1.1 Issues for clarification

There are a number of aspects of innovation that still cause confusion. Issues which require clarification include the distinction between radical and incremental innovation (4.2), technological versus non-technological innovation (4.3), the innovation process (4.6), the distinction between continuous improvement and innovation (4.4), measurement (4.5.2), the distinction between innovation and invention (4.5.3), the importance of the idea (4.5.5) and the role of the environment (4.5.6).

4.1.2 Causes of confusion

Deficient knowledge and competencies contribute to organisational confusion about innovation. An individual's inability to be clear is reinforced by the frequent, incorrect use of the word in all forms of media. It is unusual for organisations to be successful in improving their people's understanding of key concepts surrounding innovation.

There are other reasons for confusion, which are peculiar to some organisations. The success of an organisation, its culture and the way it prepares itself for the future can promote confusion. Some organisations promulgate an image of being innovative and being committed to innovation, but are not, for they are more committed to following existing work practices which have led to their success. While the word 'innovation' is mouthed and written frequently, all individuals give innovative activities a low priority compared with existing activities. These issues will be considered when dealing with organisational creativity (6.3, 6.4, 6.5, 6.6).

4.2 Radical versus incremental innovation

The pace and style of innovation has fascinated many. Schumpeter[11] distinguished one form of innovation as involving a 'jump', there being a clear discontinuity, with consequences that were often irreversible and not fully appreciated at the time of the change. This radical type of innovation has had other words associated with it including exciting, dramatic, unpredictable, revolutionary, qualitative, creative, originative and technological. In contrast to this radical type, there is another form called incremental innovation, which is much more drawn out. All the usefulness of a prior radical change is squeezed out. Other words that are associated with incremental innovation have included adaptive, intensive, humdrum, predictable, evolutionary, quantitative, and technical.

The distinction of radical versus incremental has been blurred. There has been a disproportionate interest in radical changes, partly because radical change has been seen as preferable. A related criticism has been that the distinction has been made imprecisely, because that which is really incremental has been viewed as radical (Clark and Staunton, 1989). Blurring has also been due to the retrospective nature of judgements and an indifference to context. Blurring also reflects real difficulties in distinguishing between radical and incremental innovation (*Example 5*).

While there are difficulties in distinguishing between the two forms of innovation, there are also some benefits, because radical and incremental innovation require different types of knowledge, different approaches to resourcing and different approaches to change (Utterback, 1979). They induce different expectations about outcomes, and have different consequences for the economy and for organisations. The imprecision in making the distinction between radical and incremental innovation can be reduced by a number of approaches. One is to view radical as being related to the replacement of existing competencies and technologies, while incremental is the modification of existing competencies and technologies. This is similar to the creation of discontinuities in production and marketing (Pavitt, 1986). Another way of differentiating innovation is on the basis of available knowledge. Thus, if the knowledge required for a change is outside that of the people involved in production, then the innovation is radical, while if those involved in production are responsible for the innovation, then it is incremental. Much innovation does not come from formal research and development and is incremental, but when research and development departments are involved in changing basic processes, the change is radical. In a similar vein, others have classified radical innovation as one needing a new factory and/or market for its exploitation (Utterback, 1979; Freeman, 1994).

While definitions are helpful they have limitations, particularly in producing that level of clarity which has general usefulness. At this point it is worth considering an example to illustrate the problems of differentiating radical and incremental innovation. The evolution of the commercial aviation engine contains many innovatory episodes (Fig.4.1). The following example attempts to partition these into radical and incremental innovations by looking for the replacement of existing competencies and technologies.

Example 5. Innovation and aviation engines[12]

The thrust of piston engines is generated by reaction to the large slipstream of the propeller, the engine rotating the propeller by converting linear motion into rotary motion via pistons, connecting rods and crankshafts. The jet engine creates a continuous mass flow of air, thrust being developed by a reaction to this mass flow as it is exhausted as a high speed jet of hot gas[13]. The first jet engines used a centrifugal compressor to provide the flow of air necessary for combustion[14], the compressor being powered by a turbine in the exhaust. This turbine removed the need for pistons and connecting rods. The knowledge and skills required for using turbines and compressors first evolved with the development of piston engine superchargers. While the jet engine that used a centrifugal compressor did not make piston engined commercial aircraft obsolete, there was a shift in the competencies and technology required for designing and manufacturing aircraft engines. The jet engine with an

35

exhaust driven turbine and a centrifugal compressor was a radical innovation in aviation propulsion systems.

Incremental innovation describes the small changes that occur in a product or process which enhance competitiveness to varying degrees. Existing technology and competencies remain viable. The use of an axial compressor instead of a centrifugal compressor[15] opened the way for a number of improvements in efficiency. Axial compressors provided higher pressure ratios, straight through flow and a smaller casing with less frontal area. The switch to an axial compressor was an incremental innovation, as existing technology and competencies were sufficient for the design and production of this type of engine.

Efficiency depends upon providing the right amounts of air for combustion, while avoiding complexity and weight. Greater efficiency was achieved by using multiple stages of air compression with two axial compressors running at different speeds. This was the twin shaft engine[16]. Having compressors revolving at different speeds avoided the complexity of altering the angle of the blades within a compressor. The multi-shaft (spool) engine was an incremental innovation.

Other changes such as the introduction of the fan of the turbofan engine have been less easy to categorise. By adding another turbine stage which powered a large fan rather than another axial compressor, it was possible to capture unused energy in the exhaust gas. Instead of passing all air through the combustion chambers, some cold air from the fan travelled in a duct around the engine to be mixed with the hot gas exiting from the turbine stage, this variant being the by-pass engine[17]. Some engines did not use a duct but just had a fan in a cowl this being the fan engine[18]. The changes in the by-pass and fan engine could be seen as a radical innovation, although the advent of the fan did not require new technology or new competencies. Again, what might have appeared as a radical innovation at the time appears retrospectively to be more incremental.

There are now multiple variations of these incremental innovations, each an exercise in tailoring many of the above elements for maximum efficiency in a given thrust range under cruise flight conditions. Since 1995, there have been three engines capable of producing more than 80,000lb of thrust. One of these is a three shaft engine while the other two are two shaft engines, all have a front fan, but different configurations in the compressor and turbine stages. One engine combines the fan and the front axial compressor. The frontal area of the widest engine is 44% greater than the area of the thinnest, suggesting that for similar thrust levels, engine induced drag is significantly different. Two of the engines use single crystal turbine blades. Thus, there are significant differences in the way innovations of the last thirty years have been combined, no one combination being clearly more competitive. Compared with the final developments of the piston engines of the 1950's, where small increases in power could only be obtained with excessive complexity and indifferent reliability, there appears to be untapped capability in the fan engine which is amenable to incremental approaches.

There are other innovations which have significant effects on the competitiveness of an aircraft propulsion system. The ability to monitor the health of an engine by sensors and boroscope examination has meant that unexpected engine removal is now rare. The design changes that have allowed this to occur are mainly examples of

36

incremental innovation. This approach, plus the resistance of engines to damage from ingested objects, has lead to extraordinary reliability. One turbofan has recorded 24,100 hours (seven years of use at 12 hours per day) of operation on a wing between overhauls[19]. This reliability is a significant competitive factor and a feature of incremental innovation.

Another area of innovation in aviation engines is in materials. Efficiency in the turbine stage depends in part upon how hot the turbine can be run. Innovation in materials has allowed turbines to be run hotter without sacrificing strength, increasing weight or impairing reliability. Innovations like single crystal turbine blades have required new technology and new competencies, yet these have not been given the radical label they probably deserve.

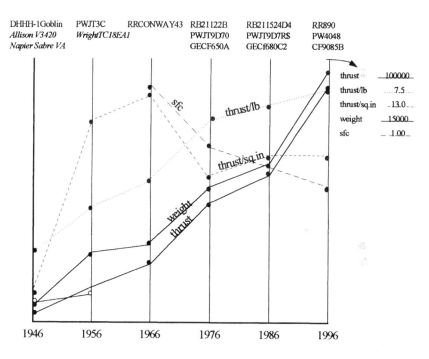

Figure 4.1 Various performance parameters of commercial aviation engines[20]. Engine types are shown at the top (piston engines in italics). Vertical axes scaling in top right hand corner. A number of innovations have resulted in more powerful, larger and more efficient engines, but no single change, including the advent of the fan (1966-76), stands out. Size increases alone have been a factor. Piston engine thrust (open circle) is calculated by multiplying horse power by 2.6. All thrust is expressed in lbs. The units of specific fuel consumption (sfc) are lb of fuel per hour per lb of thrust.

The distinction between radical and incremental innovation in civil aviation engines is blighted by imprecision, even when carried out retrospectively. If the distinction between innovation types is carried out concurrently, inaccuracy is inevitable. For example, bleeding high temperature air from the core of a turbofan engine and passing it over the casing is being considered for controlling engine shape and hence fan blade clearance. This is ingenious and is yet another innovation for improving engine efficiency[21]. It is not clear that it requires different competencies in materials and computational design. Whether they are, or are not needed, it is likely that this innovation will be viewed as incremental, because the changes induced in many performance parameters are likely to be comparatively small (Fig.4.1).

In summary, while there may be some benefits in being aware of the distinction between radical and incremental innovation, the difficulty of accurate, concurrent identification suggests that focussing on one at the expense of the other should be carried out with considerable caution (Utterback, 1994). At best, being clear about the distinction might allow resourcing to be altered to reflect the mode which is desired, yet it is unlikely that such an approach is either efficient or effective.

4.3 Technological and non-technological innovation

Much of the literature on innovation has been condemned as inadequate because it has been limited to a consideration of technology. The limitations of this view have been discussed at length (Kingston, 1977; Clark and Staunton, 1989) Wider views of innovation, where innovation is the finding of a successful solution which uses new knowledge, or uses knowledge in new ways, also encompasses areas which are non-technological (3.4).

Knowledge about a new non-technological area can relate to the environments in which the innovation must exist, or to new operating procedures. Other non-technological areas of innovation involve people, and include innovatory approaches to their selection, their work environment and how the complementary capacities of individuals are mixed and enhanced. The following example illustrates innovation and improvement occurring simultaneously in non-technological areas.

Example 6. Innovative strategies, people and technology[22]
Electricity generation is becoming increasingly competitive, with the technology underlying the burning of fossil fuels a factor in industrial and national competitiveness. Power stations are usually built where coal is abundant and accessible. Because coal differs in its chemical make-up, its ash content and its calorific value, it has been usual to design and build the furnace of a power station such that it suits the local coal type. These furnaces are extraordinary structures, being twenty five stories high, running continuously, and consuming thousands of tons of coal per day. Many of these furnaces generate enough steam energy to drive turbines, which are amongst the most powerful devices designed by humans (upwards of a 1,000,000 horsepower generating 660MW of electricity). The following example started with the need of one of these power stations to burn coal which was mined from outside the local area. Although this coal was analytically the same as the local

coal, it produced quite different ash, being much bulkier and glass like. The lava-like material glazed vital parts of the furnace, impairing its efficiency and complicating routine deashing.

The task of making the furnace function effectively without altering the furnace structure was given to a group of people brought together specifically for the task. This sort of grouping was new for the organisation and consisted of people from all parts of the furnace operation, those involved in the coal conveyer systems as well as the coal suppliers. This group adopted a quality improvement philosophy (QIP).

The idea for restoring furnace efficiency applied the concept of coal blending to their furnace, such that the lava-like property of the ash could be altered. Coal blending had been carried out overseas in power stations where all coal had to be imported, but it had not been done in a furnace designed for a specific coal type. Some coal blending had been carried out at this power station using bull-dozers, but this had not been systematic. The QIP team leader asked for and was provided with a mentor, an innovation at that time in that organisation. The leader also realised that being able to know the effect of each blend of coal on furnace performance was vital, both for achieving the objective and for motivating and obtaining contributions from the team. He placed great store on the motivating and unifying effects of feedback, though many other managers saw it as a theoretical approach and difficult to translate practically in their industry. In this activity, the leader was acting as a 'champion', although at that time the importance of such a role in innovatory activities was not realised.

A unique method of high-speed data transfer was developed which allowed high quality graphs to be automatically produced within 2 hours of each coal blending test. This system, combined with an extensive array of sampling sites at different parts of the furnace, displayed a very complete picture of the heat exchange process in an attractive form to the QIP team. Producing the different blends of coal was not practical with bull dozers as the amount of coal required was 6,000 to 7,000 tons per day. Blending was cleverly solved by the operators of the coal conveyer system. Instead of using one or another conveyer at the appropriate feed speed, the operators ran the required conveyers at fractional speeds, the speeds being in the ratio of the desired blend. This solution was relatively costless and very efficient.

Initial studies established the baseline performance with a reference fuel which was one of the local coal types The rapid presentation of data quickly allowed the effects of blending to be tracked and an optimal blend to be properly trialed. Very soon the bulky, glassy clinkers were minimised and the furnace performance improved such that it matched that achieved with the reference blend. With time there were other achievements which allowed the QIP team to exceed the original brief. It became possible to obtain the optimal furnace temperature as desired, something not readily achieved with the reference blend, there were improvements in the use of spraywater for controlling the furnace environment, and the amount of unburnt fuel decreased significantly. In part, these continuous improvements resulted from the motivating effects of being involved in a team which was constantly able to appreciate the consequences of its endeavours.

Manipulation of blending with the measurement system in place made it possible to modify the ash even further. Without affecting the improved efficiency obtained by blending, it was possible to alter the ash such that it could be used as a base in cement manufacture. This blending trial resulted in all four furnaces shifting to the technique as routine practice, resulting in significant reductions in the cost of power production.

In this example, there were a number of technological and non-technological innovations. These were innovations in that there was little prior knowledge or competency, there was significant risk and there was a need for new measures and new ideas (4.4). The non-technological innovations involved people. The decision of senior management to encourage a group of their operational people to experiment with a major problem in a critical public enterprise was innovative. The use of measurement as a motivational device, the presence of a 'champion', the provision of a mentor for that champion, were all innovatory initiatives.

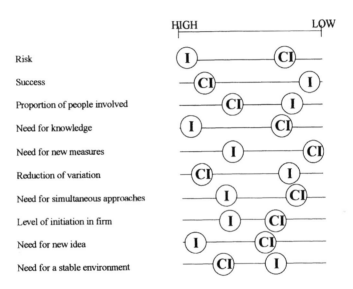

Figure 4.2 A comparison of some features of continuous improvement (CI) and innovation (I)[23]. Comparison of differences between features (for example, success versus need for new idea) is subjective. There is a tendency for differences to become less from top to bottom. Each feature is considered in 4.4.1.

Many events in this example occurred because the participants were trained in and had a commitment to a quality improvement philosophy. It is tempting to view the above example as one which displays the prowess of the continuous improvement approach. The use of the new measurement system to convert the ash into the base material for cement production is a typical outcome of the quality improvement approach. However, many of the activities in this electricity generating plant were far removed from typical continuous improvement initiatives. Thus, the leadership already mentioned, the efforts to motivate and achieve contribution, the level of resourcing, the strategic necessity of the task, the orchestration of this task from above and not from below, and the presence of new measurement methods were all atypical. The distinction of innovation from continuous improvement in this example is worth reviewing after considering how innovation and continuous improvement can be differentiated (Fig. 4.2).

4.4 Continuous improvement versus innovation

The distinction between continuous improvement and innovation is operationally important in organisations, yet some remain unclear about it. In the most obvious examples, these two initiatives differ so clearly in risk and rate of return that they appear not the least comparable. However, there are areas of overlap that bring these entities closer together. For example, innovation that provides competitive advantage is characterised by multiple, rapid, pilot projects[24]. Similarly, continuous improvement has multiple plan-do-check-act cycles that are like pilot projects, each new cycle being a 'miniature' innovation. However, these common features cannot blanket out the many facets of each activity which are distinctive. As the concurrent distinction between radical and incremental innovation is not a useful one (4.2), the following discussion delineates between continuous improvement and any form of innovation.

4.4.1 Key distinctions

A global distinction between innovation and continuous improvement is that continuous improvement implies that concepts are largely intact, while innovation relies on a concept or concepts being substantially changed[25]. Another global distinction is that the starting point for continuous improvement is a process, but the starting point for an innovation is a purpose (Long and Vickers, 1995). Areas where innovation and continuous improvement differ include, the degree of risk, the chance of success, the proportion of people involved, the importance of knowledge and competencies, the approach to measurement, the treatment of variation, the presence of simultaneous approaches, the source of the change initiative, the importance of a new idea and the need for a stable environment (Fig. 4.2).

Risk and success Continuous improvement has relatively low risk, a high chance of success and often provides small benefits. Innovation has relatively high risk, a low chance of success, but occasionally provides large benefits.

Number of people involved Continuous improvement involves more people in an organisation than innovation. Innovation is narrower or more focussed, because judgement about risk affects the choice about when and where to innovate. Successful innovation requires appropriate knowledge and skills, and organisations often have these only in core business areas. Innovation in areas where there is inadequate

41

knowledge or skill runs the risk of being trivial, unimplementable or a duplication. While continuous improvement can be carried out broadly, it is vital that innovation is focussed strategically, within which it should deal with fundamentals, be 'lateral' and broad.

Continuous improvement is touted as an activity that should be organisation wide, although this smacks of an 'evangelical' approach which some are questioning[26]. Undoubtedly, there are indirect benefits from having widespread continuous improvement, one being that it prepares people for innovatory change[27]. However, as resources are limited and rate of return is an issue, strategic issues should also affect the choice of where continuous improvement is carried out.

Knowledge and skills It is possible to carry out continuous improvement with a limited range of skills and moderate knowledge. Innovation that impacts competitiveness is unlikely to occur in such circumstances (see 3.4, Fig. 3.2). Knowledge is central to innovation and an excess of knowledge and skills must be brought together for success *(Example 5, 6* and 4.2 and 4.3).

Measurement While measurement is an essential element for the iterations of continuous improvement and in knowing whether an innovation has the potential to be beneficial, the types of measurement are quite different. For continuous improvement, the measures, the measurement process, and experience with the measures will have all been documented, displayed and will be familiar to everyone. For innovation, the measures and the measurement process can be, but need not be, as new as the innovation (4.5.2).

Variation Quality management has created a practical and rigorous approach for reducing variation, using the continuous improvement methodology. This permits processes to be brought into control and then to undergo process improvement. Innovation is more about process definition than it is about process improvement and variation reduction is not of prime importance. In innovation, variation is poured over rather than being removed, for it can point to a solution, or a new opportunity.

Simultaneous approaches Innovatory endeavours are characterised by simultaneous and different approaches for idea development and problem solving (3.3, 4.6.2, Fig. 3.1). Continuous improvement is carried out sequentially, the same people often being part of many iterations. Innovation more often has parallel activities, while continuous improvement is more likely to have serial activities.

Level of initiation While not as distinct as some of the other features, the level within an organisation at which decisions are made about innovatory activity is usually higher than the level at which decisions are made about continuous improvement. This does not apply to where ideas come from, but more to where risk and resource allocation decisions are made.

Idea The idea is the key part of innovation (3.1). While ideas are used in continuous improvement, they are not essential, nor do they have to be original. The relative neglect of the idea in innovation is considered later (4.5.5).

Environmental stability The discrimination of common cause variation from special cause variation is at the heart of the continuous improvement process, and if special cause variation dominates, it becomes more difficult to detect common cause variation. Hence, continuous improvement requires relative stability in the environment. Innovation only requires that level of environmental stability which is sufficient for designers to generate and develop ideas.

Summary There are significant differences between innovation and continuous improvement. It is unclear how the two activities interrelate or should coexist, but clarity in distinguishing them is important. The two activities can be carried out simultaneously, but with the risk that if factors like knowledge, skill, measurements, ideas and others are poorly defined, and ill understood as inputs, both innovation and continuous improvement can end up being blunted.

4.5 Other innovation issues

There are other issues related to innovation which are less explored.

4.5.1 Uncertainty and control

Innovation is steeped in uncertainty. In contrast with most sources of uncertainty in organisations, innovation creates more internal rather than external uncertainty. There remains considerable confusion about the extent to which the uncertainty of innovation should be, or can be controlled (Spender and Kessler, 1995). It has been suggested that uncertainty surrounding 'upstream', or creative innovation activities should be managed by using shared values and a strong culture. These result in personal involvement and control over the whole person[28]. At the same time, 'downstream' or implementation activities should be controlled mechanistically, or bureaucratically, with the individual entirely subordinate in achieving an organisational purpose. The latter approach is more effective where there is less uncertainty, but fails when goal related knowledge is absent or incomplete. Various models of these controlling forms and their role in innovation have been discussed (Spender and Kessler, 1995). This is an important area when innovation is considered in environments that are highly automated (11.1, *Example 15*).

Some attempts have been made to categorise major causes of uncertainty in the 'upstream' part of the innovation process (Burkart, 1994). These uncertainties are seen as items that must be addressed before a project can enter the next stage in its evolution. Key areas of uncertainty in many industries relate to the failure to define customer requirements and delays in decision making. Some large organisations with many concurrent projects have been able to be more specific about factors altering project approval and project cancellation[29]. Innovations in human resource management are marked by considerable uncertainty. In this area, the capability of the innovation 'champion', and the champion's position in the organisation, are key interacting factors in coping with this type of uncertainty (Wolfe, 1995).

4.5.2 Measurement

Measurement of innovation is difficult because of the multiplicity of factors involved in the innovation process (3.3, 3.4, 3.5, 3.6, 4.2, 4.3, 4.4). It is not possible to consider measurement of innovation without mentioning the costs incurred from foregoing the opportunity to innovate, or even the costs of being slow in innovating. Similarly, the view that innovation is a cost, instead of viewing it as the start of a revenue stream, requires different measurement approaches. Another measurement issue in an organisation involved in innovatory activity is the simultaneous need for normal trading and the preparation for future trading.

An important measurement issue is the perspective used to analyse the degree and extent of innovatory change. Analytic approaches have included technological or scientific merit, the enhancement or disruption of firm's competencies, whether the market has positive perceptions of the innovation, or whether the competitive position of the firm is altered. Differences in analytic perspective underlie the unsatisfactory nature of measurement, with the ad hoc characteristic of many approaches reflecting a failure to understand innovation in process terms.

It has been accepted practice to use indicators or indirect measures of innovation, particularly in tracking national performance. These measures give some idea as to the input to and the output from innovation. Inputs at a national level[30] have included the level of research and development expenditure and the type of research and development activity. More specific inputs include human resources and payments to outsiders for technical knowledge. Disagreement about these input measures reflects their lack of applicability to current models of the innovation process, apart from the conventional linear model (4.6.2). There is also disagreement on the need to differentiate industries and firm measures from national measures. At an organisational and an industry level, it is possible to expand the range of input measures to those that better reflect input factors for the innovation process (3.3, 3.4, 3.5, 3.6, 4.2, 4.3, 4.4).

Outputs at a national level have included the number of scientific publications, number of patents and patent applications, rates of citation of publications, numbers of degree and diploma completions, net migration rates of academics, engineers and scientists, use of new manufacturing technologies and the proportion of manufacturing output which involves new products or processes. Many of these measures are obviously specific to an innovation process and cause confusion and disagreement. In particular, these types of measure can shape views on innovation because they are being used as performance indicators by the public sector for resource allocation, reward and recognition. Another source of confusion and disagreement is the appropriateness and precision of individual measures like patents, if used as indicators of inventiveness or innovation[31].

It is not surprising then that there is disagreement about measurement, because the complexity of even the simplest process approach to innovation is forbidding. For example, diffusion is part of the conventional linear model, but itself has multiple, potentially parallel paths, such as positive disclosure, inter-personal networks, labour mobility, product availability and reverse engineering. Each of these is a cause of significant measurement debate. It may be that innovation will remain poorly measurable because it has some of the properties of an intervening variable. Intervening variables exist in the mind and mediate responses to environmental stimuli, but cannot be accessed, observed or measured (Muir, 1994). Perhaps, innovation exists in the organisational and national 'mind', and, in being a link between the environment and human creativity, will never be observed or measured in any precise or particularly useful way.

4.5.3 Invention versus innovation

An area of contention in understanding innovation is the importance placed on creativity, inventiveness and the invention, versus the importance placed on the development and commercialisation of an idea. This is also confusion of invention with innovation.

Innovation is the successful embodiment of ideas, while the idea alone is of prime importance in invention. Invention makes innovation possible but remains steeped in uncertainty and imagination. Innovation is quite distinct in this respect, in that it is not only a mental activity, but also involves rearrangement of the environment such that ideas become tangible, useable and useful. Some would disagree with this simplistic approach, in that they see innovation in terms of human contribution via individual experience, unconventional interpretation and being able to use individual uniqueness (Steiner, 1995).

The confusion of invention with innovation in part reflects the dissonance between the cultures of two groups, those that have vested interests in research of a more pure and basic form, and those that see commercialisation as the only point of idea generation. This disagreement is more prominent when, in the extreme case, the research community has been elitist, self-serving and poorly accountable, while the business community has been anti-academic, poorly skilled, and with a short term view. These polarisations are often artificial and trite, but there are real difficulties. Medical charities, some of which represent affected families with genetic disabilities, have had a significant role in directing local, innovative, medical research processes in the United Kingdom. This research has been at the forefront of new product and new treatment development and has involved research units in teaching hospitals. The public hospital system, with its associated research laboratories and staff, is now struggling with policy which is restricting the adoption of unevaluated new treatments. In correctly trying to corral uncontrolled activity, with its attendant leaching of limited resources, policy makers are threatening research and development, despite it being a key to organisational survival. In addition, they are putting in place a centralised and expensive control process which reduces benefits for multiple players (Bower, 1994).

The partitioning of invention and innovation is also important because transition between them, if orchestrated and managed, can provide multiple benefits. Career movement between industry, academia and government, and between basic and applied research is broadly beneficial to individuals and organisations. Invention is not at odds with innovation and ideally both should be viewed as being on a continuum, any point of which should be accessible as required.

4.5.4 Inventor versus innovator versus other

The innovator has been proposed to lie midway on a spectrum of human pursuits that have at one extreme the artist, the dreamer or visionary and at the other, the trader, or the archetypal official (Kingston, 1977). This distinction has been the cause of disagreement and is of questionable value.

There has been a lot of interest in detecting differences in individuals with respect to their style of handling change. The simplest distinction has those at the artistic end of the spectrum with an internal vision quite different from reality. This is difficult to communicate, is often isolating, is driven by the need for change and is highly creative. At the official's end of the spectrum there is often little to no vision, and this is supported by ordered and predictable communication, an absence of the need for change, the effective completion of a number of routine tasks and often an aversion to the creative solution. At either extreme, change in the way of doing things is unusual, for the former's activities deal predominantly with intangible things, while the latter sees no need to alter anything. Between the official and the artist are everyone else, including the inventor, the innovator and the entrepreneur. The entrepreneur and the innovator have a lot in common, and, if they are to be distinguished, the key difference lies in the entrepreneur's view as to the utility of ideas, which primarily translates into their ability to make money. The innovator's embodiment of ideas can have, but does not have to have, the element of financial return.

Much effort has gone into clustering individuals by their preferred ways of bringing about change (Kirton, 1994). It is not clear that this issue is as important as its proponents make out, nor is it likely that innovation can be orchestrated by manipulating people. There has been an underlying wish to detect 'innovators', which presupposes that successful innovation is person specific. This is almost certainly too simplistic, because everyone can be creative given an appropriate environment (5.2.3, 5.2.4, 5.3, 5.4).

4.5.5 The idea

The idea is the fundamental building block in innovation, yet this is rarely emphasised. It has been a growing subject of research. Thus, there have been descriptive studies of the sources of external information for small business managers, how personalised and how accessible these were, and how these sources affected planning and performance[32]. Idea generation and the effectiveness of idea generating processes are being measured (6.3.2). Elements in idea generation include knowledge (5.6), the motivation for challenging existing knowledge (5.3.2), mixing knowledge from associated and dissociated fields (5.4), recognising temporal attributes of idea generation (5.5) and others (5.7). There are some organisations which recognise these elements and investigate them[33]. Creativity is central to idea generation and is considered in some detail in the next chapter.

It is unclear why the idea has not been viewed as fundamental. Ideas can make organisations anxious (6.4). Organisations do not harness all human capabilities, perhaps because some are viewed as falling into the 'too-hard' basket. Thus, affection, narcissism, dependence and transference are attributes that are not rigorously explored or used. In defence of organisations, this may reflect organisational commitment to the separation of work from non-work and to a non-manipulative position in relation to the psychological well-being of their employees. Hence, idea generation may be something to be hoped for, but not something to be tampered with. Some organisations actively gather the ideas of individuals, but many do little to enhance idea production, apart from using ineffective, team-based approaches (6.3.2, *Example 7*).

4.5.6 Innovation and the environment

Environmental factors are important in successful innovation. Environmental factors can be partitioned into those outside the organisation, those within, and those that are perceived by the individual. Only the first two will be mentioned here, the last being considered later (Chapter 6).

Outside the organisation The presence of a National Innovation System is significant (3.5), but only one piece of the environment that affects innovation. For some organisations, interacting with elements of a National Innovation System is essential, but for others, success depends upon the ability to recruit useful individuals or groups. Organisations are located in institutionalised frameworks that proscribe organisational structure and how structure evolves. Some frameworks even institutionalise organisational ideas[34]. The competitive constraints and opportunities of the overarching institutional structures act as a backdrop for organisational innovation (6.7.2). Broader social attributes that affect organisational structure and its impact on innovation are part of the socioeconomic infrastructure (Lewis and Seibold, 1993). These include physical characteristics (geography, housing stock, public utilities), economic characteristics (markets, level of employment, types of industry) and social characteristics (demographic patterns, class and ethnic patterns).

The internal environment Organisations can create an internal environment that either facilitates or inhibits innovation, no matter what the state of the external environment. There are numerous legacies, cultural attributes, performance management systems and structural characteristics that can make the internal environment unconducive to innovation (6.6, 6.7.1). Conversely, the potential for an organisation to produce an internal environment that facilitates innovation is not fully appreciated. The commitment to knowledge (3.4.2), the experience and comfort with new technology (3.3, 3.6), and to an uncertain, but probably vital extent, organisational leadership (3.6) can all combine to make a suitable internal environment. The technical environment, how technology-centred automation is (7.3), how much real human-machine sharing actually occurs (11.2-11.4) are factors in the internal environment that are considered in later chapters.

4.6 Innovation models and processes

There are many innovation models and processes, reflecting variation in the environment (4.5.6), operators (4.5.4) and measurement (4.5.2) Some innovation practices or models have been mentioned already (3.3, Fig. 3.1). In seeking to have an uncomplicated approach, but without losing essential elements, this section considers three entities, a model of the innovation process, the evolution of an innovation process model, and the subprocess of diffusion.

4.6.1 A model of the innovation process

There are many models of the innovation process, and they usually have elements like sources, drivers, barriers, behaviours and outcomes. These elements interact (Fig. 4.3). In this book, creativity is equated with the sources of innovation (Chapter 5), springboards are equated with drivers or catalysts (Chapter 6) and millstones are equated with barriers (Chapter 6).

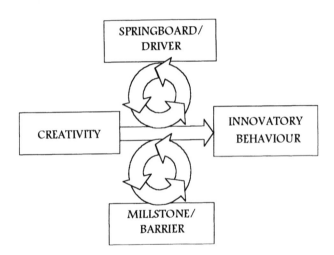

Figure 4.3 A model of the innovation process[35]**. Springboard and millstone refer to organisational rituals which are part of the behavioural environment in which an individual's creativity is facilitated or inhibited (Chapter 6).**

4.6.2 Evolution of the technological innovation processes

Several versions of the technological innovation process have been described (Rothwell, 1994; Industry Commission, 1995). While all descriptions of processes appear superficial, the evolution of this process is instructive.

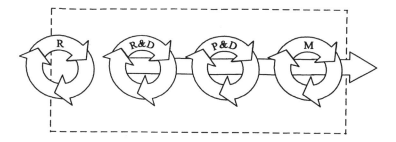

Figure 4.4 First generation model of the technological innovation process.
This is a linear model with research occurring in isolation.
Some development occurs within the organisation (dotted line)
but marketing has to work with what it is given. R = Research
in isolation: R&D = Form and researcher development: P&D =
Production and development: M = Marketing of product.

First generation In this simplest form, there is a linear, technology-push model, where the emphasis is on research and development, and the market is merely a receptacle for the output of research and development (Rothwell, 1994). This model appears applicable to some industries, even though it is open ended, and lacking technical or strategic feedback. Many of the features of competitive innovation (3.3) are not evident. In general, the push type of linkage between research and innovation is generally discredited with the approach being seen as simplistic. This first-generation innovation process was dominant for the 20 years after the Second World War. Its basic assumption, that 'more research and development in' results in 'more successful new products out', is still prevalent in some industries[36].

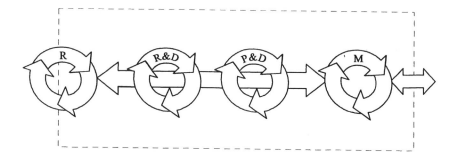

Figure 4.5 Second generation model of the technological innovation process.
This is a linear model with marketing groups directing most
research and development. Letters in circles are the same as in
Fig. 4.4.

49

Second generation An evolution, classified as a second generation model, still has a simple, linear, sequential process from research, development, production through to marketing, but here the market is the source of ideas for directing research and development. Research and development has a reactive role. This model has been described as a 'market-pull' (need-pull) model. A key danger in this model is the neglect of long term research and development programs, because of the need to keep modifying existing products to meet current changes in user requirements (Rothwell, 1994).

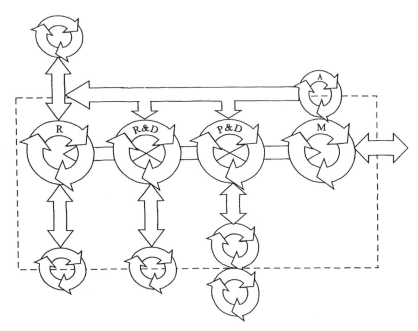

Figure 4.6 A third generation model of the technological innovation process. The emphasis here is on interaction within the organisation and external to the organisation. Each circle is also a site for knowledge and idea interaction, with information flows occurring between groups. There is still a sequence to the innovation process. A is for agency groups with other symbols as before.

Third generation Innovation models have evolved as the understanding of innovation has improved and as the need to reduce wasteful failures has increased, particularly during the period of resource constraints in the early and late 1970s. This model (Fig.4.6) is the interactive or 'coupling' model of innovation in which a logical, sequential, though not necessarily continuous process, is divided into a series of functionally distinct but interacting and independent stages (Rothwell, 1994). There are now a complex net of communication paths, both within and outside the organisation, which link various in-house functions and link the organisation to the broader scientific and technological community, as well as to the marketplace. The complexity of the model allows success and failure to be appreciated from many more points of view and demands much more from organisations, both in the creative and implementation phases. A key feature of this model is that success is associated with widespread competent task performance. Idea generation and development spread over many corporate areas. Success with innovation depends on balance, coordination, and key individuals who are able to look after the innovation process.

Fourth generation[37] Leading Japanese companies have developed a product development process which emphasises teams and speed. In developing new products more rapidly and more efficiently than their international competitors, innovative Japanese organisations have been integrating suppliers into the new product development process at an early stage, while integrating the activities of in-house departments so that simultaneous activity (in parallel) is the feature rather than sequential activity (in series). This has been labelled the 'rugby' approach to new product development (Rothwell, 1994). When innovation is very science dependent and simultaneous exploration and development is not possible, there is still functional overlap with intensive information exchange.

Fifth generation Attempts are being made to identify what will be the fifth generation innovation model. The core attribute may well be the speed of development, with 'fast innovator' being increasingly seen as the label of competitive companies (3.3). This is particularly so when rates of technological change are high and product cycles are short. New process features may relate to information exchange systems and electronic fora for idea generation and decision making. It is not clear that the need to master electronic design and information processing capabilities in the fifth generation model will prove beneficial. The use of this type of technology-centred approach (7.3) in an activity dominated by human creativity may not be innovation promoting, nor is it clear that it is a major process change.

4.6.3 Other global views of innovation processes

Existing views of organisations have efficiency as the implicit behaviour and innovation as the deviant case. Innovation pundits want to shift this to innovation as the focus and efficiency as an adjunct. This implies that all organisational processes should be recast in terms of innovative change. Such zeal is misplaced and potentially damaging to innovation activities. It ignores the need for focus and choice, which should be driven by risk, knowledge, competencies and strategic intent (4.4, 4.5).

Other global views of the innovation process have market-focussed detection, description and analysis of innovation opportunities as the key process feature. In the second generation innovation model (4.6.2), the importance of customer input and the translation of customer needs into product and service features is promoted as an integral part of all innovation processes. There is not complete agreement on the importance of knowledge of customer needs, as speed of new product development is being seen as a more potent factor in competitiveness (3.3). There are exceptions and these relate to situations where the innovation, whether it be a material for a group of technologies, or a molecule with broad implications in agriculture and human health, makes a fundamental shift in the knowledge position of organisations and their customers. In these situations, the knowledge change precedes intense development of interactions between customers and organisations.

Some see the innovation process in terms of protecting and growing an idea, followed by the preparation of the internal environment of the organisation for fostering the idea. Processes are more detailed than previously described (4.6.2). Thus, there are processes which support 'champions' (Scott, 1994; *Example 6*), processes underlying 'skunk' works[38], and processes of 'internal marketing' which are used to prepare an organisation for a new idea[39].

4.6.4 Diffusion process

Diffusion has been viewed traditionally as a process which spreads a specific innovation through a population of potential users or purchasers while the innovation remains unchanged by its spread into the market. This view is simplistic and does not reflect practical aspects of the innovation spreading process.

One dimension of the diffusion process is specific to the innovation itself. The diffusion process reflects the attributes of the innovation, whether the innovation be technological, methodological or regulatory. The spread of an innovation can reflect how well the innovation fits an unmet need, further coloured by factors like price and volume. The state of the innovation, how evolved it is, and what compromises are required in using it, are also reflected in a diffusion process. In each situation, the innovation itself dictates a dimension of the diffusion process.

A diffusion process has a knowledge dimension, as well as dimension specific to the innovation itself. The importance of knowledge for achieving competitiveness has already been mentioned (3.4). The knowledge dimension comes in several forms and is a key part of the diffusion process. Knowledge can be embodied in the physical object (the knowledge that could be obtained on being given the innovation), or it can be disembodied, in which case it may be possible to document it. Documented knowledge can be in the form of a patent or blueprint and also can be part of human capital. The latter type of knowledge is carried in the brains of individuals and can be codified, meaning that it is know-how that can be written down or otherwise communicated to others, where it is called tacit knowledge. This type of knowledge results from formal training and informal learning by doing and is relatively difficult to articulate. Tacit knowledge is also called person-embodied knowledge, in contrast with equipment-embodied knowledge. Thus, a diffusion process, either within an organisation or an industry, has dimensions which facilitate the transfer of embodied and disembodied knowledge in its various forms.

The knowledge dimension of the diffusion process is a vital one, because innovations are not stable. Innovations evolve quickly as knowledge accumulates. Organisations change to take advantage of an innovation, driven as much by new knowledge as by the innovation itself. Indeed, the success of some organisations has been dependent in part upon the speed with which knowledge is developed and becomes useable. In contrast, other organisations continue to incur considerable expense while grappling with new ways of functioning, the benefits always being some fraction of what was envisaged. Often, the knowledge dimension associated with an innovation has not been considered.

Knowledge is cumulative and this is usually irreversible. This means that the diffusion process can take an organisation on a 'trajectory', which is advantageous, but not necessarily optimal (Pavitt, 1986; 3.2.3). The irreversible nature, which is almost entirely due to the knowledge dimension, occasionally results in organisations having significant difficulty in extricating themselves from developmental 'cul-de-sacs'. Thus, information technology has resulted in massive knowledge accumulation in organisations about the technology, but this has not been accompanied by knowledge about the use of the technology. It is not clear that there is a significant pool of tacit knowledge which can help organisations. Organisations in some industries have already had to extricate themselves from expensive commitments to technology, because of the mismatch between person-embodied and equipment-embodied knowledge.

4.7 Innovation processes for the individual

The interest in innovation processes has been burgeoning, but most have focussed on processes at a national, industry or the macro-organisational level (4.6). For competitiveness to be significantly altered, individuals and groups must be involved in the sub-processes which embody the key pieces of innovation, namely the generation and development of ideas (Fig. 4.3).

In organisations, the first part of the innovation process for individuals involves identification of the need for innovation. The environment, external and internal and how it is perceived (4.5.6), provides a critical part of the need, as does the leadership of the organisation, through its capacity to clearly define and communicate goals. For individuals and groups, the acceptance that there is a need leads to knowledge acquisition, which can be as individuals, or by internal groups, or by judicious mixing of individuals across the boundaries of the organisation. This first part of the innovation process is considered again in Chapter 6 and Chapter 13.

The next step in the innovation process for individuals is idea generation, which requires creativity, a human attribute that is poorly understood and infrequently thought of in process terms. Wisely or not, the next chapter attempts to incorporate creativity into the innovation process. The creativity of interest is the creativity of everyone, rather than gifted individuals, and is very dependent upon an environmental context. Finally, there are parts of the innovation process which relate to the recognition of an idea, the sorting of ideas for their usefulness, and the well-recognised steps of trial and modification.

4.8 Summary

Innovation is not a new or complex concept, but it still causes confusion. There are multiple reasons for this, some due to real uncertainties with the innovation process and related issues, and some due to deficiencies in organisations. In this chapter a range of issues have been addressed and positions taken for this book. Some will have sympathy with these positions and want to apply them more generally. Caution is required, for innovation is dependent on context (Utterback, 1994) and what it is at present, free of all the layers of cant and personal opinion, is not what it will be in the near future or after the next stage of the information technology revolution.

Positions that have been taken include the following. Distinguishing between radical and incremental innovation is neither efficient or effective and this conclusion can be projected to all attempts to subdivide such a diffuse entity as innovation. The assumption that non-technological innovation was important for competitveness was questioned in Chapter 3. Despite this, the more non-technological innovation is examined, the more essential it appears. It may be that our attempts to take a process view of innovation are at fault, for although the process approach has evolved, it is simplistic, mechanistic and fails to incorporate the meaningful steps of human contribution. It may be that the process approach is at an infantile stage, as process models tend to be altered without supporting measurement.

Other issues have been aired without taking a position, either because they are a facade, or it has not been possible to develop sufficient clarity. Thus, measurement of innovation remains elusive, with the possibility that it is a type of intervening variable which will always be unmeasurable. The distinctions between invention and innovation, and inventor and innovator, are facades as they are parts of spectrums, the whole extent of which should be of interest to modern organisations. The idea and the environment are of such importance that mentioning them in this chapter is more to introduce the reader to these elements early, because they are vital for innovation in technologically complex environments. They will be returned to many times in the rest of this book.

Another issue that deserves more attention than has been given is the distinction between continuous improvement and innovation. The lack of clarity in organisations in making this distinction, and the importance in being able to do both activities well cannot be overstated. The tendency to blur these or choose one rather than the other as a preferred activity are mistakes that are widespread. There are issues in distinguishing between the two, and many of these issues are easy to resolve. It is time now to turn to the other source of confusion with innovation, namely deficiencies in organisations. This will also serve to introduce other parts of this book.

A concept like innovation presents difficulties, because of organisations' technological and behavioural 'environments' or culture. For example, organisation's tendency to rush to action is at odds with what is required for innovation, which, like other idea-centred activities, requires a 'pause', some thought and significant reflection. This difficulty is a feature of some organisational cultures and is independent of whether people are 'innovative' or 'adaptive'. It is also independent of whether idea generation is seen as a key piece in altering competitiveness, or whether the organisation is adept with innovation or continuous improvement or both. The behavioural 'environment', or culture of organisations, is often not suitable for innovation (Chapter 6). Innovation has been made complex by those who have tried to partition it into different types, or cover over its uncertainties. Too often this has been due to the desire of many to control the uncontrollable, measure the unmeasurable, and herd people into an activity that probably needs to be individualised (Chapter 6). The centrality of creativity has also not been acknowledged (Chapter 5).

Similarly, the technological components of the environment are far from propitious for innovation. The capacity of technology to impair creativity, and impair innovatory capacity when humans and machines share tasks has been little considered. The technological 'environment' is becoming inimical to innovatory endeavours without most even appreciating this, and this will become evident in the chapters to come (Chapter 7-10).

Notes

1   See pp. 101-105, Koestler (1964).
2   Only some areas of the genetic code change frequently, while most are relatively resistant. See pp. 372-376, Kelly (1994).
3   Some are expressing doubt as to whether this advantage is real or not. See Quinn (1992) and Flannery (1994).
4   Not found in the The Shorter Oxford English Dictionary.
5   Innovation subtypes have been proposed. For example, generic, epochal, altering and entrenching, Clark and Staunton (1989).
6   See Barnard and Wallace (1994).
7   See Carr (1994) where there is deliberate blurring of creativity, invention and innovation. See also Kirton (1994) where the commonly held links between innovation and creativity, and adaptation and non-creativity are refuted.
8   Personal observations. See also Zhuang (1995) for a preliminary survey in which there was significant variation in peoples understanding of the issues surrounding innovation and pp. 358-359 of Van Gundy (1987).
9   Market research in submission by the Australian Graduate School of Engineering Innovation (1995).
10 The pharmaceutical industry struggles to justify pricing, which has an unspecified component for covering the cost of developing new products.
11 See pp. 81-82, Schumpeter (1950).
12 Data obtained from Janes (1945-46, 1955-56, 1965-66, 1975-76, 1985-86, 1995-96).
13 See Chapter 1, Archer and Saarlas (1996).
14 See Fig. 1-2-10 of Archer and Saarlas (1996).
15 See Fig.4.4, Davies (1979).
16 See Fig.4.5, ibid. Note that the word 'shaft' is used in the example instead of 'spool'.
17 See Fig.4.6, ibid.
18 See Fig.4.7, ibid. See also pp. 19 of Archer and Saarlas (1996). Note that the distinction between a propeller and a fan becomes complex with propfans. The distinction relates to whether the aerodynamic load of an individual blade is influenced by that of its neighbours.
19 See pp. 41, Doyle and Pite (1995).
20 See note 12 above. Data obtained for the highest thrust commercial engines (non afterburning) in year shown. In 1945-46 there were no commercial aviation engines and military types in current service have been used. In 1955-56 the only type in regular service (Boeing 707) had not had its details released. Data obtained from a later edition.
21 See pp. 29, Norris (1996).
22 Material for this example provided by the team leader and mentor in the example.
23 Material for Fig. 4.2 comes from interactive sessions with 25 managers of a major bank, 24 employees of a multinational pharmaceutical company (all levels), from electronic bulletin board discussion with seven managers in the same company and feedback from four senior evaluators of the Australian Quality Awards Foundation.
24 See Section 4.6.2 and description of fourth generation innovation process from Rothwell (1994).
25 Personal communication, C. Russell.
26 See pp. 26-28, Carr (1994).

27 See Hewitt (1995), for comments on operating a new process with respect to Kaizen in the Xerox supply chain.
28 Spender and Kessler (1995) call this type of control 'organic'.
29 See Burkart (1994) and recommendations from ALCOA.
30 See pp. 13 in Innovation: A concept to market. Report by the House of Representatives Standing Committee on Industry, Science and Technology.
31 See notes on pp. 16-18, ibid.
32 See the literature review of Hartman et al. (1994).
33 See attempts to measure the use of technical reports by NASA and American Department of Defence in Pinelli et al. (1995).
34 The institutionalised framework of the health system, with its initiatives like capitation, the move to disease management and evidence based medicine alter ideas and the translation of ideas of all health system suppliers.
35 See diagram on pp. 4 of House of Representatives Standing Committee on Industry, Science and Technology Report (1995). For some other models, see:
    1. Fig. A1.2, pp. 67 and Fig. A1.3, pp. 68, Industry Commission (1995).
    2. Fig.1, Woodman at al. (1993).
    3. The Innovation Cycle of the Research Development Corporation of Japan.
    Other models and approaches are driven by specific disciplines. Hence, economists deal with the economics of innovation via stages like invention, commercial innovation (prototypes) and diffusion. Enthusiasts of macroorganization behaviour see two paths, one being innovation diffusion as corporate culture, while the other is innovation design as corporate culture. See also Van Gundy (1987).
36 One industry that exhibits many features of the first generation model is the pharmaceutical industry. Despite statements which propound that innovation in the pharmaceutical industry is current and best practice (see Hale 1996), much of the innovation process is predominantly research driven. Many new therapeutic compounds only provide marginal improvements over existing therapies. Marketing groups must deal with the products as they appear and have limited opportunities to influence early stages of innovation.
37 This is not displayed diagrammatically because of its complexity.
38 Skunk works describe the 'secretive' approach to some types of innovation in some organisation, where different measures, different forms of resource allocation and different ways of carrying our performance management are used in special areas (4.5.1).
39 Internal marketing of an innovation is common, although often not done that well. Often this is best done by a team taken from the group that was involved in the birth and development of the innovation. As a minimum a team must have a sponsor, the champion and the most persuasive communicators. Many involved in 'internal marketing' make the mistake of viewing this as a transient task, though it rarely is.

5 Creativity issues and attributes

Creativity, ideas and innovation are intimately linked and vital for changes in organisations. Creativity in organisations is highly modulated because of the perception that ideas are a threat (6.4). Humans have an abundance of ideas, but most are culled as they are generated with the remainder having a very limited existence. In organisations, the few ideas that survive are often controlled by putting them into holding pens where they have an uncertain future. The creativity that is controlled in the work place is the creativity of all rather than of a select few, and the creativity of creatives, like the artist, comic and scientist, may not be relevant.

Creativity, like many other human capabilities, has attracted a multitude of interpreters and their explanations. Approaches have been diverse, as have been outputs, but a number of themes occur recurrently and some of these are considered in this chapter. Reference is made frequently to the work of Wallas (1926), Guilford (1950), Ghiselin (1952), Koestler (1964), Gruber (1981), Perkins (1981), Isaksen (1987) and Kirton (1994).

This chapter defines creativity by considering various previous approaches, including the 'genius view', before describing a number of issues like insight, motivation and personality. This is the starting point for considering the key attributes of creativity, namely the environment (5.4), temporal features (5.5) and knowledge factors (5.6).

5.1 Approaches and definitions

There are many views on the definition of creativity. Consensus on the nature of creativity has fluctuated, with discussion on definition having a prominent place in a number of articles. Many approaches view creativity in the context of other topics such as cognitive style, imagination, motivation, intelligence, conformity, intellect, inheritance, gender, personality, selection, persuasion and mental disease. Creativity is a topic in psychology. Areas of dominant interest include the role of training, creativity in thought disorders, creativity in women, the place of hemispheric specialisation, the role of different states of consciousness, the inheritance of intellectual and personal traits, the place of the environment, the place of politics, and understanding creativity from generational analysis of the genius and the highly creative. Creativity has also been defined without being associated with other topics.

Definitions have been clustered, being divided into those which focus on the creative product, process, person, or on the environment in which creativity is manifested (Mooney, 1963; Simonton, 1988). This scheme is as useful as any other (Tardif and Sternberg, 1988), with the caution that it is not necessary for one definition to be selected or for there to be adherence to one view on how creativity should be understood. There will always be an element of vagueness and incompleteness about each individual treatment[1] of creativity. This book deliberately considers a range of views, because it is more likely to be relevant for those trying to understand creativity in organisations.

5.1.1 Product

The characteristics of the product have been used in definitions of creativity[2]. Newness is often an essential feature but there is debate about whether it is sufficient for the newness to exist in the creator's eyes alone. Some have suggested that newness should apply to the creator within a culture (Stein, 1953; Hennessey and Amabile, 1988), but others have been quite adamant that the individual alone is the focus in assessing newness (Stewart, 1950; Johnson-Laird, 1988). The essential nature of the interaction between the environment and creativity in any innovation suggests that creativity free of context is unlikely to be useful (5.1.4). The interactions between creativity and the environment are considered later (5.4.2, 5.4.3). Newness also includes the element of surprise in the context of what is known at a point in time[3].

The U.S Patent Office requires more than newness. One must have originated something of merit that others, having ordinary skill in the art related to the subject of the invention, would not have thought of, or would not have achieved if they had thought of it. The invention should overcome some prior failure or some special difficulty, offer something remarkable or surprising, overcome prior scepticism about possible success, or meet an unfulfilled need[4].

5.1.2 Person

Characteristics of people have been used in the definition of creativity. Specific characteristics have been combined into types, which are supposed to have different amounts of creativity. The cultural context of the assessor has been seen as important[5]. One approach has involved the recording of behaviours that are 'likely to be found' in a creative person (Sternberg, 1988). Thus, six major elements from one study were lack of conventionality, integration and intellectuality, aesthetic taste and imagination, decisional skill and flexibility, perspicacity, and drive for accomplishment and recognition. Some elements[6] have been combined into orchestrating factors, like intelligence, intellectual style, personality and motivation, though there is disagreement as to the validity of such approaches. It is not apparent that personal characteristics provide much practical help in defining creativity. Value and judgement sets of observers produce a diffuseness which is at odds with defining anything. As well, some aspects of the person are important for creativity but may not have a place in a definition. Motivation (5.3.2), personality (5.3.3), and cognitive style (5.3.4) will be considered later as they are important in creativity in organisations.

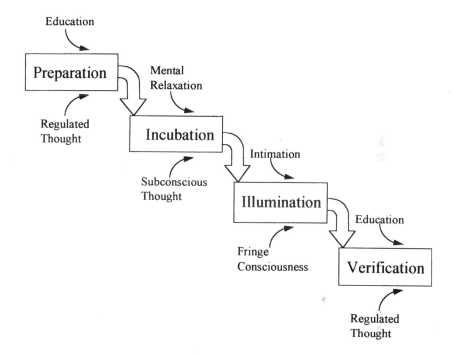

Figure 5.1 A diagram of the creative process using the process approaches of Wallas (1926) and Hadamard (1945). Some of Wallas' moderating factors have been included[7].

5.1.3 Process

Many definitions of creativity use a process approach, although the proposed processes have varied widely. Thus, creative thinking has been seen as the process of seeing or creating relationships, using both conscious and subconscious systems (Spearman, 1930). Wallas (1926) dissected the creative process into the stages of preparation, incubation, illumination and revision[8] and included a range of moderators (Fig. 5.1). Guilford (1950) conceptualised creativity by the mental abilities involved, while Koestler (1964) characterised patterns of thought, and postulated paths for the information processing underlying creativity (5.7). The process approach helps clarify creativity issues. These include the time required for each step, the place of insight, the overlap between the creative process and what is actually produced, variation and how accessible and controllable the parts of the process are in conscious awareness. The process approach to defining creativity is easy to communicate and is well suited to this book.

5.1.4 Environment

It has been proposed that defining creativity as a process occurring in a single person at a particular point in time should be superseded by definitions which see creativity in terms of context and interactions with larger networks of social systems. These provide the inputs that must be in place for creativity to occur as well as the means whereby the creative output is identified, acknowledged and dispersed (Stein, 1953; Csikszentmihalyi, 1988). Process is still a feature, although of much greater complexity (Fig. 5.3). For organisations, defining creativity in terms of context is an approach which is useful because contributions are sought from groups rather than individuals. The environment is also important in this book, because of the effect of the technologically complex work place on creativity. The environment and creativity is considered again in greater detail in a general sense (5.4) and in organisations (Chapter 6).

5.1.5 Summary

There are many approaches to defining creativity, but definition remains elusive, as with many other cognitive functions. It is likely that broader definitions are more useful. Many of the approaches have provided alternative ways of viewing creativity which have been beneficial. While no one approach is clearly superior, a process focussed definition[9] that is appropriate for this book is:

> *Creative thinking is the process of sensing difficulties, problems, gaps in information, missing elements, something askew. Ideas are generated which lead to guesses and hypotheses about these deficiencies. These guesses and hypotheses are evaluated and tested, revised and retested. Finally the idea is communicated.*

5.2 Self report and the 'genius' approach

A variety of analytic approaches have been used to examine the creativity of famous creatives. The 'self report' approach seeks to find what creative individuals thought of the processes underlying their creativity. Another historical approach tries to reconstitute the creative person in their particular environment, as well as analyse what they wrote. While many articles make reasonable reference to famous creatives, others have gone much further.

5.2.1 Self report

The self report is obviously biased as to who and what is mentioned. While this decreases its value, self report has been useful, because many occurred before structured views of cognition had been widely disseminated, with their unprocessed views providing the real benefit. Thus implies that self-reports by current creatives may not be as useful, because they are tainted by today's widely disseminated and highly popularised comments on creativity.

Some doubt the validity of the circumstances and contents of a proportion of the often quoted self-reports[10]. Thus, Coleridge's description of the creation of 'Kubla Kahn' has been doubted, some suggesting that the circumstance of the self-report was created to make the composition more interesting to the public. Self-reports by Mozart and von Kekule on their own creativity have also been doubted. Some scientists at the end of their experimental life have revealed that their creative moment of greatness lacked the grand orchestration that was part of the self-report near the time of discovery.

The self report also suffers because of its inability to incorporate environmental factors. In some societies there have been times of intense creativity in an number of disciplines (Simonton, 1984), such as occurred in Vienna at the turn of the century and Florence in the first 25 years of the fifteenth century. It is not clear that an individual could have appreciated the environmental factors at the time.

5.2.2 The 'genius' view of creativity

The analysis of the creativity of famous individuals, plus their own reports, has been a feature of many articles on creativity (Ghiselin, 1952; Koestler, 1964; Gruber and Davis, 1988). This approach has been labelled the 'genius' view of creativity, with the case study method being its most developed form. Support for the 'genius' approach comes from aggregation effects, issues around sampling, and the importance of context.

Aggregation removes key features If there is only one type of creativity in humans, then the 'genius' approach may be valuable, even though a cognitive activity is being sampled in a particularly biased way. The bias stems from the interpretative stance, as each case study has to choose a few foci and commit many significant omissions[11]. Advocates of the 'genius' approach propose that this bias is acceptable. They posit that the seeking out of the common features of creative people is pointless, in that the creative 'edge' of famous individuals will not be found in any aggregated view.

Trait measurement Some doubt that multivariant measurement techniques should be applied to measuring a particular trait in a relevant population in studies on creativity. Relevant populations have been of particular concern, because school children, psychology students, and U.S. Coast Guard trainees have an unknown quota of people who 'are functioning creatively'. In focussing on a decision making style in a person widely agreed to be creative, proponents of the 'genius' approach believe they have circumvented measurement and sampling criticisms. They suggest that it is essential to tailor the appreciation of variables to the circumstances of the life under scrutiny.

Contextual features The examination of the famous individual at their own work captures the effect of the environment, which is lost once aggregated measures are used to any great extent. This is true for factors like relationships, and their immediate physical surroundings, but does not apply to global environmental factors reflecting the state of a society.

5.2.3 Objections to the focus on the creative individual

Some have a particularly jaundiced view of the approach and values inherent in the 'genius' approach (Weisberg, 1988). Objections relate to the validity of the historical record (5.3.1), the value of retrospective investigation and the value of single case studies. These are all valid, self evident and important objections. While many creativity attributes can be gleaned from the study of creatives, and these can be generalised, it is important to try and appreciate how the creativity of the 'less-creative' manifests. To say it is less across all attributes is glib. In the next chapter the creativity of those not recognised as creatives is considered in a number of ways (6.2) and is summarised (6.2.2).

5.2.4 Summary

Up to this point some of the approaches which have been used to organise thinking on creativity have been described. Many of these schemes make some contribution to our understanding, although they are complex and difficult to generalise. In the rest of this chapter, issues and attributes will be discussed, using some of the observations already considered.

5.3 Creativity issues

A number of creativity issues must be mentioned before attributes are considered in detail. These include insight, motivation, and personality.

5.3.1 Insight

In process terms, insight is equivalent to the illumination stage (Fig. 5.1). Insight is a popular topic in creativity research, but not all see insight as critical to creativity. Some (Gruber and Davis, 1988) believe that the key processes in creativity are much slower and time consuming. Others suggest that most creative acts in many fields occur in small steps and large 'insightful' leaps are a myth (Weisberg, 1988). They propose that insights are frequent occurrences, with a single incisive event being rare.

Indeed, an insight may only be the last of many small, associated steps, but because it is tied to the solution of a problem, it becomes enlarged and embellished when the individual reviews their own creative process[12]. The preoccupation with insight may reflect fashion which biases interest in many human endeavours, particularly in human research. Despite this, there are a number of ways of considering insight, including the process view, a restructuring approach, familiarisation and forgetting, and an analogy-based approach.

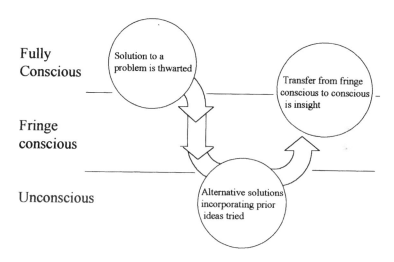

Fully Conscious

Fringe conscious

Unconscious

Preparation   Incubation   Illumination

Figure 5.2 A scheme for insight[13].

A process view Wallas' four staged creative process has been used by others for understanding insight. Thus, Hadamard (1945) has proposed that scientific insight recurrently exhibits preparation, incubation, illumination and verification. In addition, these process steps have been cross linked to different levels of consciousness (Fig. 5.2). Hadamard's theory of insight has three levels of mind, the fully conscious, the fringe conscious, and the unconscious. Thus, the preparation for insight, where the intense effort to solve a problem is thwarted, occurs in the conscious. The unconscious is 'stirred up' during the incubation phase and alternative solutions incorporating prior ideas from the preparation phase are tried. The occurrence of a very promising option leads the unconscious to deposit it in the fringe conscious, where the mind seizes upon it, the process of insight being the transfer into the conscious.

A restructuring approach An entirely different scheme underlies the approach which integrate ideas from Gestalt psychology with the problem space hypothesis. In the Gestalt paradigm, all situations are characterised by mind structures which are prey to forces. Unbalanced forces produced by a disparity between desired and achieved goals result in gaps which if pronounced result in reconstitution, with mind structures restructuring into a new configuration (Langley and Jones, 1988). In the problem space hypothesis, problem solving is associated with a search through a problem space. In cross-linking these areas, Ohlsson (1984) suggested that Gestalt restructuring can be explained in terms of information processing theory and current theories of memory. The emphasis on the description space for the development of a disparity implies that restructuring, or creativity, depends upon finding a different way to look at the problem, rather than trying to solve the problem directly.

Familiarisation and forgetting Hadamard's (1945) scheme has been altered using models of problem solving and memory. In Simon's theory of familiarisation and selective forgetting, the preparation stage involves the 'chunking' of information (Simon, 1977). Chunking is proposed as a process which circumvents the severe restrictions on item number in short term memory by the expansion of the size of each item. The expansion of the size of each item requires extensive exposure to the relevant field of information. This is labelled familiarisation and occurs in the conscious. The goals of a search through a problem space are held in short-term memory, but the chunks are stored in long-term memory. Selective forgetting is where the goals of a search in the problem space are often lost or displaced, while the chunks remain. The search in the problem space might occur again much later, but the original search strategy has been lost and there is the potential for the chunks to be joined or approached differently. The retrieval of remote chunks presents a major task for memory and some suggest that search is carried out by an unconscious memory retrieval process as a background activity occurring in the incubation phase (Keane, 1991).

Analogy-based approach The persistence of analogy in the descriptions of major discoveries has led some to give it a central role in creativity (Dreistadt, 1968). Computational models of reasoning by analogy exist, as do approaches for the indexing and retrieval of analogy-based findings and for distinguishing useful analogies from poor ones. Others have proposed that analogy-based retrieval does not result from a search through a problem space, but is a memory-related phenomenon, being very rapid and often cued by an external event. In this approach, there is no incubation stage and no place for the concept of unconscious reasoning (Langley and Jones, 1988). The predominance of conscious search has been supported by the failure of the literature to show that subjects spontaneously retrieve analogies in the absence of explicit direction to do so (Keane, 1991). Thus, creativity, and particularly the insight component, depends upon conscious search with focal attentive processing in a state of conscious awareness being essential. This approach has insight explained as a memory process rather than a search method, with the initiation of an unconscious memory search requiring conscious instigation.

Summary It is understandable that insight has been seen as a key feature of human creativity. Insight is fascinating, is sought after, and always has been a more fashionable facet of creativity than verification or incubation. However, prevailing views have suffered from a lack of balance and the deficiencies of self-reporting. At present, most see the place of insight as being a small but necessary component of creativity (Perkins, 1981; Tardif and Sternberg, 1988).

5.3.2 Motivation

There have been a variety of observations on those classed as being inquirers or creators which identify intense interest, extreme persistence, and a driving absorption in their work as key features (Simonton, 1988). Very high levels of motivation have been a feature of those who stand out as creative individuals. It has been proposed that the creative tend to be more intrinsically motivated. The more motivation is biased towards extrinsic factors, the less creative will be the outcomes (Amabile, 1983). In a variety of tasks, school children have shown that the perception of a task as a means to an end is the crucial element for creativity decrements in task engagement (Hennessey and Amabile, 1988). When reward or evaluation is perceived as controlling performance, creativity suffers and this has been observed in all age groups. Performance assessment significantly decreases subjects' intrinsic motivation for that activity, as does surveillance, deadlines and an expected evaluation. Motivation appears to be important for creativity, but vulnerable.

5.3.3 Personality

Some have suggested that personality is not a distinguishing feature of the creative, and that there is no one personality characteristic that is useful in identifying a creative individual (Tardif and Sternberg, 1988). However, some personality characteristics are repeatedly mentioned, suggesting that clusters of characteristics may indicate the presence of a creative predisposition. Frequently mentioned characteristics include perseverance, a willingness to confront hostility and take intellectual risks, curiosity, openness to new experiences, discipline, commitment, being task-focussed, dismissive of external constraints, and having a high degree of self-organisation. There is evidence that the creative personality is an enduring entity, but that creative temperament fluctuates during periods of peoples lives (Helson, Roberts and Agronick, 1995).

Some have attempted to synthesise the key dimensions of personality that are relevant to creativity. Tolerance of ambiguity, willingness to surmount obstacles, willingness to grow, willingness to take risks, and individuality expressed as an unwillingness to yield to group norms have been selected (Sternberg and Lubart, 1991). The problem with these approaches is that paradoxes are too readily apparent. For example, examples of individuals failing to enmesh well with their surroundings abound, but significant social integration and richness in the environment have been a feature of the lives of many famous creatives. Conflict appears to be an important feature, yet permissiveness, support and external tolerance also appear essential.

5.3.4 Cognitive characteristics, capacities and style

Just as there are a large range of personality factors which may have some relevance to creativity, there are an equally large range of cognitive characteristics. High intelligence, originality, verbal fluency, metaphorical thinking, flexibility and independence of judgment have all been seen as important cognitive characteristics[14], and many of these relate to cognitive capacity. Kirton (1994) has pointed out that cognitive capacity issues in creativity, such as intelligence, are quite distinct from cognitive style characteristics. Thus for intelligence, the consensus appears to be that some level of intelligence is necessary, but intelligence is not a sufficient condition for creativity.

Cognitive style is a different matter entirely, for while judgements about capacity can be made in terms of good and bad, judgements about a style make far less sense. There is ample evidence that that there are different cognitive styles, they are stable, and they reveal the way individuals prefer to change (Kirton, 1994). A cognitive style does not mean an individual cannot operate in other ways, but only points to a preferred way of operating. The different styles are equally beneficial or detrimental depending upon circumstances. Hence, using style differences to choose people for a task, and thereby orchestrating a specific mix of styles, may have a place though this type of approach is almost always simplistic. There is likely to be a much greater benefit in recognising preferred creative styles in a group chosen using other criteria, optimising them, and facilitating their interactions.

5.3.5 Laboratory based research

The creative individual's contribution is dependent upon a variety of external factors in addition to their own creative ability. Science, cognitive science, artificial intelligence and organisational sociology approach creativity differently, but all take account of the context (5.4) in which creativity occurs. The psychological approaches used to understand creativity have only recently begun to incorporate contextual factors and the whole issue of environment. Environment, an umbrella term intended to capture all contextual factors, is considered in more detail later.

Research on creativity that ignores context is of dubious value. Research findings from solving laboratory problems are unlikely to tell much about creativity as it occurs in everyone, or in the genius, particularly in the situation where their creativity is modulated. This type of research will be useful in understanding how people solve problems in creativity research laboratories, but that is likely to be the full extent of its usefulness (Weisberg, 1988). The research laboratory is also not a place where the attributes of creativity (5.4 -5.6) are likely to be usefully duplicated. Subjects in research laboratories are unlikely to exhibit deep knowledge in the area where their creativity is being assessed. There is unlikely to be time for gestation, motivation will be inappropriate and the intimate involvement with a problem, which appears to be so essential, is probably lacking. It is likely that genii, or those deemed to be creative, would not be particularly adept in laboratory problem solving. It is also likely that making a laboratory mimic a particular creative environment has little point except in some specific circumstances[15].

5.3.6 Summary

There are many issues in creativity that require greater understanding. Some of these are important for organisations that are attempting to make their internal milieu more conducive for innovatory behaviour. Currently, psychology is the discipline that provides the knowledge and competencies for furthering this understanding. Most contemporary psychological accounts of creativity appear unsubstantial, if not irrelevant, because they routinely draw on a single disciplinary lens (Gardner, 1988). Cognitive psychology is also troubled by the diversity and undisciplined nature of many of its contributions in many of its fields and creativity is no exception. The useful work on creativity is in danger of being drowned by the multitude of articles which desire to produce an original approach, which is clever in its structure, is predominantly laboratory based, and which distinguishes its author. There is little doubt that pragmatic and theoretical approaches, which are not self indulgent, and which are carried out in work places, would help immensely with understanding issues like personality, cognitive capacity, cognitive style, motivation and insight.

5.4 Environment attributes

Factors external to the person affect creativity (5.1.4, 5.2.1, 5.2.2, 5.3.5) and this has been called influence. In this section, influence is briefly discussed before considering environmental attributes using a process approach (Csikszentmihalyi, 1988).

5.4.1 Influence

Simultaneous discovery has been a persistent feature of human creativity, even when communication processes have been primitive. There have been too many examples of simultaneous discovery for it to be dismissed. Many examples have occurred in science, but it would be wrong to think that simultaneous discovery has only occurred in science. Simultaneous discovery has been attributed to 'ripeness', or the readiness of different areas of human endeavour for change. This readiness reflects motivation, plus the presence of items in the environment which are essential building blocks for a particular creation. The propitiousness of the environment can be considered in a number of ways, one simple approach being an analysis of influence.

Influence is made up of a multitude of personal, social, cultural and technological forces of great complexity. One approach to appreciating influence is to partition these environmental factors by the proportion of people who might be expected to be affected by each factor. Thus, factors related to the standard of living, security and politics are broad and quite distinct from the factors involved in a composer facilitating a master class. Divisions used in the following brief consideration of influence are the society, the group and the individual. These all have equivalents in organisations (6.7.1, 6.7.2).

Societal influence   Simonton (1984) observed that political instability in one generation depresses the likely number of major creators in the next generation in discursive fields such as science, philosophy and literature[16].

Group influence   Studies of those acknowledged to be creative reveals that a significant proportion of the output of great musicians, artists and successful humorists is influenced by the work of others. Many artists have belonged at one time or another to various 'schools' and deliberately have used specific composition and style structures. The same applies to novelists, composers and humorists. Group influence is a factor in science, with many research areas having clusters of researchers interacting via very complex interrelationships.

Individual influence   There is controversy as to how much prior work has affected an individual's contribution in music, literature and humour. Many famous works have been analysed extensively for occult influences. In addition, there is a large literature which considers the work of a creative and identifies individual effects. In science, the influence of an individual is overt and acknowledged.

Biographies of famous authors such as George Orwell, Patrick White and Samuel Johnson document the multiple influences present when their masterworks were created (Shelden, 1991; Marr, 1991; Wain, 1994). Many of these influences were at the level of the society and the group, but there were also significant influences from individuals[17]. Similarly, musicologists have looked for influence in most of the major classical works, as well as in the life of the composers. Some suggest that it takes approximately 10 years of composing experience before the influence of specific individuals disappears, and a composer becomes capable of creating a masterwork[18]. Biographies of humorists also show the extensive effects of others.

Influence has a role in creativity because existing thought patterns and frameworks provide both a 'starting point' for a new player, as well as a stable base for newness. However, the analysis of influence is flawed, for it seeks primarily to identify one or more external factors, and misses much of the two-way relationship between the individual and the environment.

5.4.2 Environment and domain

The splitting of sources of creativity as either inside or outside the individual should be avoided as there is a combination of the internal and external in many new developments[19]. The key feature is the interactive nature of the environmental effect, in that it is composed of the individual's reaction to the environment and often the environment's reaction to the individual. Environmental attributes have been described (Fig. 5.3) in terms of domains and fields (Csikszentmihalyi, 1988).

Domains are stable, cultural attributes that transmit the selected new ideas or forms to the following generations. The domain is the symbol system of a culture. It is the storehouse of the information from which, and with which, new ideas are created. Access to the domain is essential for creativity. The literature of science, the art gallery in painting, the ability to write music, the recordings of humorists, the skills required to use materials in the visual arts all reside in the domain. In viewing domains as a repository, it appears as if it has been expanding for several thousand years. However, domains are very vulnerable. At a societal level, political 'cleansing' of history, the burning of books, the loss of language by assimilation and merging of cultures all contract domains. In families and other small groups, the death of an elder can remove key parts of the group's domain.

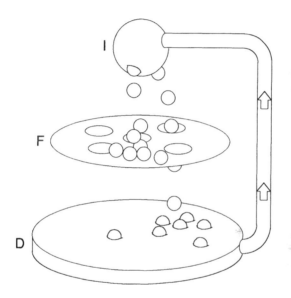

Figure 5.3 The environment attributes of creativity. An individual's (I) creative contribution is altered by the field (F), a portion of it becoming part of the domain (D). The domain provides an interactive resource for the individual (much modified from Csikszentmihalyi's 'map'[20]).

5.4.3 Environment and field

Fields are a set of social institutions which select and retain some individual's outputs. Fields are embedded in specific social systems and their importance is very evident in a variety of creative activities. In art there have been numerous examples where a creative contribution only came into existence after a rediscovery, or following some streaming or selection process. The field in art includes art teachers, art historians, art critics, collectors, gallery owners, museum curators and peers (Csikszentmihalyi, 1988). There are similar fields in music and in humour, with an individual's creation often being bypassed until a selection or recognition event moves it into the mainstream. The music or humour remains unaltered through the process of recognition (Fig. 5.3), but creativity is not deemed to be present until the recognition process is complete.

Science is similar, a 'creative' contribution requiring recognition by a group of scientists. Hence, Harvey's concept that blood circulated, rather than being produced and consumed, was not supported by the research establishment[21], with the result that this truly creative contribution languished for a while. In science and other areas of creativity, some creations are eventually judged by different fields. In science, the longer term field tends to be new scientists rather than the existing 'judges' of science. Some scientists have been aware of the importance of the field. Realising the likely enormity of their contribution and the likely resistance, they have attempted to prepare the field and make it more receptive, or at least less antagonistic. Darwin waited and devoted considerable effort to this preparation (Brown, 1995). Unfortunately, some current scientists, with contributions of much lesser stature, may have devoted too much of their time to this activity[22].

5.4.3 Summary

Precise measurement of the environment attributes of human creativity is unlikely. Nevertheless, the environment is a key factor in the creativity of individuals and must be incorporated into any consideration. Organisational equivalents of domains and fields are vital in harnessing the creativity of individuals working alone or in teams.

5.5 Temporal attributes

The environment attribute of creativity is complex, variable and difficult to measure (5.4). Temporal attributes are also surrounded by uncertainty and disagreement (Perkins, 1981). Three temporal attributes that stand out are insight, gestation and incorporation. These are considered in turn.

5.5.1 Insight

Insight appears to involve processes that occur rapidly, but this may be exaggerated by the excitement surrounding insight. The mechanisms that have been proposed to underlie insight have been considered in some detail previously (5.3.1). The self-reporting literature abounds with descriptions where there has been a creative leap, the sudden insight, the flash, the 'eureka' episode. Speed is a common feature of all the schemes proposed for insight. However, some mental processes may be even faster, particularly those that occur in situations where the perception of the rate of events appear to slow. An acceleration of mental events could cause this apparent slowing, but an acceleration effect has never been reported in descriptions of insight. Indeed, the opposite is true. Early descriptions described a state of intimation (Wallas, 1926, Ghiselin, 1952), where there is a premonition surrounding the occurrence of insight. Insight is rapid as far as the processes underlying creativity are concerned, but insight itself may not be as quick as some have suggested.

5.5.2 Gestation

Whatever the importance of insight, creativity has another longer temporal attribute called gestation, a name which suggests a slow and hidden maturation. In the anecdotes of genii, gestation has been seen as being quite distinct from insight (Ghiselin, 1952). Given the relative rapidity of insight (5.5.1), and the agreement that creativity takes time (Tardif and Sternberg, 1988), it is likely that gestation dominates the time domain.

Gestation must have a number of processes occurring within it (5.1.3). Thus, gestation is the period of incubation (Fig. 5.1), which is initiated by the thwarting of an attempt to solve a problem, or the presence of a problem awaiting restructuring, or an unconscious memory retrieval process, or a search process occurring as a background activity (Fig. 5.2). None of these are rapid processes. Indeed, some see the retrieval of remote analogies as a major task for memory, suggesting that gestation is relatively slow. Others see no place for gestation, incubation or related activities (Perkins, 1981), but the need to allow for the natural pace of creativity and the poor return from forcing the process are well documented (Ghiselin, 1952).

5.5.3 Incorporation

Another temporal attribute of creativity is the time lag to the incorporation of the new contribution. Incorporation is interesting in that it is quite distinct from insight and gestation, because the temporal properties are not determined by an individual's nervous system. Incorporation is determined partly by the attributes of the individual, but largely by the field (5.4.3). The individual's effect on incorporation has been appreciated for a long time, many creative individuals accepting some obligation for the shaping of consumer acceptance[23]. Incorporation is a critical attribute in harnessing creativity in organisations, because it can be orchestrated.

5.5.4 Summary

When creativity in organisations is considered, it is useful to have some appreciation of the temporal profile of insight, gestation and incorporation. Thus, if insight is considered to occur in seconds, then gestation occurs in weeks to months, while incorporation occurs in years. A different frame of reference might have insight occurring over several minutes, gestation occurring over a year or more and incorporation requiring decades. Similar temporal relationships appear to exist between insight, gestation and incorporation.

5.6 Knowledge attributes

There is considerable agreement that creativity requires knowledge, although there are limits to these effects because excess knowledge may be detrimental[24]. Most accept that an absence of knowledge impairs creativity. Periods of history where access to knowledge has been curtailed, or the time for acquiring knowledge has been limited, have been associated with declines in creativity. Conversely, increase in the capacity to collect and to disseminate knowledge, as well as giving people the opportunity to absorb it, appears to have been associated with increases in creativity. These are gross associations. The following sections consider the links between knowledge and creativity.

5.6.1 Knowledge and creative criteria

The interrelationship between knowledge and creativity depends on how creativity is defined (5.1). If newness is not required, then any individual solving a problem on their own, even though it has been solved by others previously, has been creative. However, a more complete knowledge would have crimped the creative endeavour early on (5.1.1). These creative acts are vital for individuals and must not be belittled, but their relationship to the creativity that leads to innovation is unclear. If an individual's creative endeavours end up in replicating something, then this is potentially wasteful. In an organisational context, the individual could be applauded, but the organisation admonished for failing to acquaint the individual with the extent of progress. The need for mastery in a field of endeavour is vital for any creative worker (Ghiselin, 1952), which means that individuals must have knowledge which is sufficient to ensure a sense of what needs to be done.

5.6.2 Knowledge and simultaneous discovery

The level of knowledge which allows an individual to be creative, but at the same time avoid the reinvention phenomenon, is impossible to define. Unwitting involvement in 'reinvention' can blur with the phenomenon of 'simultaneous' discovery, where different individuals are involved in identical creative acts synchronously, but independently (5.4.1). The phenomenon of simultaneous discovery may partly reflect the vagaries of information systems, with well-disseminated preliminary knowledge aligning creatives on the 'starting blocks'. A triggering point may not be obvious as multiple common factors in the domain and field are in play (5.4.2, 5.4.3). It is unknown how much simultaneous discovery is being enhanced as information transfer improves, though it is likely to be significant. Simultaneous discovery has been a feature of science, not withstanding the extraordinary capacity of exceptional people to create newness[25]. On a lesser scale, but vital to organisations, is the realisation that knowledge dissemination is such that simultaneous discovery is likely, and that a reliance on 'discovery' for competitiveness may be necessary but not sufficient.

5.6.3 Knowledge areas and boundaries

Koestler (1964) provided an analogy for the interrelationship between knowledge and creativity using linkages and matrices[26]. Each matrix is a collection of associations around an activity, which can be equated to knowledge and can be thought of as a subset of a domain (5.4.2). Creativity occurs when two matrices are linked simultaneously by an individual. Thus, an unresolved issue in one matrix may remain, even as the 'beam of consciousness is drifting' onto another matrix. Illumination occurs when two matrices are momentarily thought of simultaneously, but at different levels of awareness (Fig. 5.4). This analogy focuses on the importance of bridging dissimilar areas of knowledge, but some feel that just two matrices is limiting (Gruber, 1981).

The analogy of creativity occurring when matrices or planes of knowledge are linked is a useful one and underlies many of the attempts to improve research productivity using multidisciplinary collaborations. Whether matrices or planes of knowledge can be as effectively linked between people as they can within an individual is a key issue in the creativity of organisations.

5.7 Combining creativities

Any practical approach to creativity must embrace the effects of one individual's creativity on that of other people. People, as the partner in a pair or as team members in a group, are a key element in the domain and field of all individuals (5.4). The following consideration of the effect of the creativity of an individual on the creativity of others is a link between this chapter's focus on the individual and the next chapter's focus on organisations.

There are too many examples of creative combinations of people for it to be viewed as some artefact, or the plain mixing of outputs of two non-interacting processes. Thus, creative pairings and larger groupings occur occasionally in science, much less than many would hope, but still often enough to suggest a shared process is present. Jazz players, advocate teams, advertising agency groups, composers and librettists, comedy writing duos, and many other groupings are all examples. What is not clear is how the creative process within each individual is modified in such circumstances.

Whatever creativity process is present (Fig. 5.1, 5.2), one step where the combining of creativities is probably occurring is the illumination stage (5.1.3, 5.3.1). Here, a critical step is the movement of incubated thinkings from fringe consciousness into consciousness. How 'creative' an environment is depends upon how much this movement is triggerable. In Koestler's (1964) approach, illumination occurs for a brief moment when two matrices of thought are simultaneously active but at different levels of awareness. This part of the illumination step may be the only point when the creativity processes of individuals can coalesce (Fig. 5.4).

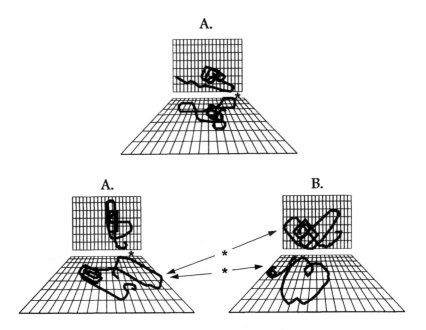

Figure 5.4 A diagrammatic representation of thinking in two matrices, using Koestler's (1964) approach. The symbol '*' is where two matrices of thought are simultaneously active for an individual (upper) and a pair of individuals (lower).

Coalesce does not mean any real fusion, but more the point where another persons explorations and incubations across a plane of thought become visible or appreciable to the individual and their own explorations and incubations. The potential for a multiplication of associations by contact between the matrices of thought between more than one person is obvious (Fig. 5.4). The necessity for the individual to be receptive to what matrices of thought are being proffered, and how the matrices are kept simultaneously active in the presence of another person may well explain the rarity of effective creativity in groupings of people. As will be discussed in the next chapter, the creativity of individuals working with others is not enhanced by just increasing the number of opportunities for coalescing individual's thinking (6.3.1, 6.3.2). Indeed, processes which aim to enhance group creativity appear to be more useful the more they keep the individual's creative process relatively separated. This is more likely to be a field rather than a domain effect. It is likely that circumstances can be created for groupings of people where field effects are not inhibitory and where access to domains requires no extra effort, but this will occur infrequently if left to chance. Motivation becomes a powerful factor when groups are put into situations where creativity becomes vital.

5.8 Summary

In this consideration of creativity, the focus here has been on individuals and interrelationships with the environment. The variety in the approaches to understanding creativity is useful and allows focus on the effects of knowledge and the environment. The variety also draws attention to issues like motivation and temporal attributes which are vital, but which are insufficiently understood to incorporate into any one scheme. Other areas where thinking is underdeveloped include insight, personality, cognitive capacity and cognitive style, but these are probably not of equivalent importance. Environment and knowledge have been given central positions, largely because this book's central theme is innovatory behaviour in technologically complex work places. The environment interactions have been divided into domain and field components, because these have practical implications. Finally, our understanding of creativity in an individual should not be transposed to groupings of humans without caution. Much of the creativity process may only be really functional within the boundary of an individual. The next chapter considers creativity in groupings of individuals (Fig. 5.5).

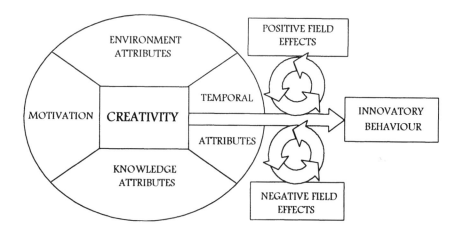

Figure 5.5 A summary diagram of this chapter's consideration of creativity in the individual. The segmented oval contains attributes and domain effects which influence an individual's creativity. The field effects which can affect the translation of creativity into innovatory behaviour are considered in the next chapter.

Notes

1   See Johnson-Laird (1988) commenting on theories of Wallas (1926) and others.
2   A product related definition from Hennessey and Amabile (1988):

> *A product is viewed as creative to the extent that it is both a novel response and an appropriate, useful, correct, or valuable response to an open-ended task.*

See pp. 12-17 for discussion on definition and judgment of what is creative.

3   A less product-orientated definition (Selye, 1962), but still not a process-related definition outlines the key characteristics of creative contributions as:

> *They are true not merely as facts but also in the way they are interpreted, they are generalizable, and they are surprising in the light of what was known at the time of their discovery.*

4   US Patent Definition is:

> *A patent is a property right granted by the United States, and by other nations, which gives the holder the exclusive right to exclude others from manufacture, use, or sale of the invention in the U.S.*

5   See Fig. 4.1 and 4.2 and pp. 109-110, Taylor (1988).

6   Abbreviated version from Sternberg (1988), pp. 128.

> *1.   Lack of conventionality - free spirit, unorthodox, makes rules.*
> *2.   Integration and intellectuality - makes connections and distinctions, recognises similarities and disparities, can reformulate old propositions in new ways.*
> *3.   Aesthetic taste and imagination - appreciates creative endeavours, is creative in other fields, has taste.*
> *4.   Decisional skill and flexibility - can change direction and use new approach, able to balance risk in decision making.*
> *5.   Perspicacity - visionary, 'swims upstream' when necessary.*
> *6.   Drive for accomplishment and recognition - goal driven, energetic and appreciates recognition.*

7   Many moderating factors discussed by Wallas reflect views and values of times past.

8   Wallas (1926) Chapter 4, Stages of control, pp. 79-107. Stages have been used by others as major elements in a process, although Wallas did not tie them together in a formal definition.

9   This is modified from the definition on pp. 47 of Torrance (1988). The very comprehensive and diffuse approach to describing/definition is the whole of the description of the creative process which makes up the introduction pp. 1-21 of Ghiselin (1952). Another version of the diffuse approach is that on pp. 360, Van Grundy (1987).

10   See pp. 13-18, Perkins (1981) and pp. 170, Weisberg (1988).

11   See pp. 246, Gruber and Davis (1988). These authors have been major proponents of the case study method and their consideration of its limitations are useful.

12   See pp. 260, James (1890).

13   Scheme is a synthesis of views summarised in Langley and Jones (1988).

14   See table 17.1 on pp. 434, Tardif and Sternberg (1988). Only cognitive characteristics that four or more authors discuss are listed.

15   It is ironic that simulators, which are designed to optimise procedures where creativity is not called for, are probably ideal for exploring creativity issues (*Example 3*). However, they are expensive to own and operate.

16   See pp. 170 and whole of chapter 8, Simonton (1984).

17   Influences of all types affected all of these authors. The body of work of each author shows influence down to an individual level, as do individual manuscripts.

18   Hayes evidence and discussion supports the importance of social conditions and differences in environmental interactions in producing differences in creativity. See Hayes, (1989).

19   See pp. 294, Feldman (1988).

20   See Fig 13.1, pp. 329, Csikszentmihalyi (1988).

21   William Harvey (1578-1657) applied unsuccessfully for a grant from the Medical Research Council to support his studies on circulatory physiology. The publication of the MRC research grant reports from more than 300 years ago reveals the honest endeavours of a group of scientists to judge the potential of the work of others in a process not too dissimilar from what occurs currently. It also demonstrates how difficult such judgements are and how fragile the 'field' is in detecting truly 'creative' events.

22   The last two decades have seen several 'science events' where making the field receptive has started with a press release. This approach bypasses the rigour of peer review and the demonstration of reproducability.

23   See comments on preparation of 'fields' as related to science (5.4.2) and note[22]. This is not just a feature of science. Hence Wordsworth's letter to Lady Beaumont:

> *Every great and original writer, in proportion as he is great and original, must himself create the taste by which he is to be relished.*

Note also that many creatives in the arts and sciences reject this.

24 There are instances where individuals feel overloaded with information. In high workload situations on flightdecks, where continual reformulation of the state of progress is required, flightdeck crew have asked for 'declutter' switches. On-line information services have the potential to saturate individuals.

25 See pp. 109-111, Koestler (1964).

26 See pp. 106-107 and Fig.8, Koestler (1964).

6 Creativity and ritual in organisations

There is growing interest in the creative process in organisations. This partly reflects the realisation that creativity and innovation are linked, though these linkages are not well understood. Another reason for interest is the acceptance of the fundamental role creativity has had in altering human existence, and that it underlies in some way the accelerating rate of change in organisational environments. As the environment looms large in understanding creativity (5.4.2, 5.4.3), knowing the effects of the organisation on people's creativity and the effects of people's creativity on the organisation, is necessary.

Creative extremes occur within most individuals on an almost daily basis, but the raw content of these mental journeys is not easily assimilated by other individuals, either alone, and particularly not in groups. Organisations are no different, with creativity posing perceived and real threats, which are countered by a variety of organisational behaviours. Some organisations appear to go further by evolving cultures in which creativity is systematically corralled and controlled. Some see technology as a means of achieving this subjugation. The extent to which creativity is dampened and is fostered in organisations is considered in this chapter.

6.1 Creativity in organisations

Many in organisations are involved in some type of creative activity, albeit relatively infrequently. This involvement is illustrated in the following example.

Example 7 Sanitising creativity[1]
John cocked his head encouragingly, and again Olivia started to speak. Again Roger interrupted and continued with the point he had been making intermittently for the last twenty minutes. John sighed. Looking into the middle distance and avoiding eye contact, he went quickly though some of the rules of brainstorming for the third time that morning. John knew that brainstorming with this group did not work as well as it once had. Perhaps it had never worked well, but as he had no real experience with any other technique, and as he had not been able to persuade his organisation to consider testing alternatives, he felt powerless. If only Roger would

not interrupt and give Olivia a chance. He suggested that the group take a short break.

Roger reflected on his attempts to improve his organisation's ability to generate ideas. About twelve months previously he had carried out a literature search on brainstorming. At that time his confidence in his facilitation abilities had been high, and he had wanted to improve the idea generation sessions that he was being increasingly asked to take part in. He was troubled by what he found, for it appeared that the least effective method for generating ideas was brainstorming. The effectiveness of all methods had been measured and all other techniques had been shown to be superior[2]. For some time he wondered why his organisation persisted in using a technique which was so discredited. The person to whom he reported, the senior manager for corporate development, seemed neither surprised nor particularly interested in his observations, but had suggested that he visit some other organisations within and outside their industry and see what they were doing.

This had been a revealing exercise. The frequency with which organisations used brainstorming as their only idea generating technique was only matched by the frequency with which the technique was used incorrectly. After five site visits, Roger also spent a day with an organisation responsible for standards, and the development and dissemination of best management practices. His conclusions had not been changed by this visit, though he thought that that organisation had played a part in making such an unsatisfactory process so widespread.

As he repeatedly confirmed the findings of his initial literature review, he had begun to realise that there must be other factors which were anchoring organisations to such an ineffective business activity. For reasons not clear to him, brainstorming was perceived as beneficial and these benefits must have been large enough to outweigh its known deficiencies in idea generation. When he told his mentor, an industrial psychologist in another organisation, of the trouble he was having in understanding the reasons for the 'brainstorming paradox', his mentor had reminded him about the propensity for organisations to act as havens for particular types of people. His mentor had elaborated this theme, saying business organisations, universities and government departments could all be considered as types of 'sheltered workshops', the key difference being that each set of employees clustered in each work place because it alone could protect them from a unique set of issues. Roger had initially puzzled over this comment but had gradually come to realise that his fruitless attempts to improve idea generation were related to the degree of certainty, and 'shelter', that his fellow employees needed from their work place.

Creativity of organisations is mostly due to the creativity of individuals who are not 'creatives'. Attempts to entrain this creativity have often floundered, as in the example. There are many reasons why creativity is not readily apparent in many organisations. Four possibilities are:

1.) A significant proportion of people are not creative (6.2).
2.) Most people are creative but their creativity is very different from that of 'creatives' and it is not readily recognised (6.2).

3.) The creativity of individuals is affected by working in groups (6.3).
4.) The creativity of people in groups like organisations is even more different because of specific environmental interactions (6.3).

The linkages between dampened creativity and other organisational factors in the example are considered later (6.4.2, 6.6, 6.7).

6.2 The creativity of everyone

While there is little doubt that there is variation in the creative capacity of individuals, in the way individuals can entrain their creative process, and in the environmental interactions affecting an individual's creativity, there is no evidence for different creative processes. This could reflect the difficulty in obtaining contrary evidence.

This book assumes that there is only one type of creativity, but has not clarified whether the creativity attributes that have been described (Chapter 5) accurately reflect the creativity of everyone. This uncertainty is due to selection bias, typified by the focus on the creative individual (5.2.2, 5.2.3). How extreme this bias can be is well illustrated by the controversy that exists between those who regard genius and its creativity as the highest expression of humanity, while others see it as a form of mental abnormality (Post, 1994).

Kessel (1989) assembled evidence which suggested that creative output only came from strengths, rather than weaknesses, in very gifted individuals, but others have suggested that there are complex links between the labelling of mental abnormality, psychopathology and creativity (Becker, 1978, Jamison, 1989; Ludwig, 1994). In a study of the lives of 291 world-famous men, Post (1994) found that severe personality deviations were unduly frequent in visual artists and writers and that these disorders might be linked to some kinds of valuable creativity. To counter this, Post (1994) also noted the juxtaposition of creative achievement with drive, perseverance, industry and meticulousness, coupled with emotional warmth, a gift for friendship and a general sociability. In a study of self image and creativity in late adolescents, subjects who were more creative had better psychosocial function, with more self-assurance and greater social confidence (Smith and Taguan, 1992).

While it is unlikely that either psychopathology or psychosocial maldevelopment underlie creative contributions in organisations, linkages to being more gifted or being more self-assured may also not apply. Thus, it is difficult to glean any clues from these polarising commentaries as to how our understanding of creativity should be broadened or otherwise modified for a more general context.

6.2.1 Evidence for differences in creativity

Most testing of creative talent points to it being normally distributed and that creative efficacy varies more in relation to motivation than to inborn talent[3]. Hennessey and Amabile (1988) suggested that there is only one form of creativity, irrelevant of the domain (art or science), and that this creativity is a continuous underlying dimension and has degrees which can be detected and agreed upon. Some have distinguished levels, but others have argued that these do not adequately describe the creative capacity of a person and other dimensions are required (Nagasundaram and Bostrom, 1995).

In considering the measurement of creativity, Langley and Jones (1988)[4] have taken an extreme view which is that humans at large possess no general creativity capability, which implies that no such component exists to be measured. Instead, they see humans possessing a wealth of knowledge structures indexed by concepts that the individual judges to be important. Thus, creativity depends on knowledge, an indexing scheme and the particular situation in which the individual is placed. Whether this is, or is not, a creativity capability seems to be unnecessarily precise in a very imprecise area. Others have proposed a variety of measures (Torrance, 1988; Kirton, 1994). None of these observations provide any real help in appreciating how the recognised attributes of creativity (Chapter 5) should be altered, if at all, for those not seen to be creatives. Some examples of creativity in everyone follow.

Humour Some forms of humour are creative[5]. While there is a large range in how spontaneously funny individuals are, those that are obviously funny occur everywhere, qualifying humour as a manifestation of creativity in anyone. This creativity can appear under difficult and at times threatening situations. Spontaneous humour is distinct from joke telling, which is a habitual form (6.5) found where less creative individuals congregate. The wide background of the spontaneously funny must also be distinguished from the narrow origin of those who use humour as a tool[6]. The creativity underlying humour does not rely on extensive knowledge and is not dependent upon critical acknowledgment, both features of the creativity of 'creatives'.

Response to chronic illness The advent of a chronic degenerative condition is as much a threat to the coping abilities of the individual and their social support systems as the disease process is to their physiology. In chronic diseases, many learn to live with symptoms even though they are grossly disabling. Yet, the same, or even less severe symptoms, occurring acutely are quite devastating in their effects. Whether these coping responses are created, or are conditioned responses, is debated. Many of these unfortunate people are able to describe and manipulate their coping behaviours, pointing to their creativity being engaged.

Many of the accommodations that individuals make are based on sound physiology, yet they know no physiology, are unselected for intelligence, have had no useful exposure to a health system, and have received no explanation or suggestion on how to make themselves relatively symptom free[7]. If these accommodations result from the creativity of everyone, then it is possible to appreciate how this creativity may differ. In making symptoms of organ dysfunction insignificant, time seems to be required, for acute dysfunction of the same degree leaves many helpless. The time required for the creative capability to be engaged can be in the order of days, but is usually much longer. Another feature is motivation, in that the dysfunction to be overcome restricts a key capability, such as mobility, nutrition, excretion, communication or reproduction. Finally, knowledge does not appear to be as prominent factor as it does in the creative activities of creatives (5.6).

6.2.2 Summary

One difference in the creativity of everyone is in the use of knowledge. It appears to be less necessary for the existing state of knowledge to be complete, and a more pragmatic and practical form of knowledge suffices. This difference is a matter of degree (5.6.1, 5.6.2, 5.6.3) and exceptions abound. Much of the knowledge important for the creativity of everyone is 'person-embodied'[8] and is not readily transferable. The domains (5.4.2) for creatives and everyone else must overlap to a great extent, although the exploration of the domain, and how actively an individual has engaged with its elements may be different There may be a greater propensity for creatives to explore the symbolic system of a domain.

Another area of difference in the creativity of everyone lies in field effects (5.4.3), or the process of acknowledgment. Field effects in organisations are powerful and often restrictive (6.4, 6.6). However, a 'make-or-break' role for the field is not present for most people outside work. Critical acknowledgment of a creative endeavour has little meaning, compared with the power that the 'field' has on creatives (Csikszentmihaly, 1988).

An area where the overlap will be considerable will be in the temporal attributes with insight, gestation and incorporation (5.5) being similar for creatives and others. Similarly, an obstruction is a powerful motivating factor for all, although this may be less apparent in the creativity of 'creatives', because their desire to progress the focal area of their creativity requires less stimulus. Taken together it appears that the creativity of everyone is less dependent upon having appropriate input and output circumstances and may be less focussed and more diffuse. The creativity of everyone is likely to have some differences to that of 'creatives', but these are small.

6.3 Creativity in organisational groups

In exploring the reasons why creativity might be muted in organisations, four possible explanations were put forward (6.1). The first, that a significant proportion of people are not creative, and the second, that most people are creative, but their creativity is very different from that of 'creatives', can be disregarded. If the creativity of organisations (*Example 7*) is deficient, and there are multiple reasons to believe that very few organisations are well placed in this regard[9], there are two remaining possibilities. The first is that the creativity of individuals is altered by working in groups, while the second has the same general explanation, but amplified by effects specific to organisations.

6.3.1 Creativity of groups

The creativity process in an individual appears relatively self-contained,

83

notwithstanding the interactions with domains and fields. A great deal of the process occurs within the individual and little of it is accessible (5.7). Thus, in a study on the lives and creative style of 291 highly creative people, Post (1994) observed that most worked in isolation. While many of the highly creative were gregarious, a significant number worked alone and preferred isolation for their creative activities.

It is rare for individuals to be able to share their creativity dynamically (5.7), and when they do it is often in a very focal area under very specific circumstances. While jazz players may be able to share at the illumination stage of their creativity (5.7), it is not clear that they share at other stages, nor do they share in other creative activities. Many 'creative' pairs of scientists share by handing each other the idea in turn, akin to passing a baton, rather than mutually holding it. It may be that in many situations where humans are being creative, the current creative output from another is distracting. One way to understand this distraction is to imagine what is happening within the individual in information processing terms.

For an individual to achieve insight, and be successful at the critical associative phase of creativity (Fig. 5.4), thinking processes may have to become more pliant, but at the same time more vulnerable to being distracted. Filters that normally are in place to maintain focus, sieve out noise and keep a train of thinking going, are turned down. Associative capacity is increased, but so is distractibility, and this trade-off is an inevitable effect of the way the cerebrum processes information. Part of the art of those that are creative may involve achieving awareness of their associative capability and honing it, while manipulating the environment so as to reduce its distracting capacity.

If it is accepted that distraction is an issue for the creative process, then organisations' attempts to combine the creativity's of individuals in group settings can be questioned. Indeed, considering how powerful and all pervasive human creativity is, and how rare really good examples of shared creativity are, it is remarkable that the insular nature of the creative process has been so ignored in organisations.

6.3.2 Group creativity techniques in organisations

Organisations have tried to tap the creative capacity of their people. Common techniques include brainstorming, nominal group and Delphi techniques, but there are many more. All of these attempt to generate ideas, though their processes are different. In brainstorming[10], individuals are asked to generate as many ideas as possible, to evaluate them uncritically before expressing them, express them, avoid interfering with the expression by others of their ideas, and then improve on or combine ideas already suggested. In the nominal group technique[11], individuals perform alone, either in the same work space but not necessarily so, all ideas being eventually displayed without modulation by others. In the Delphi technique, individual's ideas are collected and amalgamated into an aggregated view, which is then fed back to individuals without the originators being known. The amount of current social interaction is highest with brainstorming and least with the Delphi technique.

There are multiple studies which have demonstrated that brainstorming is the poorest of the above techniques for idea generation. Whether it be the number of ideas or their quality, brainstorming fares badly and this has been observed in a number of studies (Lamm and Trommsdorff, 1973; Diehl and Strebe, 1987; Mullen, Johnson and Salas, 1991). Mullen, Johnson and Salas (1991), using a meta-analytic approach, concluded that brainstorming was most counterproductive when the brainstorming group was comparatively large, when an authoritative observer was present, when group members vocalised their contribution, rather than wrote them down, and when the comparison group was a nominal group of individuals who were 'alone', rather than a nominal group performing together. As might be expected the reasons for the poor performance of brainstorming have been argued about, with the poor productivity being attributed to procedural mechanisms like production blocking (having to wait one's turn, interruptions by others, distractions), economic mechanisms (free riding, poor motivation, laziness) and social psychological mechanisms (evaluation apprehension, drive arousal and peer acceptance) (Mullen et al., 1991). Whatever the explanation, and with the possibility that different mechanisms will affect an organisations ability to generate and capture ideas dependent upon circumstances, the overall picture is clear. Idea generation in many organisations is flawed, with the brainstorm technique, which is so prevalent, failing to mix the creative capacity of individuals. The prevalence of brainstorming suggests that other factors in organisations must be in play, for it to be retained as an idea generating process (*Example 7*).

Manipulation of the idea generating process has occurred, with some techniques being able to produce more ideas which have particular characteristics. Some techniques are purportedly capable of generating ideas that are consistent with the prevailing activity, paradigm or strategic approach, while others generate ideas that are less supplementary and more tangential and modifying (Gryskiewicz, 1987). Hence, guided fantasy appears to generate less ideas than other approaches, but those that it produces tend to break away from existing assumptions (Nagasundaram and Bostrom, 1995). These techniques are not well known and while they may be used by 'creative' groups in organisations, their impact appears minuscule. Group decision support systems, which use computer based technologies, are being promoted for brainstorm like activities with little evidence of general effectiveness or efficiency. It is likely that some individuals can derive some benefit, but the circumstances may be limited (Connolly, Jessup and Valacich, 1990; Benbasat and Lim, (1993)).

6.3.3 Existing views on creativity modulating factors in organisations

There are multiple organisational factors that have been associated with high-creativity projects. Freedom and autonomy, challenge, sufficient resources, encouragement via the organisation, support via supervisory or work group systems, trust, and openness all have positive associations (Amabile, Conti, Coon, Lazenby and Herron, 1996). Factors that occur more frequently in low-creativity projects are intrusive organisational politics, excessive and harsh criticism of new ideas, an atmosphere of risk avoidance, and extreme workload pressure. The single most important creativity promoting factor appears to be the sense of challenge presented by the task (Nagasundaram and Bostron, 1995). Other associations have included the amount of autonomy and trust in the supervisor-subordinate relationship (Scott and Bruce, 1994). All of these are consistent with the creativity attributes that have been described previously (5.3.2, 5.4, 5.5, 5.6).

6.3.4 Summary

There are a number of factors that dampen organisational creativity. While it is very unlikely that people in organisations are non-creative, or have a form of creativity that cannot be recognised or appreciated, there is real doubt that everyone's creativity is optimally used when the creative unit is a group or team. Whenever a group approach has been used, the challenge has been to try and reduce the creativity decrement suffered by the group, compared with people working alone. Although the evidence is piecemeal and insubstantial, it is sufficient to question whether the current approaches to idea generation in organisations make much sense. In seeking explanations for why creativity is muted in organisations, it is likely that both general group effects and group effects specific to organisations are in play (6.1). These are considered in the following sections.

6.4 The threat from creativity

The threat posed to an individual by their own creativity is occasionally very significant, but for most people this threat can be reduced by a variety of ploys (6.5). Individuals are accomplished at this type of self-regulation. An individual working with others must cope with another's creativity, which can interfere with their own creative process. Intertwining another's creativity is not as straightforward as regulating one's own (6.3.4). Hence, creative activities can threaten individuals and groups within an organisation, and these threats are in addition to the threat posed by any 'newness' to organisational norms, interpretative stances and power structures. These threats are often hidden by organisations in their programmatic approaches[12] to coping with routine and change.

6.4.1 Threats and programmatic responses in organisations

Organisations are adept at keeping 'newness' corralled and controlled. Even an item as simple as a procedures manual can be inimical to individuality, a means for exerting control and a way of inhibiting creativity (Cohen, 1996). Part of the programmatic approach to change (Beer et al., 1990) is about keeping the size of change digestible for key internal and external groups, including shareholders. For example, theoretical views on quality management have workers creating solutions for the quality and value problems produced by managers and executives. However, much of the day to day practice of quality management has spared senior people. Their mouthing of 'quality mantras' has spared them from engaging with 'newness' and has allowed them to face only small amounts of change. The safety provided by the programmatic approach to quality management has made it difficult for decision makers to use 'newness' when they might want to. Other programmatic approaches based on teams, empowerment and culture change also control 'newness'.

6.4.2 Another view of the buffering of creativity

Underlying the programmatic approach to the control of creativity are more fundamental individual, group and organisational behaviours which have more direct linkages to creativity. In this book, these are called rituals (6.5). Individuals use rituals most effectively in their own lives (6.5.2-6.5.5) and rituals are widespread inside and outside organisations (6.6). In *Example 7*, the brainstorming approach was not really successful. The facilitator's supervisor and his mentor both knew that the work environment was extensively permeated by complex behaviours which limited creativity. In that organisation, the approach to idea creation had been sanitised by rituals. These rituals were part of the organisation (6.6), the system that it existed in (6.7), and the people that were attracted to that particular work place. Ritual will now be considered in some detail.

6.5 Ritual

Few humans devote themselves completely to creative pursuits, for most spend considerable time in routine activities. Some of these are given their constancy by our physiology, while others are stereotyped because of the benefits derived from existing behaviours. Even child behaviour is marked by scripts and scenarios which capture regular features of many endeavours[13]. While 'creatives' and their creativity are noteworthy, even they devote considerable time to habitual activities.

Humans are gregarious. Groupings of all types have both habitual and creative activities. Long term healthy relationships of all sorts abound with habitual endeavours. These are characterised by a plethora of productive and enjoyable habits which are spotted with episodes of individual creativity. Sharing occurs in the exploration of ideas, but considerable time is devoted to both useful and pointless routines. These routines provide a matrix for all relationships, with the matrix acting as a glue for many couples.

6.5.1 Ritual, rite and creativity

The routines that bind groups of people together are collections of non-creative behaviours. The word 'non-creative' is cumbersome and negative, particularly when applied to behaviours which are necessary and meaningful for individuals. The opposite of creative, 'destructive', misses the mark completely. A solution is to equate non-creative to an absence of creativity, rather than its opposite. In this book, two terms will be used for behaviours where there is an absence of creativity. For those that are unremarkable, customary and routine the word 'rite' will be used. For those whose orchestrated characteristics have links to creativity, the word 'ritual' will be used (Fig.6.1).

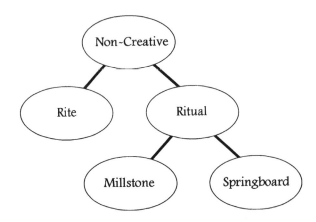

Figure 6.1 The approach used in this book to differentiate non-creative behaviours. Millstone and springboard rituals are behaviours that provide settings for non-creative or creative activities.

Rituals are themselves non-creative but some act as starting points, or platforms, or linkage behaviours for creative and non-creative activities. It is useful to distinguish two types of ritual. One type promotes creative behaviours and these can be thought of as springboards (Fig. 6.1). Those rituals that are linked in someway to non-creative behaviours are millstones (Fig. 6.1).

Some association between rituals and creative human activity has long been entertained. Thus, the ritualised mourning songs of the Rauto people are thought to transform socially disruptive grief and anger into culturally creative emotions (Maschio, 1992). The ritualism of religion, and perhaps religion itself, has the capacity to inspire and create, as well as to deceive and dampen (Ross and Ross, 1983).

In contrast, rites lack creative association. There are a variety of rites that are clustered around the constraints and demands produced by human physiology. Thus, rites abound around sleep, feeding, excretion, and reproduction. Although these rites are culturally coloured, their recurring presence attests to their importance[14]. Psychological needs also underlie a number of rites. Among many, the need for control and the need for a worthy internal image of the self drive individual rites, rites in relationships and the rites of larger groups[15]. Rites also abound in all societies. Birth, marriage, death, mourning, aging, retirement, family occasions, entertainment, worship, initiation, military service, education, sport and many other activities are peppered with rites.

There are many occasions where ritual and rite are mixed. For example, modern sporting activities are complex admixtures of rites and rituals involving players and spectators. The distinction of ritual from rite needs no further consideration here, because ritual and its relationship to creativity is the key issue. 'Ritual' is not an ideal word, but it is connected with rites[16], both encompassing custom, practice and particularly habit, the latter implying a 'customary manner of acting'. Thus, 'ritual' in this book is defined as ,

A customary manner of acting, a complex behaviour which is linked positively or negatively to creativity

This use of 'ritual' ignores Freud's link between 'ritual' and oedipal conflict[17], though it is not at odds with 'ritual' having negative consequences. It is consistent with the 'liminal' aspects of 'ritual', namely its creative, playful and spontaneous elements[18]. Some differentiate 'rite' as being concrete, particular and referring to an action, while 'ritual' is general, abstract and referring to an idea[19]. Elements of this distinction are apt, particularly the concreteness of the former versus the pliability, depth, richness and complexity of the latter. However, the key differentiating factor for 'ritual' in this book is the presence of a negative or positive link between 'ritual' and creativity (Fig. 6.1).

6.5.2 Locus-of-control and ritual

In this consideration of ritual and its capacity to act as a springboard or a millstone for creativity, a scheme is required (Fig. 6.2) to clarify the effects of ritual that impinge upon the innovative capacity of organisations. One dimension for considering rituals is the separation of rituals by their capacity to act as springboards or millstones for an individual's creativity. Another dimension relates to the locus-of-control that individuals have with respect to a ritual.

Locus-of-control ranges from an internal locus-of-control where the individual actively initiates, manipulates and controls the ritual for its capacity to enhance creativity, to an external locus-of-control where the ritual is not orchestrated or controlled by the individual and the involvement is relatively passive (Fig. 6.2). Locus-of-control has not been seen as a useful concept for understanding creativity (5.4.2) where the environment has a much more complex interrelationship with the individual. However, in looking at rituals as stages or linkages to creativity, the locus-of-control concept is useful, both generally and for understanding organisational rituals. Some general examples follow.

6.5.3 Internal locus-of-control rituals

In general terms these are the rituals that individuals use to initiate or continue creative activities. They are behaviours which enable people to be creative. Thus, artists, writers and composers often have patterns surrounding the place and time at which they can work creatively. The rituals are very much orchestrated by the individual and many of these have been documented (Koestler, 1964)[20].

Groups also orchestrate rituals which provide platforms for creative activities. Thus, advertising agencies are adept in how they form groups and how they have their groups work. Again the locus-of-control is internal, even though the advertising brief is an externally generated task (Fig. 6.2).

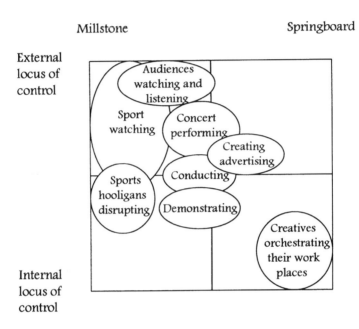

Figure 6.2. **The horizontal dimension separates rituals by their capacity to act as millstones or as springboards for creativity. The vertical dimension separates rituals by the locus-of-control of the person involved in the ritual. In general terms, individual's rituals become more likely to enhance creativity as the locus-of-control becomes more internal (6.5.3, 6.5.4, 6.5.5).**

6.5.4 External locus-of-control rituals

Rituals surround the appreciation of the creativity of others. Looking, watching and listening are ritual behaviours within which an individual uses their own creativity in assimilating new material. Rituals regulate the amount of material which might be assimilated. They are not generally orchestrated by the individual and have an external locus-of-control (Fig. 6.2).

Watching rituals A goal of a gallery is to display art in a way which allows it to be fully appreciated by many types of people, and which ensures that the art itself is not degraded by this activity. Many art galleries achieve the latter, but in so doing they induce viewing rituals. There is a diligence, almost a homage from viewers, which is conducted in relative silence. The quiet deference of most viewers may be part of their assimilation process, or may be their adherence to rules, but there are also ritualistic elements which are induced by the mode of display, the structure of galleries and the behaviour of gallery staff.

Audience participation rituals Opera, ballet or concerts are arenas of ritual for performers and audience alike. The form of such occasions is relatively stereotyped. Thus, in a concert there is an introductory item, followed by a lesser known or slightly experimental piece before the interval. After, there is a major work from a relatively limited set. In creatively engaging with the performance, the audience does so in a passive way that is controlled. Undoubtedly, a significant factor for encouraging these mass rituals is the need to optimise the process of appreciation for as many people as possible. The behaviour of performers during and at the end of opera, ballet and concerts is also highly patterned and ritualised. There is a linkage here with the relatively muted way in which any performer can alter a role by their own creativity. Both the performer and the audience are passive participants in a series of complex rituals which they find enjoyable.

6.5.5 Mixed

There are rituals where the locus-of-control is mixed or of a more intermediate type.

Demonstrators and public display rituals Demonstrations have become arenas of ritual for demonstrators and spectators. Repetition and rigidity in the form of the demonstration have anaesthetised spectators to the implications of the demonstrators' different point of view. Control of the form of the demonstration has relegated spectators to being just another audience and limited the capacity of a demonstration to recruit. The rawness of the dissent of the demonstrator has also been channelled or corralled by the rituals involved in the modern form of street demonstration. The mixed nature of the locus-of-control in demonstrations reflects the use of ritual by authorities to dampen engagement by audiences and the use of ritual by demonstrators as a means of exhibiting their unique way of grappling with an issue. The format of demonstrations allows 'control' and 'voice' simultaneously. Thus, the ritual displays of dissent by demonstrators give some expression of their creative engagement with an issue, but the overall structure of the demonstration cocoons the display and dampens its impact on others.

Sports watching rituals Sporting occasions are remarkable for spectator rites, before, during and after an occasion, and for player rites within the game itself. Rituals also abound at sporting occasions. Part of the attraction for spectators is the occasional 'play' which, because of its ritualism, produces something long remembered, spoken about, and which creatively engages watchers. The same ritual elements have been applied to bar room scenes in cowboy movies and the antics of human-machine combinations in current major film releases. The locus-of-control is mixed. The linkage of sports teams to groupings of people, either locally or nationally induces other rituals which are much less orchestrated than those of normal sports watchers. These rituals can be damaging to the individual and to society. Potentially more harmful is the capacity of these rituals to divert individuals from creative engagement with issues of substance.

6.6 Ritual in organisations

There are many rites and rituals in organisations. Some rituals exclude individuals from making unique contributions, while others, ostensibly designed to facilitate creativity, consume time and produce little that is new (*Example 7*). This section describes some rituals related to repetitive work, leadership and the alignment of behaviour[21]. Others have described organisational initiation rituals which limit a newcomer's contribution (Bolman, 1991).

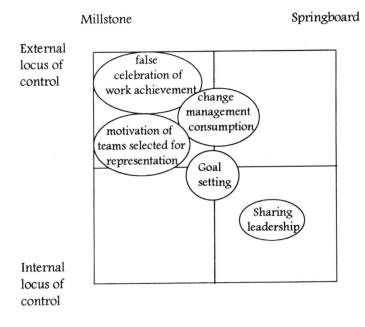

Figure 6.3. The separation of ritual behaviours in organisations is along the
same dimensions as in Fig. 6.2. Interorganisational variation is
large. For example, sharing of leadership can be ritualised in a
way which will promote creativity, but it can easily be
ritualised in a detrimental way (6.6.2).

6.6.1 Rituals associated with repetitive tasks

A key concern of an organisation is the achievement of an optimal level of employee motivation, and contribution to continuous improvement in the face of repetitive tasks. This is particularly an issue when the work of an individual is highly ordered, with little opportunity for the individual to make a unique contribution and with the organisation unwilling to recognise the value of well-performed routine work. Rituals may be used to cover over this sameness by the false celebration of achievement, the consumption of change management rhetoric and the formation of dysfunctional teams. Underlying these is a failure to recognise the value of work that is repetitive, resulting in activities which misrepresent routine.

Achievement rituals There are a series of rituals in some organisations which relate to the way work achievement is presented. Any work, which is meaningless, has little fulfilment, and is marked by sameness, can be given a heroic dimension by a ritual (Hopfl, 1994). Rituals can actually trivialise work and numb people to the implications of sameness. Thus, work achievement which is relatively mediocre can be celebrated with a recognised ritual. For the organisation, this ritual worsens the return on investment of an unsatisfactory activity, while the 'false achiever' is distanced from learning and contributing to improvement. These ceremonially blessed artifices[22] can deceive on-lookers and produce an insidious from of self deception. False celebration is a significant ritualistic barrier to creative contribution and is an orchestrated activity outside the control of the individual (Fig. 6.3).

Change management rituals There are organisational rituals related to change which involve all individuals. Most organisations regularly flirt with management evangelists and prophets of change management. These travellers engage in rituals, with an unreflective and opportunistic approach related to mastery of individuals (Hopfl, 1994). Many of their offerings have a recognisable and extensive religious rhetoric, although it has been suggested that they are more related to magic than religion[23]. A proportion of individuals in organisations appear to ritualistically consume this change management material, many seeing it as part of their yearly activity. The ritual consumption of change management reassures, but it is expensive and its effects are transient. Instead of change initiatives being tailored to an organisation, the process of consuming the offerings of visiting change agents allows individuals to wall change off. Creative engagement by individuals is made less likely by this ritual, despite them having a semblance of choice (Fig. 6.3).

Team motivation rituals There are rituals related to team motivation which can obstruct the essential advantage of a team, namely the mingling of knowledge, skills, personalities and behaviours, such that in combination there is a greater and more unique contribution than the sum of the contributions of individuals. Teams selected for reasons of representation, rather than for complementary capabilities, are potentially dysfunctional, either in terms of productivity, creativity or both. These teams abound in rituals which dampen an individual's willingness to contribute.

Similarly, team celebration can be steeped in rituals, which too often fail to give the individual something truly desired, and too often leave emptiness and doubt about each individual's contribution. Under a guise of being a grouping that brings about improvement, teams can be just another means of achieving repetitive work, with detrimental rituals being partly responsible. Teams do not necessarily shift the locus of control for individuals from external to internal, particularly when teams are selected for reasons of representation (Fig. 6.3).

6.6.2 Rituals and organisational leadership

Leadership tasks can be divided into design and implementation components (Fig. 6.4). Rituals abound around leaders with some being orchestrated by the leader, but others arising from employees or outsiders (6.7). Two leader dependent and one employee dependent leadership rituals are considered.

TASK	DESIGN	IMPLEMENTATION
Clarify/focus	Goal setting*	Achieve buy-in
Resource -capital	Provision	Allocation
-labour	Selection	Empower
-processes	Systems	Integration/improvement
Motivate	Create values	Model behaviour
Acquire new technology	Detect	Mix with strategy/people
Bring about learning	Processes/systems	Monitor and use
Innovate	Innovation process	Facilitate champions
Share leadership	Complementary team*	Team decision making
Focus on customers	Customer interface	Direct contact/monitoring

Figure 6.4 A matrix[24] which breaks up leadership tasks into design and implementation components. Two design components (*) are discussed in the text.

Goal setting rituals Leaders give clarity and focus to an organisation by goal setting and persuading people to make these goals their own. The design component of this task is the setting of goals. The leader must create an unambiguous form of a goal which engages people and resides comfortably within the values of the organisation. Leader ratings are linked very specifically to the achievement of organisational goals, but many of these are largely orchestrated by markets. The narrowness of these goals can be numbing, with leaders having little room to move. Despite the leader creating the goal, the locus-of-control can be relatively external, such that goal setting becomes ritualised in a way which dampens leadership creativity and makes the designing and communication of goals humdrum and routine.

Sharing leadership rituals Leaders broaden their leadership capacity and give their organisations the capability of coping with external variation by sharing their leadership. The design component of this task involves the leader creating a complementary team. The leader must blend people competencies, knowledge and motivational patterns to compensate for the leader's and others' deficiencies. Few leaders create leadership teams de novo, many being faced with the task of blending new people into the existing leadership team. There are many ploys that are used to make people's differences visible and valued. Some use assessment tools which can enhance the appreciation of differences[25], but judgment is required in employing these devices as their use can easily be ritualised. Once ritualised, the value from differences becomes lost in 'boxed' descriptions of people that stunts a leaders capacity to bring about higher levels of functioning. The complexity of these tools, their capacity to give an external locus-of-control, the temptation to interpret them quickly and in an ad hoc manner, can swiftly dampen a leader's capacity to design an effective team (Fig. 6.3).

Employee leadership rituals There is another set of rituals surrounding leaders which has less to do with the leaders themselves, and more to do with followers' beliefs, perceptions and expectations of leaders. These have a mixed locus-of-control. Thus, the perception that leaders are adverse to experimentation and are uncomfortable with messages about failure occurs in some organisations. This perception leads to rituals which keep innovations 'secret', thus directly impairing the creative capacity of an organisation. Beliefs about 'superhuman' capabilities of leaders produce rituals which have employees exaggerating a leader's physical and mental capacities, and unnecessarily exaggerating the loneliness of the leader. Loneliness in a muted form is a feature of good leadership, but excessive isolation can remove some of the stimuli which leaders require to be creative (6.4).

6.6.3 Rituals surrounding the alignment of behaviours

From the time of induction to the time of dismissal or retirement, alignment of each employee's behaviour is a significant issue for an organisation. Codes of behaviour, statements of values, rules, vision, mission, guiding principles and goals are all outcomes of behavioural alignment activities. In time there is a tendency for behavioural alignment activities to be ritualised. There is always the risk with behavioural alignment that instead of providing a common base from which individuals can express their individuality, the base position increasingly stifles and inhibits. This need not be a passive process, for some behavioural alignment activities, such as the procedures manual and vision development occasions are very ritualising. These entities, and the way they are produced, can be key elements in rituals, which primarily constrain an individual's creativity in the work place (Cohen, 1996).

Repetition is part of the reason why a behavioural alignment activity loses its freshness. This applies to those presenting and those participating in the behavioural alignment activity. Those carrying out the alignment activity are aware of the shift to less useful rituals and try to counter it with the continual introduction of new programs. Even these can become a restricting ritual, because the 'newness' of each program eventually causes employee cynicism and disengagement. External behavioural alignment programs are difficult to tailor to any organisation and this 'foreign' character reinforces ritualised disregard.

6.7 Background factors in organisational rituals

There are factors internal and external to organisations that make rites and rituals more likely.

6.7.1 Internal to the organisation

Organisations can be prone to activities which reinforce a person's organisational identity without defining their work. These have given rise to terms as the logic of confidence (Meyer and Rowan, 1992) and 'face work' (Goffman, 1967). Together, these activities maintain the plausibility and legitimacy of the organisation. Goffman (1967) has identified facets of 'face work' which ensure that an individual's goals and the organisations purpose can remain dissociated[26]. An unwanted consequence is that the dissociated nature of these rituals is a powerful inhibitor of creativity.

This dissociation is also visible in the tension that exists between groups, units or departments and their achievement of technical excellence, and the need for sharing of this excellence in cross-functional activities. Again, dissociation between a group's goals and organisational purpose can give rise to rituals which inhibit creativity. This tension is inevitable, but if it is not surfaced and managed, it leads to rituals which are counterproductive and anti-creative.

New technology in work places, whether it be it's development, selection or its implementation is also surrounded by rituals, some being harmless but many being counter productive (Landauer, 1995). The goals of much office automation are productivity related, but 'face work', in terms of giving an organisation legitimacy and plausibility, often drives the presence of machines, rather than any specific advantages that they might provide. While technology will be considered in detail later (Chapter 7), it is important to realise that some goals surrounding the acquisition of new technology, particularly office technology, can be poorly aligned with organisational purpose. This dissociation drives rituals which stunt creativity.

6.7.2 External to the organisation

Organisations operate in environments where success depends in part upon how closely the organisation aligns itself with the rules of the overarching bureaucracy (Meyer and Rowan, 1992). These rules can create conflicts and inconsistencies for organisations, because the 'ceremonial' rules related to meeting technical and efficiency requirements come from poorly aligned parts of the bureaucracy.

Common examples include the university that maintains a department which is deemed to be appropriate, because of the 'ceremonial' rules of a tertiary education system, but which functions independent of student need. Similarly, hospitals acquire an expensive technology for a prestige 'myth' (Meyer and Rowan, 1992), but current health services largely do not require it. This results in some costs being factored into services and the device being committed to a type of research which is unsatisfactory, because research direction is dictated by technology. Health systems are rich in examples, for multiple groups have legitimately placed a technical or efficiency demand upon a hospital or community service, without taking into account others' parallel demands.

Companies are also prey to the need for alignment with either a local bureaucracy or, in the case of multinational subsidiaries, the additional task of aligning with the centre of their organisation. These situations promote rituals, because the structural and functional inconsistencies produced by variations in the bureaucratic environment distort values, goals and roles. These confuse and obstruct individuals in their attempts to make unique contributions. The need for certainty has meant that many organisations try to influence how much alignment they have to make with the varying and inconsistent demands of their operating environment[27]. In some cases, these external efforts are as much about making an organisation's internal environment less ambiguous as they are about ordering the external world. The need to reduce ambiguities often result in rituals, many of them shackling creativity in a way not easy to resolve.

6.8 Summary

This chapter has moved from the general effects of an environment and other factors on an individual's creativity (Chapter 5) to the specific effects within an organisation. For the individual at work, the organisational environment looms large as a determinant of an individual's creativity in the work place. This chapter has emphasised that the environment does not solely consist of domain and field elements, but is also the behavioural milieu of an organisation.

The creativity of everyone, in contrast with the creative, probably differs a little, being less demanding about what is required for creativity and its acknowledgment, as well as being less focussed. A key factor in organisations is the effect of other's creativity on the creativity of the individual, with both general effects and specific effects from groups in organisations. While the domain and field are assumed to have the same importance for individuals outside and inside the work place, the effects of groups in organisations imposes behavioural filters that dominate the work environment, positively and negatively, and orchestrate individual's creativity.

The behavioural 'filter' imposed by the organisation has been explained using the complex behavioural entity of the ritual. The features of this use of ritual are its positive and negative linkages to creativity with locus-of-control being a key factor (Fig. 6.5). In general, an internal locus-of-control promotes rituals that are creativity promoting and an external locus-of-control promotes rituals that are creativity inhibiting. In the external world, rituals are powerful orchestrators of creativity and the world within organisations is similar. The organisational rituals that are described in this chapter have generally been those that dampen creativity, as few organisations would say that their creativity is sufficient, or is sufficiently expressed. The next section focuses on one part of the organisational environment, namely that which is dominated by complex technology which requires humans and machines share tasks. The importance of rituals and their capacity to modulate creativity in technologically complex environments is addressed in the last section.

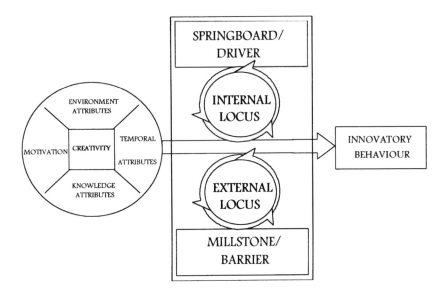

Figure 6.5 The 'ritual filter' in an organisation (large box). This produces field effects and is capable of promoting or inhibiting innovatory behaviour.

Notes

1   This example is fiction. It reflects an aggregated view from experiences in many organisations in Australia in period 1992-1997.
2   See 6.3.2 for a limited review on efficacy of brainstorming compared with other organisational idea generation techniques.
3   See pp. 14, Osborn (1953). Osborn does not provide evidence.
4   See pp. 199, Langley and Jones (1988).
5   See pp. 93-96, Koestler (1964).
6   Humour is used as a tool by some leaders. This form of humour is not universal nor manipulative but is part of the way some grapple with motivation.
7   There are degenerative disorders of the nervous system which particularly damage the body's capability to keep blood pressure at an appropriate level. See pp. 468-469 of Adams and Victor (1993). These disorders are rare, take a long time to evolve and can afflict any human in middle age, unrelated to socioeconomic class, upbringing, training, occupation or known environmental factor. The following coalesces a number of clinical encounters of the author and demonstrates how some health care consumers (patients) achieve partial symptom resolution:

The first manifestation of poor blood pressure control is usually associated with changes in posture. Normally, any postural change which alters the height of the brain with respect to the heart (from lying to sitting or standing) results in a rapid sensing of blood pressure decline due to gravitational effects on the level of blood pressure. This sensing of blood pressure decline is carried out by the nervous system. It results in nervous system responses which restore arterial pressure such that the amount of blood entering the brain is once again sufficient to meet the brain's needs. When this reflex control system becomes damaged, consumers experience 'fainting' like symptoms with postural changes, most commonly in getting out of bed in the morning. Consumers often develop novel solutions to the problem of not being able to buffer the blood pressure drop that occurs.

Almost all learn without instruction that symptoms can be ameliorated by slowing the speed at which they get up. Some consumers first seek medical help for unrelated problems. It is only on detailed questioning that the difficulty they have had with arising from bed comes to light. They admit to increasing difficulty over several years in getting up without feeling faint.

Their ability to create novel behaviours related to body posture results in them remaining symptom free. Postural plays include getting up in a staged sequence or sitting on the edge of their bed reading for a while. Arising from bed can last up to 20 minutes rather than up to 20 seconds. Sometimes when disability is more pronounced and in situations where there is little time, consumers will leave their bedside in seemingly bizarre postures. Thus, some start moving by walking around bent at the hips with their trunk nearly horizontal. This posture is physiologically appropriate, because the spatial relationship between the heart and the head is maintained at that of the recumbent position and gravitational effects on blood pressure in the head are minimised..

8   See pp. 62-63, Industry Commission (1995).

9   Personal observations from being an Australian Quality Award Evaluator from 1992-1996.

10   See pp. 96-100, Morgan (1993), or pp. 24-27, Howell (1995).

11   An appreciation of the different techniques and others is best obtained by reading the references in section 6.3.2.

12   See Beer et al., (1990) for a criticism of the programmatic approach to change. See also pp. 361-363, Van Grundy (1987).

13   See pp. 27-28, Gardner (1995). See also discussion on pp. 121-123, Reason (1987).

14   Some examples of physiologically bounded rites include those related to sleep onset and excretion.
Sleep onset rites
The importance of episodes of rapid eye movement (REM) sleep is well recognised. REM sleep is vulnerable to many factors including light, noise, discomfort, time zone shift and medication. Many of the rites surrounding the start of sleeping can be interpreted as REM promoting. These are very variable, and can include washing, praying, meditation, reading, noise and light reduction. Rites have been observed in significant numbers of adult American college students, either in the form of a preparation behaviour or in the use of a 'sleep transition object'. See Markt and Johnson (1993).
Excretion rites
Habitual behaviours are a feature of excretion. The ability to store urine and faeces allows individuals choice with the use of their time. In some species excretion is a time of vulnerability. In many species, physiological systems have evolved which allow some control over the period of storage, and thus some choice as to the time when the storage function is changed to an excretion function. For this control to provide the greatest advantage, excretion, when it is chosen to occur, must be as complete as possible. In some humans, rites used to assist in making emptying as complete as possible, include isolation, timing related to meals, and a variety of diverting activities such as reading and contemplation.

15   Psychological needs underlie rites. Examples related to exercise (individual), consumer and doctor (diads), and groups (scientific meetings) follow:
Exercise preparation
For some, there is significant enjoyment in preparing for exercise which is in addition to the pleasure obtained from physical exertion. Windsurfing, skiing and cycling are sporting activities where the rite of donning special clothing can be a key attraction. There are also rites related to the 'warming up' before many exercises, which are as much an opportunity for display as they for inducing suppleness and flexibility.
Consumer-doctor behaviours
There are behaviours exhibited by consumers and doctors which are a combined rite, requiring

inputs from both for their contact to be successful (See pp. 47-95, Goffman (1967); see pp. 95 and chapter, Farr and Markova (1995)). The examples given by Goffman are mainly from psychiatric ward situations, but they are directly applicable to all doctor-consumer encounters. In those consumers where belief in the 'magical' part of medicine is important for symptom resolution, this partnering rite may be a factor in achieving the desired outcome. Some clinicians have been able to play their part in this combined rite, being able to use their and their consumers' capabilities to great effect. Other clinicians have sheltered in less productive rites, for reasons of dependence, control and doubt of self-worth.

Communication in science meetings

Communication is an important part of the scientific process and this often occurs in scientific meetings. In some meetings, the communication of new science is riddled by rites, people responding to a presentation in an order which reflects both their seniority and the time they have worked in the topic area. When abused, this combined rite ensures that all communication remains in a form which is controlled by the most senior person. In ideal circumstances, this combined rite can efficiently provide the context for appreciating new thought

16 See The Shorter Oxford English Dictionary.

17 See Ross and Ross (1983) for a consideration of Freud's view and its expansion.

18 See ibid. and the combination of Freuds approach with that of Winnicott and Turner.

19 See pp. 11-12, Grimes (1995).

20 See pp. 317-319, Koestler (1964), particularly A.E. Housmans description of how he created his poetry and the methods of Schiller, Turgenev and Balzac.

21 The choice of organisational rituals is based on those that have been obvious to the author and no weighting should be given to their choice or order.

22 See pp. 37, Grimes (1995).

23 Hopfl (1994) makes the point that management evangelists promise immediate reward (magic) rather than a deferred reward (religion). In reality there is a spectrum of promises and these alternatives are more colourings.

24 This way of looking at leadership reflects discussions with Professor G Eagleson of the AGSM. This model has not been validated and should be viewed more as a framework for partitioning out the creative components in a leader's tasks. The concept of complementary leadership and its implications is currently being explored (Waldersee, Simmons and Eagleson, 1995).

25 Tools used for describing individual's characteristics, or preferred actions, include Myers-Briggs, MAP and others.

26 See also 'Decoupling and Ritualization', pp. 211, Meyer and Scott (1992).

27 See pp. 125 in particular of Scott (1992).

Part B
Automation

7 Technology-centred and human-centred automation

Automation is the replacement of human activities by machine activities. Early machines were exquisitely simple in the way they multiplied or replaced human force. The lever, nail and screw remain pre-eminent machines to this day, their capacity to alter human existence largely taken for granted. By the time human force could be amplified with stored energy, using machines like boilers, waterwheels, windmills and cannons, humans had became the dominant consumers, predators, and combatants.

Machines have infiltrated human lives in the developed world. Discrete, simple machines have become complex, integrated and automated. Despite their sophistication, efficiency and performance, these automated machines are still machines (Jordan, 1963), but machines which have evolved. This evolution in capability now has machines doing more than just enhancing an individual's ability to exert physical force, or do repetitive tasks rapidly and accurately. Automated machines can now do things human are incapable of, such as the sampling of Jupiter's atmosphere, the visualisation of the deepest sea floor, and measurement within a nuclear power plant. Human existence in homes and work places is now so dependent upon automated machines that their contribution is seen as essential and reversion to human labour is no longer an option.

Where an automated machine has replaced a human, or has done a task outside human capability, the costs and benefits have been predictable, though sometimes obfuscated. In contrast, when automated machines have been required to share work with humans, benefits have been less obvious (Landauer, 1995). An underlying factor has been the expectation that automation can amplify human cognitive capabilities. Cognitive enhancement provides automation with a greater challenge than that presented by task repetition and force multiplication. There are instances where cognitive enhancement has improved productivity, improved safety, and increased effectiveness and quality, but automation has also had little, none or unwanted effects. This chapter considers some of the uncertainties associated with sharing cognitive activities with machines.

The current approach to automation is a stage in an evolutionary process for machines. In orchestrating this process, humans have ventured into and retreated from cul-de-sacs on an evolutionary path[1]. In addition, there probably have been some significant defects in the way this evolutionary path has been generally approached, some of which have not been rigorously addressed[2]. As sharing with machines becomes more prevalent and as cognitive enhancement becomes the goal, these unresolved defects may become impasses rather than cul-de-sacs.

7.1 Definitions

There are many definitions of automation. The introductory definition,

> *Automation is the replacement of human activities by machine activities.*

is similar in form to[3],

> *A device that accomplishes (partially or fully) a function that was previously carried out (partially or fully) by a human.*

Other definitions[4] emphasise control of processes with multiple stages[5],

> *A system or method in which many of the processes of production are automatically performed or controlled by self-operating machines, etc.*

but fail to mention human involvement. The emphasis in this book is on automation which partially replaces human beings, but which has, as a defining feature, the optimisation of the human contribution. In many industries, automation is prevalent, but explicit statements about how tasks are allocated to machines, humans, or shared[6], are not available. Whatever definition is fancied, it must be remembered that this book is specifically focussed on the sharing of work by humans and machines.

7.2 Types of shared automation

There are various types of automation where humans and machines share. A useful approach to partitioning automation by tasks has been described for aircraft automation (Billings, 1991; 1996). While automation that completely replaces humans is not the focus of this book, much of this type of automation does not replace humans as completely as has been thought. This so called autonomous automation is considered later (10.1.6). Automation can be partitioned by task (7.2.1) and by behaviour (7.2.2), and these can be further divided as described below.

7.2.1 Task clustering partitions

While most commonly applied to aircraft, control, information and management types of automation (Fadden, 1990; Billings, 1991) are apparent in many other situations where humans and machines combine.

Control automation Control automation assists or supplants a human in guiding a machine through the manoeuvres necessary for safe performance. Control automation has a major role in looking after machine sub-systems. In transport systems, control automation provides power assisted braking, anti-skid braking, fuel delivery and electric power. Control automation plays a major part in the sub-systems of modern manufacturing operations, diagnostic technology and energy generation and supply.

Information automation This type of automation is changing very rapidly. It is the automation which provides humans with information about the well-being of the machine and the progress made in achieving the shared task. In an aircraft, information automation consists of all the displays about the machine, the displays and avionics devoted to navigation and environmental surveillance, as well as all the displays related to communication with the outside world. In ground vehicles displays are simpler, the most obvious being the odometer, but now being supplanted by trip computers and ground positioning systems. In industry, information automation has become vital for displaying the progress of an activity, the level of satisfaction at the customer interface and the evolving nature of environmental threats and opportunities. In health delivery, information automation abounds, though it remains poorly focussed[7].

Management automation Management automation allows humans to exercise strategic rather than tactical control over a joint human-machine activity. Management automation is goal directed rather than function directed. In an aircraft, a pilot might set a goal for management automation which involves flying between two points in the most fuel efficient way within some airspace constraints. Management automation directs control automation as to the best way to do this, as well as orchestrates information automation to keep the pilot informed. Fuel refineries, nuclear power plants, and some forms of automated manufacturing use management automation.

7.2.2 Behaviour orchestrating partitions

Another way of partitioning automation is in terms of the machine's intention to alter the behaviour of its human partner. Machines can intentionally or unintentionally alter the behaviour of those that are sharing a task, and this can be prospective, concurrent or retrospective behaviour. Thus, some automation assists quality assurance and is periodically performed, usually long after the activity. Other automation reduces variation in behaviour and is performed soon after the behaviour occurs, while the most orchestrating automation attempts to control behaviour as it occurs or is about to occur.

Assurance automation There are forms of automation which assist humans to make use of information, but at the same time leave a trail as to the information that has been used. This provides a means of carrying out quality assurance or audit. In this book this is called assurance automation. Hence, electronic prescribing allows medical practitioners to prescribe more efficiently and more effectively, but each therapeutic decision, and the related use of stored information for making the therapeutic decision, can be retained for review by the practitioner or an outside agency. There are many issues with this type of automation which are unexplored[8].

Variation reduction automation There are forms of automation which track the performance of the human-machine combination. The purpose of these monitoring systems is to flag performance variation which is outside a predetermined range. Thus, most modern, large, commercial aircraft have the capacity to record, via a quick-access, flight-data recorder (QAR), a variety of performance parameters which are down-loaded at the end of each flight. Such systems allow detection of variation in flight operations, aircraft performance and engine performance. Optimally used, variation in flight operations which exceeds that specified, or is part of a trend which may result in limits being exceeding, is detected and fed back into training (Phelan, 1996)[9]. Retrospective drug utilisation review, or drug use evaluation, serves a similar function in the medical prescribing environment[10].

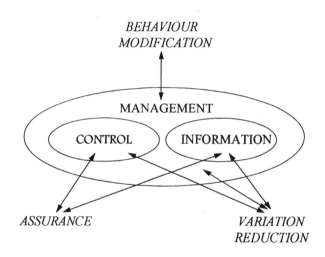

Figure 7.1 Some of the obvious linkages between task related types of automation (circled) and behaviour-orchestrating types (italics). See 7.2.1 and 7.2.2 for explanations of the partitions.

Behaviour modification automation Improvement in the capability of automation has resulted in some machines having multiple purposes, even including the control of human behaviour. In its most innocent form, this automation provides a reminder, presents the next step in a sequence, provides options, or is an 'aide-de-memoir'.

However, there are more controlling forms, with machines having a specific purpose of corralling behaviour as it occurs. Thus, automation has always been associated with standard operating procedures (SOP), check-lists and guidelines. As the prowess of automation management systems has evolved, the need to orchestrate the human partner with SOPs, check-lists and guidelines has increased (11.4.2). Even this process of orchestrating behaviour is being automated, with flightdeck check-lists and consulting room therapeutic guidelines becoming electronic. There are many other examples, including automation which alters attentional states in transportation systems (*Example 8*), and drug utilisation review systems which alter clinical decision making (*Example 14*).

7.2.3 Partition interrelationships

The task-clustering and the behaviour-orchestrating partitions of automation are interrelated, the latter often providing a behavioural constraint to the former. It is as if the power and flexibility given to the individual by sharing tasks with sophisticated automated systems has resulted in designers and owners developing other layers of automation which at their best are facilitating, but are equally capable of being controlling (Fig. 7.1).

7.3 Technology-centred automation

Technology-centred automation is automation in which the machine contribution to achieving a task and the needs of the machine for achieving the task are of prime importance. All of the types of automation described so far (7.2.1, 7.2.2) can be technology-centred. Technology-centred automation is automation which reflects a manufacturers capacity to automate, that is when the technology allows it, rather than when automation should occur (Parasuraman, Bahri, Deaton, Morrison and Barnes, 1990; Billings, 1991; Sarter and Woods, 1995). Thus, the role of the operator remains unconsidered, considered late in the design phase, or even later in the implementation phase.

Our lives are littered with machines which have been created using a technology-centred approach. A well-known example is the video cassette recorder, but more prevalent, and perhaps more flawed, is the personal computer. Much current personal computing hardware and software reflects what is possible and not what is desired, with much hardware capacity remaining minimally utilised for the life of the machine. Many attributes of the software reflect the whims of suppliers, rather than the results of a concerted co-development by the supplier and users to meet the latter's needs (Landauer, 1995). Devices such as ground positioning systems, new types of telephone[11], some electronic kitchen devices, modern sewing machines and many others have had their designs compromised by the technology-centred approach. Some of the consequences of the technology-centred approach in aircraft are considered later in more detail (9.1.4, 10.4, 10.5, Chapter 11).

When automation became practically feasible, the fact that the machine's needs dominated design, training and use was acceptable, as this evolutionary step for technology required many compromises from designers, owners and users. While the need for compromise has lessened, an approach which balances better human needs with machine needs has failed to materialise[12]. The recent advent of human-centred automation (7.4) may be the next stage in machine evolution. Technology-centred automation does not appear to have been the consequence of a specific philosophical position, or a specific school of designers, but is both generational and evolutionary. It currently dominates human-machine developments.

7.3.1 Autonomy, authority and feedback

A feature of technology-centred automation is its autonomy, meaning its capacity to carry out long complex sequences of actions, without requiring human input, once the sequences have been pre-programmed and engaged. This autonomy reflects the capacity of modern systems to alter their performance in response to inputs from various sources. Coupled to autonomy is a capacity called authority, which is the capability of modern systems to control and command actions. Significant coupling of autonomy and authority is inevitable and leads to the machine performing in a new role, that of an agent (Sarter, 1994). While automated systems which perform as 'perfect' agents are a desired end in the technology-centred approach to automation, there is disagreement as to how to orchestrate autonomy and authority so as to achieve an optimal agency relationship between humans and machines. This manifests in many forms.

In aircraft, designers have differed markedly in their approach to the level of authority and autonomy, some electing for high levels (10.4.1), while others have chosen simplicity with continuous human involvement (Wiener, 1993). System management, which involves humans giving 'consent' (10.1.4), is another approach (Billings, 1991; 1996; Sarter, 1994). Pilots want more automation, but also want to maintain authority. Their wish to uncouple autonomy and authority presents a challenge to designers, trainers and users, which currently requires resolution (Tenny, Rogers and Pew, 1995).

Many have identified the inevitable consequence of increasing authority and autonomy, namely the increasing need for feedback (Norman, 1990; Billings, 1991[13]; 1996; Wiener, 1993; Sarter and Woods, 1992; Sarter, 1994, FAA, 1996). As the prowess of technology advances, the need for feedback increases, until either the human is swamped by feedback and is unable to receive it, or the feedback must be so cropped by the machine that it is no longer an impartial supplier[14]. Either way, the quality and extent of the sharing between human and machine is threatened (9.1.4, 12.5), and the nature of the agency relationship changes. Feedback in the technology-centred approach to automation has not evolved 'pari-passu' (Fig. 7.2) with the capacity to achieve autonomy and authority (Sarter and Woods, 1992; FAA, 1996). The technology-centred approach has been happy to allow its prowess in achieving authority and autonomy to outstrip its capacity to provide feedback (9.1.4, 10.4.2, 11.2.1). As yet, there has been no real attempt to redefine the nature of the agency relationship between humans and machines when feedback becomes inappropriate, either in the way it is supplied or received. The consequences of impaired feedback between humans and machines (Chapter 8) require a new approach (Chapter 12).

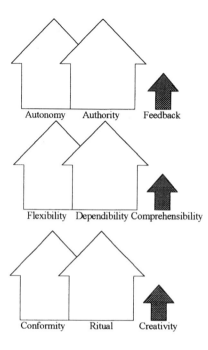

Autonomy   Authority   Feedback

Flexibility   Dependibility Comprehensibility

Conformity   Ritual   Creativity

Figure 7.2 Technology-centred automation has altered many aspects of automation, including associated behaviours (bottom row, 7.2.2). Changes have not been matched.

7.3.2 Flexibility, dependability and comprehensibility

Technology-centred automation is very capable at increasing the flexibility of human-machine sharing. Flexibility means automation that allows adaptation to a variety of environmental, operational and human variables (Billings, 1991). In this book, flexibility and adaptability are considered to be similar, though others have differentiated them (Billings, 1991). Technology-centred automation produces flexibility via transitions between the multiple, automated, operating modes which many machines now have (Sarter, 1994[15]; FAA, 1996[16]). Tightly coupled to flexibility is dependability, which is the capability of a machine in any of its operating modes to be relied upon or trusted (Billings, 1991). Dependability is similar but not identical to predictability (12.3.1), both being facets of trustworthiness. Users, owners and designers seek flexibility and dependability because they are desired facets of an agency relationship between human and machines. Technology-centred automation is adept at delivering flexibility, adaptability, dependability and predictability.

Aircraft once required very precise procedures, but the flexibility of technology-centred automation has altered the amount and type of procedural activity required on flightdecks (Degani and Wiener, 1994). Training pilots to take advantage of this flexibility is very time-consuming and has not been as straightforward or as successful as many would have liked (Sarter, 1994). The flexibility given by multiple operating modes mean that aircraft can be flown at various levels of human-machine sharing (9.1.4, 10.1). However, these levels have not resulted in machines being tailored to the individual differences of operators in the technology-centred approach. The flexibility given by multiple modes has bred uncertainty amongst many airlines and the approach they should employ (11.4.2) in using the automation they have purchased (Billings, 1996). There have been doubts expressed about how predictable users find much technology-centred automation (Billings, 1991; 1996; Sarter, 1994; FAA, 1996). It is likely that technology-centred automation is very predictable and dependable, but whether it justifies the faith that it engenders is questionable[17].

An inevitable consequence of a surfeit of dependable operating modes is the lack of a deep comprehensibility of each (Fig. 7.2). The more technology-centred automation improves flexibility and dependability, the greater the likelihood that the full functionality of a particular operating mode cannot be appreciated (9.1.4). While simplified models of automation modes might help pilots understand the functionality of more modes, they ensure decreased comprehensibility when a problem occurs. An antidote is that automation be simplified to the point where it is always comprehensible, but this has not been part of the technology-centred approach.

7.3.3 Conformity, ritual and creativity

Technology-centred automation cannot cope with much behavioural variation in its human partners (Fig. 7.1). The technology-centred approach relies on procedures to produce the behavioural conformity that machines must have when tasks are shared with humans. Machine needs dominate the procedural sequences of human actions required for machine interaction. Ritualised behaviour is another consequence of technology-centred automation and this is loosely coupled to procedure-related, behavioural conformity. The propensity of automation to induce rituals (6.5) is distinct, in that it occurs spontaneously, while the procedures needed for behavioural conformity are constructed when the machine is being designed and developed. The rituals mainly have an external locus-of-control, because the policies driving procedures are those of the owner and designer (11.4.2). As such they are more likely to suppress an operator's creativity (6.5.2, 11.4). This can be appropriate for normal operations, but can hinder performance in unusual circumstances (*Example 15*).

7.4 Human-centred automation

Human-centred automation is evolving as an alternative to technology-centred automation. Its key difference is that the starting position in designing shared systems begins with the human and with human capabilities, rather than with the machine and its capabilities (Billings, 1991; 1996). Complementing human capabilities is the key feature of the human-centred approach to automation (Jordan, 1963; Billings, 1996). It has much in common with the 'user-centred' approach to designing and using technology, and has been invoked as a solution to automation problems in aircraft. In this section, the principles of human-centred automation will be described. How successfully human-centred automation is in meeting its goal of achieving complementarity between humans and machines is considered elsewhere (10.2, 10.3, 10.6).

7.4.1 Responsibility and command authority

Human operators bear heavy responsibility for safety in transportation and other shared systems, and while there are many regulatory and procedural constraints, the operator's authority to do what has to be done, particularly in unforeseen circumstances, is generally accepted as being unlimited for all practical purposes. It is possible for the machine to limit the extent of human authority (7.3.1) but the human-centred approach limits this exercise of authority to only the most compelling situations, and only after users have been extensively consulted and options tested (Billings, 1996).

In practice, command authority can be compromised in a human-machine sharing environment. Thus, indecisiveness by operators can result in humans assuming roles when they should not have them, or relinquishing authority when it is inappropriate[18]. Another way that command authority can be compromised is when the linkage between humans, machines, policies and procedures becomes inappropriate. It is not easy to produce policies and procedures which result in an ideal authority gradient between humans and machines (11.4.2). The variation that exists between owners[19] in promulgating policies and procedures is direct evidence that some operators must have compromised command authority. In addition, machine design can compromise human authority (10.4.1).

A centrepiece of the human centred approach to automation is giving direction in the area of responsibility and command authority. Whether this is an appropriate goal in the context of complimentary sharing between human and machines is considered later (10.6, Chapter 12).

7.4.2 Operator involvement

Another area of automation that the human-centred approach seeks to change is in the degree that operators should be involved, or 'drawn in', to operations when humans and machines share. The human-centred approach proposes that humans should be actively involved (Billings, 1996). This implies humans are engaged

111

actively in either control, decision making, allocation of resources, evaluation of alternatives, or combinations of these. In contrast, the technology-centred approach promotes passive roles like monitoring.

The human-centred approach has produced a number of suggestions for maintaining involvement, particularly under low workload conditions. These have included giving people continuous tasks which are unrelated to the primary purpose of the shared activity, to reducing the amount of machine assistance under low workload conditions. In practice, these suggestions are not very practical, nor is it certain that they would pass any test of being 'user-centred'. It is possible that the human-centred approach is correct about the need to promote involvement, but is currently unclear about relevant processes.

The human-centred approach to automation also focuses on machine attributes that can easily reduce involvement. Predictability of automation is seen as a central issue. Involvement suffers quite markedly if a mental model of a machine's contribution cannot accommodate a machine behaviour. Currently, involvement is made vulnerable because of the complexity of current automation, even when systems are performing faultlessly[20]. When a fault or unexpected event has occurred, the poor predictability of automated systems can rapidly overwhelm even the most proficient of human partners. At present, this type of predictability requires either disabling the machine[21] or coping with it by significantly increasing the human resource[22]. The human-centred approach promotes simplification to address the predictability issue (Billings, 1996).

7.4.3 Operator information

The technology-centred approach to automation has advanced the autonomy and authority of machines, without paying sufficient attention to the vital, but less coupled need, of providing the human with feedback (7.3.1). The human-centred approach redresses this by requiring that designers, owners and users make the provision of information, in a form which is easily assimilated into knowledge by any operator, a key role for the machine. There has been limited progress in providing information that is meaningful to all operators, especially average operators when they are fatigued (Sarter, 1994; Billings, 1996). It is not clear that the human-centred approach to providing operator information has been really centred on humans, for most 'improvements' concentrate on the properties of displays. This machine focus in part reflects what can be changed, rather than what should be changed, and leads to uncertainty in the whole area of information provision in the work place. Hence, the value of electronic libraries on flightdecks and information systems in corporate settings is unclear, suggesting that owners, users and designers have yet to achieve a common understanding.

A specific information element that is central to the human-centred approach to automation is feedback about the status and activities of the automation itself. Studies have demonstrated operator doubt about automation status (Sarter and Woods, 1992; Wiener, 1993; Sarter, 1994), partly because automation is capable of dependably carrying out tasks, but is not capable of telling people what it is doing[23]. This fuels the inadequate understanding of automation in normal operations, despite significant investment in training (FAA, 1996).

7.4.4 Machine monitoring of humans

In critical human-machine systems, the contribution of one human has been monitored by other humans. The technology-centred approach has attempted to have the machine monitor the human contribution, mostly with respect to the performance of tasks. Machines are quite capable of doing this and as long as the machine's capacity to alert the human to inappropriate performance is not impaired[24], the technology-centred approach has worked well. However, this approach can become inadequate. For example, the complexity of modern systems produces entanglements (*Example 15*), which can end up as having warning systems to detect problems in warning systems. In addition, the excellence of machines at monitoring human physical performance is not matched by their capacity to monitor human cognitive performance.

Thus, technology-centred approaches have had great difficulty in monitoring human contribution when the human task has been one of monitoring and no physical actions have been required of the human. Machine systems which monitor human alertness have been incorporated into cars, trains and aircraft, but these have not provided significant benefit, because their design reflects a preoccupation with physical rather than mental performance (Satchell, 1993). The human-centred approach has set automation designers the task of upgrading the capacity of machines to assist and monitor cognitive human involvement or, make the inevitable human errors less damaging. At present, there has been little progress in these difficult areas.

7.4.5 Comprehension of purpose

The human-centred approach to automation has recently identified that the two-way communication of intent[25] between humans and machines is an underlying and fundamental need for successful human-machine relationships. In this book the communication of intent is called the sharing of purpose. This is considered in detail elsewhere (12.2). At present, comprehension of purpose of machines by humans and of humans by machines is seen to be a cross monitoring task. Thus, the intentions of the automated systems and the human operators must be obvious and must be communicated to each other and all other intelligent agents in the system. Many automation related incidents and accidents demonstrate a misunderstanding of purpose on the part of the human or the machine, and this applies particularly in abnormal circumstances (Sarter and Woods, 1992).

7.5 Summary

It is probable that the technology-centred approach to automation, which basically consists of automating as soon as the technical capacity becomes available, is not so much a cul-de-sac in the evolution of machines, but a necessary diversion. One reason for this diversion is the advent of behaviour-orchestrating types of automation, which have sat for sometime, albeit unrecognised, alongside the different task-orchestrating types of automation. The inability of much technology-centred automation to enhance human cognitive activities is another reason for the approach to automation straying. The evolutionary diversion will deliver a better definition of its successor, because the failure of much technology-centred automation to deliver what has been required, particularly in areas of cognitive enhancement, will produce clearer definition of problem areas. It is not clear that the human-centred approach, as it is currently framed, is the successor to the technology-centred approach. It appears to have been diverted by issues of authority and control, anathemas to real partnership in human terms. What is encouraging is that the human-centred approach, which started from the position of asking whether automation is required, has an evolving character. The most recent and exciting change is its recognition of the importance of communicating intent, or the sharing of purpose. This is an essential first step for creating human machine partnerships based upon the way humans naturally share, rather than some machine dependent hybrid. This book views the sharing of purpose as a starting point for the development of the successor to the human-centred approach (Chapters 12, 13).

Notes

1 The evolutionary path of most types of machine has cul-de-sacs. See Parkes (1970) on British Battleships and the advent of the ironclad ram (pp. 175-186). Also reflect on the wrist watch fitted with a miniature keypad calculator, each key too small for a finger, and the R101 Airship, designed by committee, which resulted in it having difficulty in lifting its own weight.

2 See 10.4 where two unresolved features of flightdeck automation, protective automation and system feedback are discussed.

3 See pp. 6, Parasuraman et al. (1990)

4 See The Shorter Oxford English Dictionary

5 See pp. 7, Billings (1991)

6 Personal inquiries in a variety of industries - there are rare exceptions.

7 Health care systems have lots of data but little of it becomes information. Hence, there is precise information on prescribing and on procedures, but these are infrequently linked to reasons for presenting or diagnoses.

8 Two imperatives in health delivery are quality and value. In many health systems there is a stand-off between doctors who deliver health and managers who would control the delivery. In recent years computers have been increasingly used to promote the manager's ends, generally with disappointing results. A feature of these efforts are machines being given multiple, non-aligned purposes (See *Example 14*). There are various solutions (See 13.3, *Example 17*).

9 See *Example 3*.

10 Retrospective drug utilisation review (DUR) looks at recent prescribing for trends and variances that are outside agreed practices. Ideally it is done by the practitioners and ideally associated with some training process which helps practitioner understand and justify variation. Although this can merge into assurance and audit, it is the time-course and the locus-of-control which distinguish it. DUR is moulded by the health system it occurs within.

11 New types of telephone, and the ground positioning units offered to general aviation pilots have many functions and levels of capability. It is far from straightforward for the average user to take advantage of what these devices offer.

12 The dilemmas are well documented. For example, see sections 1.4 on opaqueness of systems, and section 1.5 on ironies of automation in Reason (1990).

13 See whole of discussion of information automation, pp. 42-48 of Billings (1991), which is excellent on feedback issues although this term is not prominent.

14 It is inevitable that feedback involves alteration of information because information must be displayed and readied for interpretation. The absence of 'impartiality' means that the machine will be more involved in altering feedback by filtering, simplifying, selecting, etc.

15 See Fig.4, pp. 19 for mode complexity, Sarter (1994).

16 See Fig.3 and 'Variation in the automation interfaces among different aircraft types' pp. 50-53, FAA (1996)

17 This comment relies on Rempel et al. (1985) and their developmental sequence for trust. See 12.3.1, 12.3.2, 12.3..3 and Figure 12.2

18 See pp. 70-71, 81, Billings (1991); pp. 8-9, Billings (1996); pp. 4-8, 97-99 Sarter (1994).

19 See comments on differences among carriers (5.4), Degani and Wiener (1994).

20 See automation surprises, pp. 28-36, Sarter (1994).

21 There has been a reluctance in incidents for crew to revert to hand flying (exemplified in pitch control incidents due to inappropriate mode selection) and also observed in simulations (Sarter, 1994). See also pp. 35-37, FAA, (1996) on inappropriate use of automation, either by not turning it off, or by turning it on to try and recover an abnormal situation.

22 See *Example 15* and descriptions of Flight 232 (Gerren, 1995) where a DC-10 centre engine failure caused loss of many flight controls, the 'unflyable' aircraft being flown and crash-landed by means of an augmented crew.

23 See pp. 63-64 , Wiener (1993), in particular comments on automation being in an intermediate stage of development and not being capable of giving feedback.

24 There have been numerous incidents and accidents, where the machines capacity to monitor human performance has been interfered with. This even goes as far as deliberately interfering with the feedback systems that the machine has, by pulling circuit breakers in warning systems, or by acknowledging the presence of the warning but explaining its presence in an inappropriate way.

25 See pp. 13, Billings (1996).

8 Humans and machines II

The technology-centred approach to automation has served well in some areas of routine work and has allowed humans to be innovative occasionally (Chapter 2). However, much of the sharing of tasks by humans and machines is currently unsatisfactory, because many human capabilities, including creativity, are dampened. The examples in this chapter show how the flaws in the technology-centred approach trap humans and make them passive and dysfunctional, or stimulate them to subvert the purpose they should share with the machine. People can become so detached from the task, that their behaviour becomes a primary factor in causing disaster.

8.1 Automated vigilance control

Locomotive cabins have changed markedly with the demise of the steam engine. The cabin of a steam engine was a dynamic and demanding work environment, with human skill and experience making significant differences to machine performance. This 'art', with its attendant manual tasks, has virtually disappeared. While modern locomotive cabins are not highly automated, the driving task has been simplified to such an extent that very little is now expected from the human. There can be a number of unwanted consequences.

Example 8. Locomotive cabin noises[1]
The Bradazon 2020 locomotive was running smoothly. Fourteen feet above the ground the driver had an unsurpassed view of the track and countryside as the heavy freight train thundered southwards. To onlookers, the turbo-charged diesels produced a sound like thunder, but within the cabin the train was virtually noiseless. There was the occasional click and hiss from the automated control systems, but this did not disturb the sound of light music from the driver's transistor radio.

An unusual sound for a visitor to a working cabin, but usual for the driver and the driver's mate, was the intermittent clicks of the alerting system. The alerting system consisted of a push button which had to be pressed within 10 seconds of a control panel light switching on, otherwise the train would start an emergency braking manoeuvre. The light switched on at a variable interval after the last button push, the interval ranging from 4 to 14 seconds. A visitor could have been forgiven for being confused by the relationship between the driver's button pushes and the presence of the panel light, because they appeared dissociated. The driver was pushing the alerting system button with an interval of 11 to 12 seconds whether the panel light was on or not.

On the driver's mate side of the cabin there was an electric jug and a small griller, but no driving controls. The driver's mate checked how close the water was to boiling, as they had just passed the Conaman road crossing, which was a point on this trip at which the crew usually had a cup of tea. The mate was pouring the water when he thought that the alerting system had momentarily changed its rhythm, but he did not look across as he was searching for the sugar. It was only as he began to hand the driver his cup that he noticed that his driver had fallen asleep. The mate had heard that drivers could keep pressing the alerting system button while asleep[2], but he had never observed it and thought it was just a pub tale.

The control cabin of modern locomotives has altered markedly with changes in technology. Noise, physical workload, discomfort and temperature extremes have all been reduced. The driving and monitoring tasks have been simplified to the point where the capacity of individuals to be vigilant is seriously impaired. Alertness assisting systems have been added, but their effectiveness is questionable, with unwanted 'automatic' behaviours being occasionally observed[2]. The technology-centred approach to automation has failed to meet the needs generated by the cognitive tasks of this work place. In addressing the need of sustaining attention by adding another layer of automation, the technology-centred approach has probably compounded rather than resolved the problem. Not surprisingly, humans become disenchanted and even less capable of providing their own solutions. The issue of vigilance and how it might be managed in the future is considered later (9.1.4, 10.3.3, *Example 16*).

8.2 Human flexibility versus machine flexibility

Flightdeck crew hope that the flight plan that they create at the start of a sector remains viable for the whole of that sector, particularly as a flight plan is shared with the aircraft's automated flight management system (FMS) which in some aircraft can be complex to change[3]. Humans can circumvent this complexity and its attendant restrictions, as described in the following example.

Example 9. Creative reconfiguration of a machine[4]
Errol scanned the instruments again. It had been an uneventful flight, with less headwind than expected. Overall the flight had gone well, considering the contingencies the crew had covered in their joint, pre-flight briefing. Then, there had been much discussion on the best way to handle what was likely to be a 'boisterous' cabin. So far, there had not been a problem, as the purser had managed the football

118

team and their doting entourage very well, while the other passengers had been particularly tolerant. More reason, Errol reflected, to make the descent phase of this trip as smooth as possible.

For this reason alone, Errol felt completely justified in altering the flight profile from that mandated by the flight management system (FMS). While he and his co-pilot were aware that the descent profile proposed by the FMS would consume the least amount of fuel, the difference between the machine version and the profile he and his co-pilot preferred was small. The benefit of their preferred descent profile was that the transition from cruise to descent was gradual, and the steepness of the machine's descent was reduced. The machine version could create a sense of unease in the cabin, and this was out of the question on this particular flight. To avoid the complexity of reprogramming the FMS, and the need to justify a non-standard flight profile, Errol and his copilot used a technique for 'tricking' the machine, with a ploy well known to those that used this type of aircraft.

During the environmental update of the FMS, both agreed to alter the prevailing wind from a slight headwind to a 60kt tailwind. They knew that this would start their descent early and give them the shallower descent profile they wanted, without them having to justify it. They were convinced this was good airmanship, that they were caring for their airline's customers, and because of the presence of the football team, for the intactness of the aircraft cabin. While they knew that placing incorrect information in the FMS was corrupting the integrity of their aircraft's automated systems, the work required to alter the profile from the optimal fuel burn mode, and the need for its justification, made their 'fooling' the system worthwhile.

There are instances where the 'control' exerted by a machine is usurped by a human, despite training to accept the machine's autonomy and authority[5]. In these situations, humans use their creativity to deviate from procedures. Well-trained, well standardised and well-motivated human operators deviate from procedures because of individualism, frustration and the desire to inject variety into some of their work practices[6]. The dependability and flexibility of technology-centred automation (7.3.2) enhances their perception that they can usurp the authority and autonomy of the machine and that there will be no untoward consequences, although this is often not true (Degani and Wiener, 1994). In this example, the flight crew have usurped the autonomy and authority of the machine in a way which corrupts it.

Flightdecks are resplendent with rituals of various types. The technology-centred approach to automation and it's attendant policies and procedures all produce external locus-of-control influences which will suppress creativity (6.6, 11.4), though, in this example, inadequately from the point of view of the designer and the owner. It is arguable whether the creativity that was used to bypass the autonomy and authority of the automated systems was misapplied, as the purpose behind misprogramming the FMS was perfectly aligned with the overall purpose of the flight. The need to 'trick' the machine reflects poorly on the technology-centred approach, because it indicates that the machine cannot comprehend purpose at more than a tactical level (12.2). In the next example, creativity is again used to bypass the autonomy and authority of an automated system, but by using other technology, rather than altering a procedure.

Example 10. Machine bypass[7]

George looked speculatively at his passenger. He had heard a rumour in the El Greco, the eating place of taxi-drivers, that their company was using 'false passengers' to ensure that the electronic dispatching system was not being abused. As the passenger dropped his suitcase and its contents spilled out over the back seat, George realised that this passenger posed no threat.

George looked at the electronic dispatch unit mounted beside the right hand pillar of his windscreen. He had come to accept it over the last few months, particularly when he realised that he was earning more because of it. Initially he had missed the interchanges between the operators and other drivers in the old radio despatch system. In that system, all taxis belonging to the one company could hear all the conversations. These had entertained him during long slow shifts, and also had allowed him to detect local occasions when many visitors were in town, particularly visitors who were generous with their tips. This had changed with the electronic dispatch system, for this one-way, digitised, data link provided the essential information about prospective customers, but failed to provide those added layers of information that could increase a driver's earnings. The company for which he drove had embarked upon a program which emphasised the need to improve customer satisfaction and had simultaneously introduced both the new despatch system and uniforms for drivers. Drivers were told that the despatch system would optimise the balance between the supply and demand for the company's services and required drivers to meet the needs of the despatch system before seeking customers by other means. While George wore his uniform willingly enough, he would not give up all the benefits of the old radio system.

George slipped the mobile phone out of its concealed pouch on the upper side of the steering column under the dashboard. He called Dorothy, his wife, who drove taxis for a competing company. He learned that her company was being used for a conference of American cardiologists, and that at present all their taxis were struggling to carry them to satellite meetings in the local city hospitals. George grinned. He realised that his current, bumbling fare would allow him to cruise into the vicinity of these rich visitor and provide customer service as if by chance.

Data link systems improve a number of communication parameters. In this example, the capacity of such a system to enhance the use of the assets of the organisation is unquestioned, and the resource issues surrounding data links do not arise[8]. The individual in this example preferred communication to be 'noisy' and personalised, but that was not the sole reason for using other technology to bypass the system. In contrast with the previous example, the taxi driver's goals were not well aligned with those of his organisation and this misalignment was enhanced by the communication technology. The machine in this example was incapable of generating a sense of partnership. In this situation, organisational success depended upon human compliance and rituals, but this organisation was feeble in facilitating these, because of its ineffective use of uniforms, rules and inspectors. Even if these had been well implemented, the potential of the human and the machine to share purpose (12.1, 12.2) was limited because of the technology-centred approach to automation.

8.3 Faultless machines and disasters

The Airbus A320 and the Boeing 757 have been involved in fatal accidents, where faultless aircraft have flown into the ground during a descent. The following gives brief descriptions of two of these accidents. Both of these aircraft have highly automated cockpits.

Example 11. Cocooning at Strasbourg[9]

Flight IT5148 had started its descent towards Strasbourg after an uneventful trip. The aircraft, an Airbus A320 had accumulated 6,316 flight hours in just over three years service and was in perfect condition. On board, there were 90 passengers, 4 cabin crew and 2 cockpit crew. During the descent to ANDLO, a point 13nm from the runway where the approach from 5,000ft commenced, the crew had made a number of minor procedural errors, related to instrument checking and turning on the engine anti-icing. Because the initial phase of the descent resulted in the plane being high and fast relative to that required at ANDLO, the air traffic control offered to take them back to this point using a racetrack pattern flight path. The crew accepted this offer and arrived at ANDLO at the appropriate height and speed. The final approach was authorised by air traffic control and the crew selected the second flap position and lowered the landing gear.

Instead of descending at a 3.3° flight path angle (a descent rate of 700ft/min) the A320 descended at a very much steeper angle, with a descent rate close to 3,300ft/min. Instead of decelerating during the last phase of descent, the aircraft accelerated, the speed reaching the configuration limit of 200kts such that the crew deployed the speed-brakes. Neither of the crew members commented or questioned the multiple cockpit displays of a too rapid descent and neither questioned their need for the speed-brake.

The aircraft entered trees with a steep flight path, some 10-12° nose down. Eight passengers and one stewardess survived in an aircraft that was technically faultless. All the evidence pointed to a mis-selection of a descent mode from one controlled by flight path angle to one controlled by vertical speed.

There have been a variety of disasters where automation has 'cocooned' humans to such an extent that the resulting behaviours have been lethal. In this example, the ability of the cockpit crew to appreciate the parlous state that was developing had declined, although it was signalled on multiple displays and by attention getting events like speed-brake deployment. The ability of humans to continuously update a relevant mental picture of their progress (Chapter 9) was impaired. There have been three A320 accidents[10] where faultless aircraft have crashed and where the pilots have been in some way insulated or 'cocooned' from developing events. These, and many other incidents and accidents involving other types of aircraft, have been attributed to problems which primarily reside at the flight crew-automation interface[11].

The next example is similar and is provided to achieve balance across aircraft types in the identification of automation problems. It is worth pointing out that the different approaches to automation of the major manufacturers (10.4) have not given either of them immunity to the 'cocooning' effect of technology-centred automation.

Example 12. Cocooning at Cali[12]

It was a calm and windless evening at Cali airport when the Boeing 757 fist called the air traffic control. Cali airport lay in a valley, with the steep mountains lying to the East and West being part of the Cordillera Occidental ranges on the pacific border of Columbia. The magnificent Cauca river ran nearly due north down the middle of the valley.

Because of the height of the surrounding terrain, there were only two approaches to Cali airport. There was a direct approach for an aircraft flying south, where the let down started at Tulua 63km northward in the valley. The aiming point in this approach was the Rozo beacon, 5 km to the north of the airport The southern approach onto the Cali beacon, which was to the south of the airport, was more frequently used, because it had an instrument landing system. On this evening all beacons were functional and the plane was faultless. This type of aircraft had never had an accident in 13 years of extensive commercial transport operation.

Because of the terrain, the position of the aircraft was unknown to the air traffic controllers and, because of the calmness of the evening, the aircrew were offered the approach onto the Rozo beacon, with the condition that the aircrew must report when they were over Tulua.

The aircraft had already passed Tulua when the aircrew accepted the Rozo approach but they did not know this. They had also begun to descend with the aircraft flight management system controlling the descent and the lateral navigation of the aircraft. The aircrew were not familiar with the approach from the north and did not have the approach charts when they asked the flight management system to take them over Tulua. Unfortunately, this occurred when Tulua was behind them and not ahead of them. Obediently the flight management system turned the aircraft to the east so as to retrace their path back to the chosen approach. The aircraft hit a 12000ft mountain at an altitude of about 9000ft, 18km to the east of the flight path.

The important points that are common to both examples are the trust placed in the machine, the faultlessness of the machine, the precision of the machine and the imprecision of the human-machine combination. In both examples, there were non-standard elements in the descent, which required incorporation into the situation awareness of the crew, but this is not a rare occurrence. In both, there were some non-standard approaches to operating procedures, but neither of these types of anomaly clarifies how technology-centred approach to automation was inadequate. Others have classified these accidents as due to problems at the flight crew-automation interface (FAA, 1996), and technical and procedural solutions have been recommended and carried out.

Flightdecks and aircraft cabins are rich in rituals, many of which help dampen the creative excesses that the technology-centred approach cannot cope with (7.3.3. 11.4). In the last two examples, it is possible that creativity dampening rituals, excessive trust, and some interface problems, came together momentarily in a lethal cocktail. It is also possible that these accidents were the full expression of the potential for disaster which lurks in the technology-centred approach to automation. Other examples *(Example 8, 9, 15)* reveal a similar, if not fully expressed, lethal potential. This potential arises from an inadequate sharing process (Chapter 12). In both examples, it appears that the purpose of the machine and the purpose of the humans had become dissociated and that there was excessive trust by machine and human in each other. When these are coupled with inadequate feedback, or the assimilation of feedback, there is potential for misadventure.

8.4 Focal automation and displaced consequence

A variety of surgical procedures have been automated. The outcomes of automated surgical procedures, many of them being forms of laparoscopy, can be similar to the outcomes achieved by traditional operative techniques, but with some alteration in operative morbidity[13]. Most laparoscopic procedures produce some improvement in the quality of life in the post-operative phase[14]. Automation of surgical tasks with a technology-centred approach provides benefits, but because the automation is limited to the surgical procedure, other factors that are important in health improvement remain uncontrolled. The following example illustrates what can happen when part of the health care chain is automated, but other parts are not altered.

Example 13. Time for change[15]
Mrs Gromes smiled as her surgeon looked at her steadily. He asked again if she had any questions concerning her forthcoming elective gastric surgery. She indicated she was content and that her information needs had been well catered for. She understood that she would be having surgery on the outlet of her stomach but, in contrast with the operation her sister-in-law had undergone, she would be able to go home on the day after her operation, and that she would only have a small scar on her upper abdomen. The surgeon described how the automated stapling device would be used to reconfigure the shape of her stomach, how it had revolutionised the surgical approach, and how it had reduced the duration of stay within his hospital. The surgeon had shown her the device, part of which would be passed down her oesophagus and part inserted through a small whole in her upper abdominal wall. She marvelled at its ingenuity and simplicity. She knew from her sister-in-law that eating would be different for some months after the operation and this had been discussed carefully by her surgeon.
The day after the operation, Mr. Gromes picked up his wife's overnight bag and both of them thanked the ward sister for the excellent care. When they arrived home, Mrs Gromes had a shower and marvelled that within 24 hours of a major abdominal operation she could be standing in her own shower, feeling in control, independent

123

and well. She knew that she would have to be disciplined about her eating with respect to quantity, frequency and content, but her morale was such that she felt completely able to manage.

The hospital nutritionist had given her some bottles of white fluid which covered her complete dietary requirements for the first two post-operative days. The nutritionist had also given her a food program for the first month at home. Mrs Gromes stuck rigidly to this program, but at the start of the fourth post-operative day had her first bout of diarrhoea. Within 24 hours her diarrhoea, related to any oral intake, had become more precipitous and violent. Mrs Gromes tried to conceal the problem from her husband but when she soiled their bed twice on the sixth night, both realised that, like her sister-in-law, and as discussed by her surgeon, she had developed a post-gastrectomy syndrome. Weakness and fatigue nullified Mrs Gromes' continuing attempts to prolong the normality of the first few post-operative days. Mr Gromes felt increasingly helpless as they together tried more and more extreme measures to quell the diarrhoea and reduce the wasting which was becoming obvious. In desperation Mrs Gromes rang the contact number provided by the ward sister and by the eighth day she was readmitted. She initially required treatment for depression before she began, with the help of the nursing staff, to evolve her own particular solution to her post-gastrectomy syndrome.

Automation in health delivery systems is burgeoning, but it is not clear that hospital costs will be consistently reduced. The need for longer operative times, disposable instruments and an alteration in morbidity means that some automated processes are associated with increased, rather than reduced hospital costs. There appears to be societal savings via reduced sick leave and better hospital turnover, although the complexity of modelling the opportunity costs borne by 'unpaid helpers' makes assessment difficult[16].

The post-operative period in a hospital ward after traditional surgery is a time for wound healing and adjusting to personal change. Rituals have a critical and powerful effect. For many health care consumers, it is a time of adjustment and assimilation, and for a few, a vital time for grappling creatively with major anatomical, physiological and psychological changes. This is particularly true if there are rare, unwanted outcomes from the surgical intervention, as occurred in the example. In the example, automation produced a satisfactory 'technical' result, as much technology-centred automation can, but a poor overall result for all those involved. Automated surgery has the potential to make the clinical result worse, if an individual's capacity to heal needs more personalised care, or there are displaced consequences which can be ameliorated by a longer admission. Because of its focus on the 'technical', rather than on the combination of the human and technical, the technology-centred approach struggles when human issues encroach.

8.5 Summary

Most automation has been designed using the technology-centred approach and this is capable of producing all that owners, users and customers could want. In the first chapter of examples (Chapter 2), automation even provided unexpected benefits and was a key contributor to innovatory behaviour in work places. The current chapter is a foil, for innovatory behaviour is not a general feature of working with machines designed by the technology-centred approach. The examples in this chapter show situations where creativity and innovatory behaviour are subdued, or if present, occur inappropriately. There are rituals in the examples which promote or hamper innovatory behaviour and they frequently accompany the technology-centred approach. The interplay of ritual, technology and innovatory behaviour is explored in more detail in the last three chapters.

There are a number of common themes in the examples in this chapter. The technology-centred approach to automation has advanced autonomy and authority to the point where some humans will not accept it and will bypass its control using their own techniques, altering procedures or manipulating technology itself. Another theme is that the flexibility and dependability of the technology-centred approach is equally able to be used for undesired or desired purposes. In the examples, the consequences of inadequate feedback are dramatically demonstrated, ranging from a work environment which is so free from feedback about task progression as to be totally sterile, to one where, despite displays accurately depicting progress, humans have become incapable of assimilating it. The behavioural state of 'cocooning' was illustrated to draw attention to the fact that there are uncertainties in human-machine interactions which defy our current understanding. These themes point to problems with misaligned purposes, inappropriate trust and inadequate use of the unique capacities of the human and the machine. Together they suggest problems with task sharing and these are addressed in the last two chapters.

Finally the current human-machine interactions have consequences on creativity. The examples show that creativity will appear, despite technology, but usually for achieving the human's purpose rather than a common purpose. At other times creativity is absent when there is a desperate need for it. Overall the technology-centred approach to automation appears inept in helping humans engage their creativity when it is required. Other consequences of the technology-centred approach, such as reduced situation awareness, complacency, inappropriate trust, and miscommunication were also present. These are considered in the next chapter.

Notes

1   Identifying features have been removed. The cabin details are accurate, as are the details of the alerting system. The use of the 'noise' theme is a concoction. Alerting systems are offered in some aircraft (Satchell, 1993).

2   Automatic behaviours in road and rail transport have been described (Peter et al., 1990; Mackie and Wylie, 1991).

3   One FMS (Flight Management System), certified by the FAA requires 164 keystrokes to program a single IFR approach. See summary of position papers A-6, in Proceedings of workshop on Light Crew Accident and Incident Human Factors, June 21-23, 1995, Office of System Safety, FAA.

4   This example is fictitious and is based on pp. 24-25, Degani and Wiener (1994).

5   It can be difficult to distinguish between techniques which allow humans to better carry out their tasks, or are examples of personal style in using the automation, versus manipulations which are prompted by 'clumsy' automation. See pp. 22-23, Degani and Wiener (1994).

6   See pp. 10-12, ibid. See also operator adaptation, and capacity of operators to 'trick' systems in cardiopulmonary bypass systems, Cook and Woods (1996).

7   This example has had identifying features removed and George and company inspectors are a concoction. The despatcher system, the reason for its use, and the addition of alternative communication technologies are real.

8   See Logsdon et al., (1995) where resource issues in data link communication relate to the need for someone to read a display which diverts an individual and takes up more time than aural systems.

9   This description is synthesised from the preliminary accident report (Alston, 1992), which provides a more detailed account than prior summaries (Learmount, 1992).

10 See Habsheim, 26 June, 1988; Bangalore, 14 February, 1990; Strasbourg, 20 January, 1992, mentioned on pp. D-2 and D-3, FAA (1996).

11 See 24 incidents and accidents briefly mentioned in Appendix D, FAA (1996).

12 This description is synthesised from a variety of accounts of the Cali accident as it was reported and as it is described on p. D-8, FAA (1996).

13 Automation of a surgical procedure currently means the surgeon uses a laparoscope or similar device rather than the traditional open surgical procedure and this applies for cholecystectomy, appendicectomy, and inguinal herniorrhaphy (Orlando and Russell, 1996; Barkun et al., 1995; Berggren et al., 1996). Alteration in morbidity for laparoscopic cholecystectomy is an increase in the risk of stricture and an increased risk of bile stones.

14 Increased quality of life post-operatively is a more rapid assumption of normal activity and more consumers satisfaction after laparoscopic cholecystectomy, Orlando and Russell (1996). There may be only slight changes after an inguinal herm laparoscopic procedure, Barkun et al, (1995).

15 The incident is a fictitious. Gastric drainage operations such as this are not carried out by laparoscope, although there are a variety of gastric laparoscopic approaches. Post-gastrectomy syndromes are rare but still occur, even after laparoscopic procedures. See Casas and Gadacz, (1996)

16 Read articles by Orlando and Russell (1996), Berggren et al. (1996) and Barkun et al. (1995) to confront the complexity of determining the benefit from automation in surgery.

9 Current automation consequences

The initial approach to human-machine sharing, called technology-centred automation (Chapter 7) has been responsible for a considerable evolution of automated machines. The human-machine relationship has also developed, although some aspects have lagged behind others (Fig. 7.2). Feedback has lagged behind autonomy and authority (7.3.1), comprehensibility has lagged behind flexibility and dependability (7.3.2) and creativity has lagged behind conformity and ritual (7.3.3). These lags are consequences of the technology-centred approach.

Human-centred automation (Chapter 7) has attempted to address some of the consequences that have been produced by the technology-centred approach. Human-centred automation has considered responsibility (7.4.1), command authority (7.4.1), operator involvement (7.4.2) operator information (7.4.3), the machine monitoring of humans (7.4.4) and the sharing of purpose by humans and machines (7.4.5). This approach has focussed interest rather than provided solutions. This is not surprising, considering that the human-centred approach is less than twenty years old and very much in an evolving state.

This chapter considers the unwanted consequences of current automation, some of which were illustrated in the last chapter. By and large these are not outcomes of a well-defined approach to human-machine sharing, but rather consequences from the absence of any approach. Some of these consequences have been collected together under the term peripheralisation (Norman, Billings, Nagel, Palmer, Weiner and Woods, 1988), which describes the role changes which accompany increased levels of automation. On the flightdeck, peripheralisation encompasses reduced situation awareness, complacency and an impairment of communication, effects believed to be important in human error production. Other consequences[1] have included primary-secondary task inversion, automation deficit, boredom-panic syndrome and 'cocooning'[2]. Reduced situation or state awareness has been identified as the most serious consequence and is considered first in this chapter.

The importance of these consequences has been realised by the military for a long time, but their effect on civilian transport, health and industry activities is only just being realised. The recent report by the Federal Aviation Authority Human Factors Task Force (FAA, 1996) on current human-machine interface performance provides the first substantial, and more importantly public expression, of doubt in the present approach to automation. The report indirectly criticises those who have had advisory roles, and indirectly expresses doubt about the overall effectiveness of the approach called human-centred automation. As will be shown in subsequent chapters, the current impetus to 'fix' the consequences is probably unwise, as a more fundamental rethink of the human-machine interface is now warranted.

9.1 Situation awareness

Researchers have yet to fully agree on a definition for situation awareness. There have been differences in seeing situation awareness as a product, namely knowledge, versus a process, namely perception. Currently, some view situation awareness as both a momentary mental model of the environment (product) plus the processes of sampling, representation and projection which produce goal-directed knowledge and behaviour (Endsley, 1995a). Others have steered clear of the mixture, and have used an environment interaction approach, with situation awareness being adaptive, externally directed consciousness (Smith and Hancock, 1995). Another group sees little benefit in a definition, and have proposed that situation awareness be considered a label for a variety of cognitive processing activities that are critical in dynamic, event driven environments (Sarter and Woods, 1995).

A definition used by many which bridges product and process includes[3]

Situation awareness is the perception of the elements in the environment within a volume of time and space, the comprehension of their meaning, and the projection of their status in the near future.

but equally good is [4],

An understanding of the meaning of events and the ability to anticipate the consequences of taking or failing to take particular actions.

The environmental interaction view encourages simplicity such that the following

Awareness appropriate for the achievement of a purpose.

could be a definition[5]. In this book, situation awareness is seen as a process, rather than a label for a cluster of cognitive activities, but a process that currently cannot be clearly demarcated. While the environmental interaction approach (Flach, 1995; Smith and Hancock, 1995) suits the biases already present in other sections of this book (Chapter 5), this chapter considers situation awareness in terms of some of the process elements that are critical in dynamic, event-driven environments.

Limitations in knowledge, sustaining attention, and processing information appear to underlie lack of situation awareness and these three will be considered briefly. This makes it possible to appreciate the effects of the technology-centred approach to automation on situation awareness, particularly with respect to feedback, machine comprehensibility and the human capacity to remain generative, or creative, with goal-directed knowledge and informed action (Smith and Hancock, 1995). Topics which are not covered include the measurement of situation awareness[6] and its interrelationship with decision making[7].

9.1.1 Some historical features

Situation awareness is an issue because of human limitations with knowledge generation, sustaining attention, and processing information. Each of these is considered briefly.

Knowledge generation   The linkage between inadequate situation awareness and incomplete goal-directed knowledge has long been appreciated, particularly by the military. The loss of HMS *Victoria* after being rammed by HMS *Camperdown* in 1893 amply demonstrated the vital role of goal-directed knowledge[8]. Various branches of the military have initiated many of the systematic approaches to knowledge acquisition, with the occasional lapse[9]. For example, the transition from land and sea reconnaissance to air reconnaissance started with military ballooning[10], which was effective in enhancing the situation awareness of the British forces during the war in South Africa at the end of the last century. The development of the aircraft during the first world war owed as much to its capacity to facilitate reconnaissance, either by aircraft or balloon[11], as it did to being an offensive weapon in its own right. Current technologies provide an abundance of goal-directed information, but there are still situation awareness problems because of the inability of the recipients to maintain the necessary attention and to process this information (Endsley and Smith, 1996).

Sustaining attention   The capacity of people to sustain attention has often proved inadequate, no matter how clear the overall tactical need for attention, nor how involved humans have been. This inattentiveness has impaired situation awareness from the time a human first attempted to mount a lookout, or stand guard. Observations on the first radar operators established that monitoring was vulnerable (Mackworth, 1950), and that the capacity to detect declined with time on the task. There have only been a few modern, air-to-surface, cruise missiles fired at ships under operational conditions, yet their success rate[12] suggests that attentional systems, and the allocation of attention, are key factors in military situation awareness.

Sustaining attention has been an issue in non-military work places as well. Many incidents and accidents in commercial aviation and road transport have revealed how much difficulty operators are having with sustaining attention (Satchell, 1993). Elegant studies in flightdecks on instrumented pilots have described the pattern of inattention and its rapid onset (Cabon, Mollard, Coblentz, Fouillot, Stouff and Molinier, 1991). The demands for sustained attention have changed as the machine environment has become more complex. Thus, sustaining attention is vulnerable

Innovation and automation

when attention has to be allocated to a number of simultaneous tasks (Endsley and Smith, 1996), and further threatened by having to allocate attention to determining how well a machine is progressing with each of them (Sarter and Woods, 1995). There has been recognition of impaired attentional states like absorption, fixation and preoccupation, and their role in errors, incidents and accidents on flightdecks[13]. There are other examples of inattention coupled to impaired situation awareness in space exploration, nuclear power plants, other transport systems[14] and anaesthesia. It is unlikely that work places, like financial dealing rooms, automated manufacturing systems, security systems, electronic broking houses, strategic control centres, traffic control rooms and many office automation systems have solved the attentional needs required for maintaining situation awareness.

Information processing The human capacity to process all the information needed for maintaining situation awareness has always been marginal. The earliest machines, though unsophisticated by modern standards, brought this vulnerability to the surface, particularly in situations where humans were required to foresee the consequences of their current interaction with a machine. Classic examples include the first overseas flight of the R101 airship[15], and the 'Battle of May Island' tragedy involving the K-Class submarines[16]. The need to obtain machine assistance with information processing was understood during the first aircraft flights and underlay the early development of stability augmentation devices[17]. The increasing sophistication of machines and their potential to overload the information processing capacity of humans is now seen as a major factor in impairing situation awareness. This is being countered by a variety of design approaches like automation modes[18], automation which is adaptive[19], and 'intelligent' interfaces[20]. The success of these approaches in sustaining attention in the automated flightdeck (Sarter and Woods, 1992; 1995; Sarter, 1994), anaesthesia (Moll van Charante, Cook, Woods, Yue and Howie, 1992; Gaba, Howard and Small, 1995; Obradovich and Woods, 1996) and nuclear plant process control (Woods, O'Brien and Hanes, 1987) is currently under debate.

9.1.2 Situation awareness processes

There is no agreed process or scheme underlying situation awareness, although some have been proposed (Tenny et al., 1992; Endsley, 1995a; Adams et al., 1995; Previc, Yauch, DeVilbiss, Ercoline and Sipes, 1995). It is unlikely that any current model or scheme will be substantiated, because of the mix of cognitive processes, confounded by the effects of individual differences. The following briefly summarises one approach.

A starting point is Neisser's expanded view of the perceptual cycle (Tenny et al., 1992). Here, current environmental information continuously modifies a model of the current environment which itself directs perceptual exploration. The outcomes of the perceptual exploration are used to update the current environmental picture, with selected pieces of information being pooled to refashion the environmental picture.

This basic cycle has been enlarged by the addition of a general exploratory cycle where higher order cognitive strategies are employed[21]. For example, anticipation at the basic perceptual level is a readiness to perceive certain information, while at the cognitive level, anticipation means the consideration of possible outcomes using knowledge intensive activities. These can include contingency planning and the exploration of those system faults that have the potential to become factors in a longer term outcome.

The layering of a general exploratory cycle around a core perceptual cycle is one way of describing processes involved in maintaining situation awareness. This description is not that useful, unless the constraint imposed by a limited information processing capacity on simultaneous tasks, is factored in. Thus, deeper processing of information is required to give a level of significance to an input, which will link it to an appropriate level of attention. Unfortunately, deeper processing comes at a price, namely a greater potential of failing to interpret other available data. The converse, less time and effort on processing, runs the risk of misconstruing the implications of incoming information. These trade-offs are part of every situation where multiple tasks are being undertaken. They become particularly evident when switching between tasks is required, with switching resulting in a significant loss in sensitivity or time that can be allocated. When the switch is to a topic that is unrelated to a current task, interpretation takes time, effort and can involve a considerable mental workload.

9.1.3 Other features

The importance of sustaining attention, information processing, and goal-directed knowledge acquisition, are unquestioned and have been considered briefly (9.1.1). If it is accepted that situation awareness is currently difficult to define, and that it must be viewed as an aggregate term for those cognitive processing activities required in dynamic, event-driven environments (Sarter and Woods, 1995), then there are two features that deserve more emphasis. These are its dynamic and creative nature and its relationship with purpose.

Dynamism and creativity The dynamic nature of situation awareness may appear as the continuous anticipation of change in a task, or it involves the continuous iteration of a mental picture or model of the environment. The capacity to continuously create new mental forms is a vital part of situation awareness. The more dynamic are the processes underlying awareness, the better the situation awareness. From giving a speech, to doing psychoanalysis, to flying a long haul aircraft, to managing an industrial project, to caring for an individual with a chronic illness, to conducting a scientific research program, to exercising stewardship for an organisation, there are benefits if those involved continuously re-shape significant tasks. Flexible and continuous re-assessment of a task distinguishes those who are skilled. However, even the dynamic, creative prowess of the skilled suffers significantly when another task is added or overlaid. In many occasions where situation awareness has been insufficient, it has not been the skill of individuals at a particular task that has been in question. Rather, it has been the decline in their performance at a task, in the face of competing task demands.

Purpose The importance of purpose alignment in complex human-machine environments is now being acknowledged (Billings, 1996) and has been linked to awareness in the adaptive, externally-directed consciousness view of situation awareness (Smith and Hancock, 1995). A persistence feature of those incidents and accidents that have been linked to both situation awareness problems and concerns about the human-machine interface (FAA, 1996), is the presence of conflicting purposes between human and machine (*Example 11 & 12*). Goal-misalignment can easily outstrip processing, attentional and assimilation capacities (*Example 15*). Thus, in work places where situation awareness has been deficient, differences in purpose are a common issue.

The FAA has produced nine recommendations for improving the situation awareness of flight crew. These address inadequate automation mode awareness, inadequate awareness of systems and status, variation in interface design, design of warning systems, uncertainty as to what is required to provide feedback, and hazardous behavioural states (FAA, 1996). All of these deficiencies impact understanding the purpose of the machine, particularly under dynamic, environmental situations.

9.1.4 Technology-centred automation and situation awareness

Viewed retrospectively, it might be thought that problems with situation awareness were almost bound to occur with a technology-centred approach. This approach to automation is characterised by deficiencies in machine feedback (7.3.1) and machine comprehensibility (7.3.2), both key factors in achieving state awareness about systems. An independent observer might even see situation awareness as an artificial construct, fashioned to meet known deficiencies in the technology-centred approach. However, deficient situation awareness antedated complex machines and technology-centred automation (9.1.1). The effect on situation awareness of deficiencies in machine feedback and in machine comprehensibility will be considered. Two other areas where the technology-centred approach affects situation awareness indirectly, are its inability to entrain human creativity and its inadequacies in helping humans sustain attention.

Feedback There are various ways that human-machine systems obtain and provide feedback. The simplest and most frequently used is system performance. Whether this is the flight path of an aircraft, the track of a road vehicle, the output of a production process, or the resolution of a clinical symptom or sign, outputs or outcomes are potent and useful means of providing feedback. This type of feedback is a feature of the technology-centred approach to automation. The benefits of this type of feedback are its relative immediacy and its simplicity, while its deficiencies are its inability to transmit information about an impending undesired outcome, either as system trends, or shifts in performance of intermediate process steps.

Many complex systems currently provide feedback about system performance, trends and the performance of process steps. Despite the display of aberrant system behaviour, humans have remained unresponsive in technologically-complex work environments (*Example 11 and 12*). This applies to many work places, as well as the flightdeck[22]. On the flightdeck, the unresponsiveness has been approached in two ways (See 10.4.2 for a more detailed consideration). One approach has rationalised the feedback paths in the new electronic environment, by providing machine certainty if feedback is insufficient or ineffective. The alternative approach has been to maintain all existing feedback paths and add others as new technology allows. While it may appear as if the provision of machine certainty after rationalising the pathways for feedback is just another form of technology-centred automation, it is unclear that adding more feedback, to feedback developed from the existing technology-centred approach, represents an advance. The lack of agreement has prompted the Human Factors Team of the Federal Aviation Authority to conclude that there is a lack of credible data and consensus regarding what constitutes effective feedback and how best to provide it[23].

A key feature of technology-centred automation, the meeting of machine needs before meeting human needs, appears to still hold sway. In part, this results from uncertainty as to what are the human's needs for feedback. It may be that the real legacy of the technology-centred approach in the area of feedback is its inability to ask questions related to these needs.

Comprehensibility In the last three decades there has been an explosion in machine capability, so much so that understanding them is now a key issue. While this has become particularly evident on flightdecks, inadequate knowledge of automated systems is also apparent in modern vehicles[24], medical diagnostic and care systems[25], and in the corporate and manufacturing environments[26]. Under normal conditions, it is not readily apparent that situation awareness suffers, but there is evidence that it is impaired when system demands are high.

The technology-centred approach to automation has been frequently associated with poor comprehensibility and impaired situation awareness on flightdecks (7.3.2). The automatic pilot of thirty years ago has been replaced with flight management systems that have multiple 'modes' for each phase of flight (Degani, Shafto and Kirlik, 1995). Each mode contains sequences of electronic actions, electronic responses, and conditional states, all orchestrated by the flux of information from aircraft sensors and the desires of the electronic controller. For example, there are many possible descent modes in an aircraft, such as vertical speed, flight level change, VNAV path, VNAV speed, and Flight Path Angle[27]. The complexities of sub-system performance and sub-system engagement within each of these modes are considerable, and together they put comprehensibility under strain.

Obviously, the first use of a mode made a great deal of sense, because it encapsulated much functionality which, up to that point, had been provided as discrete elements. The mode allowed the human and the machine to know and use these capabilities within a functional block. In their initial form, modes helped comprehensibility, information processing, goal-directed knowledge acquisition and situation awareness. However, when machine capability increased further and multiple modes became possible, designers failed to appreciate that the benefit of using modes could easily be reduced.

Each mode makes significant demands on pilot knowledge, with the consequence that pilots must restrict the modes they use, if they are have to sufficient goal-directed knowledge within each mode. The flexibility of the technology-centred approach (7.3.2) has made it almost inevitable that there would be a multiplicity of modes. As the number of modes has increased, their ability to cluster functionality has declined. In addition, the capacity for modes to mean different things under different operating conditions[28], and for modern aircraft to switch their modes without pilots providing consent, further increases the likelihood that the machine and the human may not share purpose, with impaired situation awareness resulting (Sarter and Woods, 1992; 1995; Degani, Mitchell and Chappell, 1995).

Creativity The human propensity to vary their approach to tasks produces problems for human-machine interactions where machines have been designed by the technology-centred approach (7.3.3). Organisations have circumvented this problem by diverting significant resources to the selection of people of particular types, to the continual evolution of standard operating procedures, guidelines and checklists and to training and certification. Together, these produce powerful ritualised behaviours (6.6, 6.6.1, 6.6.3, 7.3.3, 11.4), which dampen individualism. Under normal operating conditions, individual creativity is neither desired or expected, and as technology-centred automation is not designed to access it, this ritualising of behaviour is entirely appropriate.

The capacity to maintain situation awareness comes under stress when circumstances become less routine (*Example 15*). On these occasions, additional demands are placed on goal-directed knowledge, information processing and creativity and these demands can be new for the individuals involved. Enhancing creativity, particularly that required for building new mental constructs of the environment in complex situations, remains outside the capacity of the technology-centred approach. So deficient is this approach in these situations that in the instances where humans have realised what is required, they have chosen to increase the human resource, rather than look for assistance from the machine[29]. At times, the machine designed with a technology-centred approach has continued to work inappropriately.

Sustaining attention The linkage between situation awareness and sustaining attention has been described (9.1.1). Automation which manages vigilance, while achieving a task, might be an ideal (*Example 16*), but a reasonable expectation is that automation should not impair the human capacity to sustain attention. Technology-centred automation has failed in this regard.

Many aspects of current automation impair sustained attention. On flightdecks, the excessive variability in displays consumes attentional resources[30], as does the diversity and poor integration of warning systems[31]. A design goal has been to reduce workload at times when it has been unacceptably high. This goal has been achieved in routine operations, but at the cost of having such low workloads in the cruise phases that vigilance has suffered. Attempts to provide auxiliary aids for sustaining attention are acknowledgments that the technology-centred approach is faulty[32]. The philosophy surrounding these systems is questionable, as is their scientific basis, for they have the potential to create new, unwanted behavioural effects. Sustaining attention in other work places suffers in a similar way.

9.1.5 Summary

Situation awareness is a complex process, which currently cannot be clearly delineated, nor will it be measured in the foreseeable future. Problems with situation awareness hover over all automation designed with the technology-centred approach, and the current responses to situation awareness incidents and accidents are reactive and focus on providing short term solutions. Limitations in knowledge, sustaining attention, and processing information underlie lack of situation awareness in routine situations, but in the more dynamic, or an unexpected environment, the capacity to remain generative, or creative, with goal-directed knowledge is vital. Currently, situation awareness is an issue in a limited number of work places. Soon, many work tasks, including strategy development and the handling of key customers, will correctly and incorrectly involve the concept of situation awareness without having a coherent philosophy for human-machine interaction.

9.2 Complacency and miscommunication

Peripheralisation (Norman et al., 1988) is the role change which accompanies increased levels of automation and encompasses reduced situation awareness, complacency and an impairment of communication. The latter two have frequently been observed when there have been problems with human-machine interfaces.

9.2.1 Complacency

Complacency has been used as a behavioural coding category in aircraft incidents. It has been defined in various ways (Singh, Molloy, and Parasuraman, 1993), including,

> *Self satisfaction which may result in non-vigilance, based on an unjustified assumption of satisfactory system state.*

Complacency and situation awareness are linked. Excessive trust generates complacency, which can interfere with sustained attention, and hence situation awareness (9.1.1, 9.1.4). With respect to automated systems, complacency inducing factors have been broken down into those which are confidence-related, reliance-related, trust-related and safety related (Singh et al., 1993). Trust is probably a key underlying factor when humans share with machines (Riley, 1989; Taylor, 1990). Trust is also a key determinant of successful sharing between humans (Mink and

Mink and Owen, 1987), and is considered later in the context of sharing between human and machine (12.3).

Pilots' attitude to automation indicates that trust is an issue (Weiner, Chidester, Kanki, Palmer, Curry and Gregorich, 1991; Tenny et al., 1995). Complacency is of significant concern to pilots as flightdecks become more automated, yet pilots want more automation, and also want to maintain authority (Tenny et al., 1995). There are contradictions here which suggest that the trust in technology is fluid and not rationally driven. Some airlines are dictating that automation be used to the maximum which, coupled with pilots high compliance with standard operating procedures, will further promote trust. Training that unnecessarily glosses over the poor feedback and the poor comprehensibility of technology-centred automation creates an ideal climate for over reliance, trust and complacency. Complacency has been publicly acknowledged as an issue on flightdecks[33].

Anaesthesia has been likened to commercial piloting with long periods of low workload and a significant monitoring task, interspersed with brief interludes of frantic activity. Anecdotally, complacency has been an issue, although most current human-machine interest in anaesthesia has focussed on situation awareness, the human computer interface, and decision making (Moll van Charante et al., 1992; Gaba et al., 1995; Obradovich and Woods, 1996; Cook and Woods, 1996). There is a considerable bias in this interest in that much of this recent work has focussed on cardiothoracic surgery. This ignores the bulk of surgery for which anaesthesia is much less demanding, both temporally and from a physiological and therapeutics' knowledge point of view. Complacency is an issue across most of anaesthesia, independent of any technology. Complacency is not helped by the design of the technology used for monitoring consumer state, as its 'clumsiness' leads to stereotyped routines and rituals which become detached from purpose (Cook and Woods, 1996). The vulnerability of rituals to small changes in the machine or the environment[34], underlies one link between ritual, creativity and technology (Chapter 11).

Complacency in clinical care has long antedated technology and is not limited to anaesthesia. The presence of technology in the form of monitoring equipment, organ support systems and infusion devices in wards and intensive care units will be increasingly coupled with complacency-related problems. These will be enhanced by both the technology-centred approach in their design, and the competing demands for attention, because staff are under resourced in most health systems.

9.2.2 Miscommunication

Peripheralisation encompasses miscommunication. It has been proposed that automation alters communication content and the communication process in situations where humans and machines share tasks. Thus, it has been observed that as the degree of flightdeck automation increases, inter pilot communication decreases (Costley, Johnson and Lawson, 1989). There have been communication flaws preceding the incidents and accidents which have generated the current concern about the human-machine interface[35]. However, it is not clear that miscommunication is due to the technology-centred approach, for it may be a consequence of subtle and general automation induced changes in crew coordination (Norman et al., 1988).

Undoubtedly communication is being altered by automation, but how harmful this is, is unknown. One area of concern is the variation in communication practices which are in part due to the technology-centred approach to automation. The uncertainty surrounding the automation of checklists and modes has resulted in significant variation between airlines in the way cockpit crew communicate and thereby share with the machine. Some airlines require their aircrews call out all mode changes as a means of the crew monitoring automation modes (FAA, 1996). Similarly, the communication surrounding checklists is relatively varied (Degani and Weaver, 1994). The need for one crew member to devote themselves to handling current flight management systems (FMS) can take them out of communication loops on the flightdeck.

9.3 Odds and ends

There are a number of other effects from current automation which are of unknown significance. These include primary/secondary task inversion, 'cocooning', automation deficit, boredom-panic syndrome and some hazardous states of awareness like absorption, fixation and preoccupation. The first two will be considered briefly while the rest have been described elsewhere[36].

9.3.1 Primary/secondary task inversion

This is a behavioural phenomenon where the presence of a backup system results in flight crew using the backup system as a primary source of information (Weiner and Curry, 1980). Hence, a number of early mishaps with Ground Proximity Warning Systems (GPWS) may have in part been due to crew inverting the importance of the normal altitude displays and the GPWS. With an inversion, the crew interpreted warning system silence as indicating that there were no altitude issues. The advent of Traffic Collision Avoidance Systems (TCAS) has the same potential, such that once it is turned on, some flight crew will no longer use the current systems and procedures on flightdecks to maintain a picture of the proximity of other aircraft[37]. The use of automated check lists also has potential for primary/secondary task inversion, because humans will be able to transfer the responsibility of the checking task to the machine (Palmer and Degani, 1991). Any backup system is able to substitute as an information source[38].

9.3.2 Cocooning

This automation dependant behavioural state is characterised by humans becoming insulated from ongoing events. It probably encompasses other hazardous states of awareness. It has already been suggested that excessive trust and over reliance on automated systems (Singh et al., 1993), plus creativity-dampening rituals (8.3), might have a role in producing this type of behavioural state. Another contributing factor is likely to be the difference in performance between out-of-the-loop monitoring versus in-the-loop monitoring (Parasuraman et al., 1996). Out-of-the-loop monitoring is a feature of the conventional technology-centred approach to automation and manifests as poor monitoring of an automated task, compared with the monitoring of the same task performed manually. This is particularly so when operators are engaged in the manual performance of other tasks (Parasuraman, Molloy and Singh, 1993). This may be due to the normal decrement of vigilance with a constant task, forgetting[39], or the allocation strategy of diverting resources to manual tasks rather than to the monitoring task (Parasuraman et al., 1996).

9.4 Summary

The last two chapters describe some of the current problems which occur in technologically-complex work environments where humans and machines share tasks. Most current automation has been created with a technology-centred approach, and the contents of these last two chapters might be seen as an unbalanced criticism of this approach, focussing on relatively rare events. The issue of balance is redressed in the next chapter (10.2, 10.3) by considering user surveys which paint a complex picture. While there is evidence which affirms the effectiveness of current automation (see also Chapter 2), there is also significant concern that current automation creates problems when humans and machines share tasks. These problems centre around situation awareness and complacency and become particularly evident when non-routine situations arise. In innocent forms, they affect all of us everyday of our lives, but they have a malignant potential which must not be ignored. The extent of this problem is unknown, but is likely to be large, particularly as our societies become totally dependent upon automation.

Notes

1 See pp. 10-13, Satchell (1993).
2 The term 'cocooning' describes the dissociated state that appears to have existed at some human-machine interfaces (*see Examples 11 & 12*), where information about the increasingly parlous state of an activity has been available but has not been assimilated.
3 See quotation of Endsley in Tenny et al. (1992), Adams et al. (1995), Flach (1995).
4 See pp. 2, Tenny et al. (1992).
5 Modified from discussion of Smith and Hancock (1995). See pp. 146.
6 Measurement is being carried out. For a review of measurement approaches, see pp. 65-70, Endsley (1995b).
7 See model in Fig. 1 of Orasanu (1995), and Fig. 1a & b in Kaempf et al. (1996).
8 See pp. 337-339. of Parkes (1970). In summary, HMS *Victoria* was rammed by HMS *Camperdown* during a manoeuvre which required two columns of British battleships to turn simultaneously towards one another. The manoeuvre was possible if the columns of ships were more than 1600yds apart (the turning diameter for these ships being 800yds), but at the start of this manoeuvrer being carried out before anchoring off Tripoli, the columns were only 1200 yards apart.
9 See 'A visit to GHQ in France, August 1917', pp. 369, Hastings (1987).

10 See pp. 10-36, Walker (1971).

11 Control of airspace over the trenches either allowed your own aircraft to carry out reconnaissance or it allowed your balloons to stay airborne without danger.

12 The sagas of USS *Stark* and HMS *Sheffield* are well known and similar. In HMS *Sheffield* there was no appreciation that an Exocet air-to-surface missile was coming towards them, even though the adjacent picket ship HMS *Glasgow* had reported the oncoming planes and the missile launch. During the critical detection period, HMS Sheffield was carrying out a satellite transmission suggesting that allocation of attention across tasks was a critical factor in the state of situation awareness in the control room See BBC Documentary, *The Falklands War*, No.3 Trusting in Luck.

13 See pp. 58-59, FAA (1996).

14 See *Example 8*.

15 The story of the last flight of the R101 is well known. It is unlikely that the information processing capacity of the crew was sufficient to appreciate how the carrying capacity of the airship was declining as the trip progressed.

16 The 'Battle of May Island' incident involved the K class submarine, a large, fast submarine, capable of escorting surface ships. On 31 January, 1918, 2 flotillas of submarines were sailing with destroyer flotillas and cruiser squadrons at a speed of 20knots on a dark night, with no lights, at the entrance of the Firth of the Forth. One submarine turned out of line to avoid fishing vessels but suffered a jammed helm and ran into another. Both flotillas were then involved in a series of chain collisions as well as being run down by their escorting vessels. These collisions were spread over some time and resulted in two submarines being sunk with heavy loss of life. Two other submarines and several large surface ships were badly damaged. It is unlikely that information processing capacity was sufficient, in admittedly difficult circumstances. See pp. 34, Lipscomb (1975).

17 See pp.16-17, Billings (1996).

18 See pp. 44-48, FAA (1996). Also see Fig.2 on pp. 45 of FAA (1996) for a Boeing aircraft and Fig.4 on pp. 19 of Sarter (1994) for an Airbus aircraft.

19 See Parasuraman et al. (1996), which presents evidence that temporary allocation to human control is beneficial in inducing system awareness.

20 See Warwick (1997) about the F-22, in particular pp. 11-12 of the supplement and the capacity of the tactical interface to alter itself, depending upon threat intensity.

21 See Fig.1-3 , pp. 4-8, Tenny et al. (1992).

22 See appendix D of FAA (1996). In many, but not all, of these incidents the machine displayed information, which was not assimilated.

23 See pp. 56-58 of FAA (1996) and see Recommendation SA-5 (pp. 63) which states;

    The FAA should encourage the exploration, development, and testing of new ideas and approaches for providing effective feedback to the flightcrew to support error detection and improved situation awareness.

    SA-6 and SA-7 are related to feedback as well. See also discussion in general and 'Intelligent Feedback' pp. 31-32, Palmer et al. (1993).

24 Anti-lock braking systems are not understood by many drivers and this becomes evident during an emergency braking manoeuvre.

25 Medical technology abounds in poor comprehensibility, particularly as it has become more automated. See Cook and Woods (1996) and Obradovich and Woods (1996). When demands are high, like in cardiopulmonary bypass, the poor comprehensibility of some medical technology and its effects on situation awareness present problems.

26 Office automation comprehensibility has declined significantly. Five years ago, organisations could have a completely capable information management group, but this no longer exists, and complex contractor or outsourcing arrangements are now required, but usually prove inadequate.

27 VNAV is Vertical Navigation. See pp. 47, FAA (1996) and Fig.2.

28 See pp. 6, Sarter and Woods (1995), and data on pp. 310-313, Sarter and Woods (1992).

29 See 1.) the 'battle' that took place in *example 15*

    2.) the use of extra human resource in the saga of flight 232. See Gerren (1995).

    3.) 12.2.1

    4.) note 15 of chapter 12

30 See pp. 50, FAA (1996).

31 See pp. 50-56, ibid.

32 See pp. 109-110, Satchell (1993), and the 'Pilot Guard' announcement, Moxon (1997).

33 See pp. 59, FAA (1996). See Table 5b, pp. 23, Tenny et al. (1995).

34 See pp. 610, Cook and Woods (1996).

35 The cockpit transcripts for both the Strasbourg (*Example 11*) and the Cali (*Example 12*) have communication faults in the period leading up to each accident.

36 For automation deficit, boredom-panic syndrome, see pp. 12, Satchell (1993) and for absorption, fixation and preoccupation, see pp. 59, FAA (1996).

37 TCAS traffic advisory warnings are trusted the least in a survey across multiple aircraft types and this may prevent TCAS causing primary/secondary inversion. See pp. 33, Tenny et al. (1995). However, some incidents suggest that the inversion is already occurring.

38 See sample narrative No.1, Palmer et al. (1993), where an aural approaching-altitude alert, a backup system, is used as a primary source.

39 This use of 'forgetting' means the degradation of an operator's mental model of a task when a task remains automated for long periods. See pp. 677, Parasuraman et al. (1996) and *'familiarisation and forgetting'* as a mechanism for insight (5.3.1).

10 Sharing with machines

Many species share. When humans share, their selflessness can be so fulsome as to be a defining feature of the species. Human sharing can also be driven by self-interest, such that its meanness reflects poorly, even in comparison with the harshest and most maligned of predators. Sharing has always suffered from the spectre of self-interest, but human bravery and self-abnegation refute that all sharing is so driven (Vasillopulos, 1987).

Sharing between humans is complex and is based on relationships. For individuals, sharing is most problematic between adults, often possible between children, quite likely between humans and animals, and entirely straightforward between humans and many machines. The fragility and artificiality of organisations makes sharing difficult in work places[1], despite the theories of academics, and the magical nostrums of management practitioners.

In the present chapter, current sharing between humans and machines is explored. When humans have shared with most machines, like cars, bicycles, and other simple devices, sharing has been straightforward. Sharing has been more questionable when the machine is automated, particularly when the automation requires that the human and the machine work together on a task. Two approaches to this type of sharing have already been described (Chapter 7). While the human-centred approach to automation is still mainly conceptual, the technology-centred approach has been able to produce useful sharing, even in cognitive rather than physical areas (*Examples 1-4*), though this does not routinely occur (*Examples 9-13*). A rather more sinister relationship between human and machine is also possible, where cognitive tussling occasionally gives way to physical struggling, as machine and human simultaneously strive to achieve contradictory goals.

The present chapter explores how sharing between humans and machines occurs at present. Currently, technology-centred automation can be separated into different levels which produce different types of sharing. Sometimes this sharing is satisfactory, but it is unusual. What is always present is the uncertainty as to how to produce useful sharing, and this is explored in some detail. Finally, the current philosophical basis for sharing with machines is described.

10.1 Levels of automation and types of sharing

Sharing between humans and machines occurs in many forms, and these can be stratified into levels of automation (Riley, 1989; Billings, 1991; Endsley and Kiris, 1995; Tenny, Rogers and Pew, 1995; Billings, 1996). At one extreme, machines operate autonomously, while at the other, there is manual control. Between these two there are many different levels which have different degrees of human involvement.

Like many issues in automation, there does not appear to be complete agreement on how the different levels of automation should be delineated. One scheme (Riley, 1989) has two dimensions, the first being machine intelligence which has seven levels ranging from presenting raw data to anticipation of operator error. The second dimension is autonomy, with twelve levels ranging from varying types of communication to varying degrees of autonomous action without human permission. In a survey of pilots and their views on levels of automation, the researchers opted for three levels, because of pilots' difficulty in understanding the differences between levels (Tenny et al., 1995). Others have used five levels (Endsley and Kiris, 1995).

The levels used in this chapter were created for understanding aviation automation (Billings, 1991). There are seven levels. Starting from the direct, manual control end of the spectrum, there is assisted manual control, shared control, management by delegation, management by consent, and management by exception, before reaching autonomous operation (Fig. 10.1). These levels have been criticised, because the distinctions between have been seen as subtle and ambiguous (Tenny et al., 1995). Nevertheless, oversimplification is as much a problem as is subtlety and ambiguity. The seven levels are useful when aviation examples are used to illustrate sharing issues, and these will be considered briefly with the two extremes of direct manual control and autonomous operation being considered together.

10.1.1 Assisted manual control

In the assisted manual control level of automation, human involvement is high. In aircraft, almost all control is assisted, from amplification of force via hydraulic systems to stability augmentation of various forms. Some of these systems can be selected and some of them work continuously and are not intended to be bypassed[2]. In the modern automobile, power steering is a simple form of assisted manual control which cannot be disabled, while a cruise control system provides assistance which is optional. Office automation abounds with optional systems, with word processing packages having concurrent spelling and formatting support. In medical practices, allergy and drug interaction alerts are features of electronic prescribing systems[3], while optional information provision about therapeutic agents is provided for pregnancy and disease states. Manufacturing of all types abounds with assisted manual systems, which control production lines, warehouses, inventory and the working environment. Similarly, service industries have sophisticated systems, with tourism operations of all types depending upon the considerable assistance providing by the automation of booking and scheduling.

10.1.2 Shared control

The A-320, the first fly-by-wire commercial aircraft, has shared control of all normal flight control modes (See 10.4.1). Pilot control is considerably modified by flight control computers with the aircraft able to ignore pilot input, if it is outside the control laws of the aircraft. The control laws are tailored to respond in ways which seem natural to the pilot, yet they are always present and much of the safety of the aircraft depends upon this 'invisible hand'. Human involvement can be extensive but at times humans are quite distant from tasks. Sharing is incomplete.

Some cars have anti-skid braking systems and traction control devices. These alter a driver's input on emergency braking and rapid acceleration, such that the safety and performance of the vehicle are enhanced. Some of these devices are not controllable by the driver, as they are a machine contribution to vehicle performance with the device interposed between the human and the machine. Organisations' electronic customer inquiry systems allow customers to exercise a limited choice in making an inquiry, but the choice is bounded, with many systems requiring entry before alternative and restrictive forms of use are provided. Second generation patient consultation systems control the opportunity for the doctor to alter the medical record. Different parts of the record remain changeable for different periods of time, with most inputs becoming non-volatile after about 30 minutes. From this point, the doctor may alter the record, but the original is kept for auditing purposes[4].

10.1.3 Management by delegation

Aircraft autopilots put the pilot into the role of manager[5]. When a pilot gives an autopilot a task to maintain a heading or hold a flight level, the machine can use a variety of performance modes to satisfy the tactical requirement. This level of automation is distinct from assisted manual control where tactical needs are met by the human, and is different from shared control, where the automation functions as a permanent partner. There are other examples of management by delegation in the hovering control of military and civilian helicopters and the ground-hugging, flight capability of some military aircraft.

In pharmaceutical manufacturing, humans delegate packaging of valuable, and potentially dangerous products, to a machine, which ensures that the pills are the right size, colour and shape, that the correct number of pills are present, and that they are properly aligned in a blister pack which ends up in a box with the correct label on it. Complete delegation occurs, but the level of delegation is selectable. The machine is capable of monitoring itself and its performance at the task. Management by delegation requires human involvement at the time of delegation, but only monitoring from that point on.

10.1.4 Management by consent

Given a goal, an automated machine can be delegated to achieve it, but stages of this task can require human consent. This is a feature of the A-320 and the Boeing

757/767 aircraft, which will not initiate a descent while in the cruise phase of flight without an enabling action from a pilot[6]. It is likely that there are military equivalents when critical phases of missions also require a human sign-off. Human involvement can be very variable.

Consent and automation is an uncertain area, because the act of consent can be perfunctory if complacency is present There are systems in railways (*Example 8*) and aircraft which require the human verify that they are alert[7]. The alerting system may not be attached to any operating system, but failure to respond in an appropriate manner causes the machine to miss the 'continuous consent'. These consent systems do not appear effective in altering alertness.

10.1.5 Management by exception

Automation which manages by exception is able to carry out a complete, complex task, unless the human intervenes. Commercial and military flight management systems conduct complete journeys, faithfully following a program put into a flight management system before the engines were started. The plan can be altered, by the pilot during the flight, but this is because circumstances have changed. Human involvement can be very low up to the point of the exception.

10.1.6 Direct manual control and the fully autonomous machine

There should be no sharing issues between humans and machines when there is direct manual control or a fully autonomous machine. In both cases, the 'messiness' of human-machine interaction is removed from operations. The number of instances where there is total manual control without any machine contribution is not as frequent as might be thought. Of even greater rarity are machines which are given complete responsibility for the well being of humans. Hence, the paradox of seeming to be able to have fully autonomous flightdeck operations, but not implementing complete machine control. The case for retaining pilots will be used as an example, as there are some logical and illogical issues in this and other work places, which are important for understanding the paradox and later considerations of roles for humans and machines (10.6, 11.3, Chapter 13).

Direct manual control There are few aircraft flying which do not have some form of machine assistance. Control automation in the form of yaw dampers, trim compensators and warning systems all reduce the direct manual component of the flying task[8]. Even when automated aircraft work in a manual mode, there is often back-up automation involved.

General features of autonomous flightdeck operation Despite the current capability to do away with flightdecks that accommodate humans, there is no suggestion that pilot free flight operations are being seriously considered. Indeed, the converse is true. The Human Task Force of the Air Transport Association of America sees humans managing and directing the air transport system through to the year 2010

(Billings, 1991). Pilots and flightdecks are central parts of all projected civilian aircraft projects, that is all subsonic, mass-transport aircraft, as well as future systems such as the Boeing High Speed Civil Transport (Alter and Regal, 1992; Palmer, Rogers, Press, Latorella and Abbott, 1995). Despite the different values and approaches to risk by the military, the human's place in the cockpit remains largely unchallenged[9].

There are some exceptions. For example, the Darkstar and the Global Hawk are long endurance, unmanned air vehicles designed for stealthy, high-altitude, reconnaissance missions. There are also a range of less sophisticated pilotless reconnaissance machines being used at present, as well as more exotic, earth-to-low-orbit shuttle replacement systems[10]. The need for endurance and keeping the airframe as small as possible are factors in dispensing with an on-board pilot.

Reasons for retaining pilots If those contributions that only a human can make are ignored (12.4.2, 12.4.3, Chapter 13), then there are still other technical reasons which have required humans maintain a significant presence on flightdecks. At present, the maturity of the technology of the aircraft is sufficient for pilot-free flight. However, as each aircraft ages, it embarks on a decay process which is relatively but not totally predictable. While failure of aircraft parts is extraordinarily rare, the aging of many parts is influenced by how they are looked after. The introduction of this human element means that the machine is capable of malfunctioning in an unpredictable way. Thus, engine failures can normally be managed by standard operating procedures, but on rare occasions when engine failure has sprayed engine parts through their own containment systems[11], pilots have faced unique situations. The aging of airframes is now an issue, with many of the first generation of widebody aircraft becoming uneconomic because of maintenance costs[12]. Sometimes these older structures have failed in use and the presence of a pilot has averted disaster[13]. While aircraft are theoretically capable of supporting pilot-free flight, they become imperfect with time, and management of this imperfection requires a human presence.

Similarly, the technical environment in which aircraft fly, that is the system which manages airspace, is very predictable, but not totally so. The non-technical environment, that is all that can occur naturally in the flying arena, is not predictable and at times appears wilful. The accommodations that pilots make from their accumulated experience and wisdom and the intuitive feel that pilots have for their aircraft and the environment are not readily mimicked.

While pilots are valued for the above reasons and for the unique contributions that they make, their presence on flightdecks is not solely based on logic and a 'unique' contribution to a mission. Passenger expectations add predictable and unpredictable elements. It is uncertain how willing the public would be to use a transport system when it is not controlled by a human. The fact that much of a commercial flight is already not controlled by a pilot is ignored or not realised. There are some ground based transport systems that are controlled remotely. The contribution to flightdeck operations by humans is probably overestimated by the public, and is in part related to the aura which envelops cockpit personnel. This aura

145

is part of the mantle of 'command', which is necessary as flightdeck personnel accept authority and accountability at the start of each flight. The mantle is deliberately amplified to passengers in a myriad of ways, maintaining the docility of most passengers for extended periods under very constrained conditions. The mantle of 'command' is reinforced by the patterned communications that flow into the passenger cabin from the flightdeck and can be vital under some circumstances.

Thus, pilot-free flight in commercial passenger carrying operations is not entertained. Yet, what is less clear, and the source of debate, is the nature of the tasks that still require human input in the face of machines that can operate autonomously. Pilots themselves are virtually unanimous in seeing themselves as responsible for the flying of aircraft in the future, but they also desire greater automation (Tenny et al., 1995). Hence, the autonomous level of automation is both artificial and elusive.

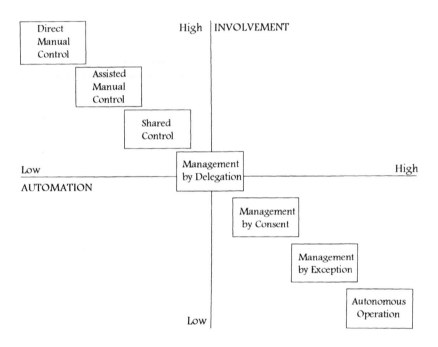

Figure 10.1 A comparison of the various types of automation with respect to the level of automation and the level of human involvement. The underlying concept for this display comes from Billings (1991; 1996)[14]. The relationship between level of automation and degree of human involvement is an idealised one. Each type of automation is a way of humans and machines sharing.

146

10.1.7 Summary

More evolved automated machines do not always operate at one level of automation while less evolved automated machines work at another level. Nor does automation move from one level to another, if one level of automation is inappropriate or inadequate (Fig. 10.1). Rather, more evolved automated machines appear to synchronously employ a number of automation levels. As each level of automation dictates a type of relationship between human and machine, more evolved automated machines have multiple, simultaneous, different types of relationships with operators.

10.2 Current sharing is satisfactory

Humans and machines share tasks to achieve outcomes. For some, the achievement of an outcome is all that matters, but for others, how outcomes are achieved is also an important issue. The means used to achieve outcomes can be a defining but subjective characteristic for individual and organisational satisfaction. Modern survey techniques have been used to probe subjective and objective satisfaction with the human-machine interface and have given some useful insights into sharing (Wiener, 1989; Wiener et al., 1991; Sarter, 1994; Tenny et al., 1995).

10.2.1 Overall measures

In an extensive survey published in 1995, pilots from a variety of aircraft (Airbus A-320, McDonald Douglas MD-11 and Boeing 747-400) felt that the different levels of automation (10.1.6) were more than sufficient for normal flight conditions and almost exactly met needs for non-normal conditions[15]. Satisfaction was also shown by the desire for more automation[16]. A 1991 survey of DC-9 and MD-88 pilots showed that only about a quarter thought that flightdeck designers had gone too far with automation, with this opinion reflecting more the view of those who flew the less automated DC-9[17]. The 1995 survey was able to detect preferences as to the type of automation, with pilots consistently supporting automation of the human-centred type rather than the alternative of 'full-automation'[18].

10.2.2 Specific areas of satisfaction

Automation can be of various types as well as at various levels. In the 1995 survey, control automation and automation which provided protection to the aircraft came closest to meeting current needs, with information, decision support and systems automation having a greater unmet need[19]. Pilots saw clear advantages in automated flight, compared with unassisted flight, in areas of workload extremes, and the detection of system errors. Pilots expressed a preference for an intermediate level rather than the autonomous level of automation as it offered nearly as much benefit with far fewer concerns[20]. None of the surveys have explored the capacity of current automation to help individuals do tasks differently, whether by choice, or forced by circumstances. The examples in Chapter 2 illustrate this capacity.

In *Example 1* about the control room, the operating procedures of the refinery allowed flexibility in the way tasks were shared. Operators were able to choose the level of automation and the supervisors' trust in the operators and the operators' level of trust in the machine were high. A sense of accord existed between humans and machines with the human-machine interface being used in novel and useful ways. How much of this had been orchestrated, and how much had occurred for other reasons[21] was not clear. The opportunity for a user to obtain benefits from automation was also exploited in *Example 2*, but individual initiative was required to overcome organisational indifference and inertia. That automation can be used formally in improvement and innovative activities, as well as provide significant benefit and satisfaction, was shown in *Example 3*. Here, the aviation industry demonstrated its prowess at using many levels of automation in a routine manner. Other long term users of information systems, such as research groups, database service providers and libraries are also able to obtain competitive advantages from current technology. In *Example 4*, the administrative assistant was able to gain considerable personal satisfaction from the flexibility of current technology and the ease with which it could promote innovative interactions in the work place.

10.3 Current sharing is unsatisfactory

The recent spate of surveys have often revealed subjective and objective dissatisfaction with the human-machine interface (Wiener, 1989; Wiener et al., 1991; Sarter, 1994; Tenny et al., 1995). Despite the desire for more automation (10.2.1), pilots have not expressed a blanket acceptance of automation. When asked whether 'the more the better' described how they thought about more automation, only 13% of pilots agreed or strongly agreed in the DC-9/MD-88 survey[22]. Similarly, the 1995 survey in highly automated aircraft showed that pilots felt there was greater virtue in shared rather than fully autonomous automation. Overall, dissatisfaction is relatively muted, particularly when it is compared with pilots' clear concern with specific features about current automation. These are covered in the rest of this section.

10.3.1 Machine induced surprises and misalignment of purpose

A recurrent report from automated flightdecks is that events occur that cause surprise to experienced pilots. In a survey of 166 Boeing 757 pilots, over 60% agreed or strongly agreed that there were aspects of that aircraft's automation that caused surprise (Wiener, 1989). In the DC-9/MD-88 survey, nearly 40% of pilots agreed or strongly agreed that there were modes and features of the automation of the newer MD-88 that they did not understand (Wiener et al., 1991). In surveys of Boeing 737 and of A-320 pilots, 67% and 80% of pilots had been surprised by automation during line operations (Sarter and Woods, 1992; Sarter, 1994). Although these incidents are being specifically sought, and only one incident is required to qualify, there still must be concern with these observations. When the incidents have been analysed (Sarter and Woods, 1995), the surprise commences when the machine's performance diverges from what is expected, but in most cases, the machine and the human have had different purposes for some time, though neither has realised this. In some situations the divergence in performance has been allowed to continue (*Example 11 & 12;* FAA, 1996) with disastrous results.

10.3.2 Trustworthiness and dissatisfaction

The conclusions by Tenny et al. (1995) on the trustworthiness of automation are of interest, in that their survey reveals a preference for simple, easy to use systems rather than for leading edge technologies. After ease of use, pilots want machines to be error resistant and able to check for typical kinds of mistakes, while their final preference is for machines that try to help after an error has occurred. In part, this reflects pilots perception that current automation levels are sufficient for normal and non-normal flight conditions, but are lacking when faced with emergency conditions (*Example 15*). Thus, trust is limited to the straightforward type of technology, with complex, advanced technology being perceived as less trustworthy.

10.3.3 Specific areas of concern

When working with high levels of automation, pilot's specific concerns include time spent working with and watching the interface, rather than looking outside the aircraft (head-down time), complacency, and degradation of pilot skills (Tenny et al., 1995). Over 60% of pilots in the DC-9/MD-88 survey agreed or strongly agreed that the head-down issue caused concern. The levels of concern decreased significantly as the level of automation moved from the fully autonomous to a more shared type[23].

In *Example 8* in the locomotive cabin, the automated systems were configured for autonomous operation during the routine part of a journey, there being little evidence that the operators were trusted to choose the manner in which automation might have assisted them. The need for a secondary system to maintain vigilance pointed to design failure, because the primary interaction between human and machine left the human incapable and almost completely peripheralised. This dismissal of the human contribution, and the consignment of humans to monitoring roles has been mimicked in road and air transport systems. In these situations, humans can re-exert their authority, but this may be at odds with the designer's and the owners' intentions. In *Example 10*, the flight crew deliberately misprogrammed a flight management system, their dissatisfaction leading to actions. This is not an isolated incident, there being an extensive 'library' of alternative ways of interacting with automation. While this human ingenuity can be admired, it is important to remember that this type of dissatisfaction is a threat to current automation, as there can be immediate or delayed consequences that are impossible to predict. Dissatisfaction can result in other behavioural states which have been considered in *Examples 11& 12* and discussed in the previous chapter. Finally, automation can be unsatisfactory because it fails to address larger system issues and their consequences. These are illustrated in *Examples 13, 14 & 15* and are discussed later.

10.4 Some uncertainties about human machine sharing

The evidence that there is uncertainty in the approach to sharing between humans and machines is widespread and is particularly easy to demonstrate using differences in modern flightdecks. This should not be taken as a criticism of flightdeck designers. Because the modern flightdeck must be automated, and because it is to a large extent an isolated capsule, there is a vital need for clarity in the design of this particular work place. Flightdeck designers have been extremely successful, and far in advance of others, in merging the capabilities of humans and machines. However, a consequence of being at the leading edge of human-machine interface design is the inevitable involvement in some design cul-de-sacs and their associated, automation-induced dysfunction.

In the last few years, there have been three major widebody civilian aircraft producers, namely Boeing Airplane Company, Airbus Industries and McDonald Douglas[24]. Some of their aircraft, the Boeing 747-400, Douglas MD-11 and Airbus A-320 have been ranked by pilots along a dimension of increasing technology, from Boeing, to Douglas, to Airbus (Tenny et al., 1995). This pilot's ranking may be influenced by training and manufacturer materials and is a survey result only relevant to a specific period. Thus the recent introduction of the Boeing 777 has probably recast the rankings significantly. The three companies have produced aircraft whose flightdecks are remarkably similar in many ways. Of interest are those flightdeck functions where there is variation in the way humans and machines share tasks. If it is assumed that this variation equates to uncertainty about human-machine sharing, then it is useful to consider some examples. Two flightdeck functions, envelope protection systems and how the machine informs the crew of its status, particularly the status of its engines, will be considered.

10.4.1 Protective automation

In order to appreciate the uncertainty in the approach to protective automation, it is necessary to understand a little about fly-by-wire control systems. It is a feature of the A-320 and Boeing 777. Fly-by wire systems signal pilot inputs with electrical signals, rather than alterations in a mechanical or hydraulic control system. The electrical signals go to electronic control devices whose outputs alter control surfaces by electrical servomechanisms or hydraulic sub-systems. The presence of electronic control devices provides designers with the opportunity to limit how far and how fast control surfaces move, independent of what input the pilot is providing. It is possible to mix attributes such that aircraft stability can be augmented, without any sacrifice of agility. These systems can change the pilot's perception of the aircraft, even allowing the attributes of different aircraft types to be mimicked. In addition, these systems allow pilots to 'fly' unflyable aircraft, although this option is not used in passenger aircraft[25]. Similarly these systems make it possible for the structure of the plane to be protected such that 'destructive' pilot commands, or those that would strain the aircraft structure, are limited in their effect. The A-320 was the first large passenger carrying aircraft to have a fly-by-wire control system.

The protective automation systems in the A-320, MD-11 and Boeing 747-400 are significantly different. In the A-320 the fly-by-wire system provides envelope protection, where certain flying characteristics of the aircraft, such as the bank angle, the angle of attack, and the degree of pitch, cannot be exceeded by the pilot, no matter what control input the pilot provides. This complete protection exists, as long as the flight control computers are on, and flying is conducted above cut-off values[26]. The MD-11 adopts a different approach to envelope protection. In this aircraft automatic protection keeps the angle of attack within limits, but can be overridden by application of additional control forces. Instead of the responsibility for overstressing an aircraft structure residing solely with the designer, as in the A-320, the MD-11 approach allows the pilot to share the responsibility. Thus, the pilot can operate to, or even beyond, aircraft limits in circumstances where a dire emergency demands it. To enhance this fusion of responsibility, the flying characteristics are designed such that if the aircraft is flown to higher limits than preferred, there is a progressive deterioration of flying qualities as these higher limits are approached.

This difference in design is probably not due to differences in the capability of structures or systems. Thus, it would have been possible for the fly-by-wire system of the A-320 to be configured as an 'incomplete' envelope protection system, similar to that of the MD-11. The Boeing 777 is a fly-by-wire aircraft which mimics the MD-11, in that pilots are able to override automatic protection mechanisms, but must suffer a degradation in flying qualities in this mode. Thus, two manufacturers have made considered, but different choices, which suggests that different cockpit design groups have adopted divergent positions related to the assignation of the protective task to the human or the machine.

Outwardly the complete protection mode appears to assume that humans cannot contribute to solutions and that the task of salvaging a desperate situation or creating a new approach, is not something that should be aided or abetted. In contrast, the incomplete mode allows for extraordinary performance under extraordinary circumstances, but must factor in the costs of over stressing structures in circumstances which are not extraordinary. It is possible that the logical and economically advantageous approach of complete envelope protection will be overtaken by the incomplete protection approach, because there have been rare instances of extraordinary human performance which have saved aircraft. These have been used as the justification for retaining human involvement in the cockpit (10.1.6). It is also possible that the presence of incomplete envelope protection leads to greater synergy between human and machine under normal flying conditions, because care of the machine becomes a continuous task of a pilot. Pilot preferences are not clear on the issue of envelope protection. In contrast to the preference of 747-400 and the MD-11 pilots for an incomplete form of protection (Tenny et al., 1995), those piloting the A-320 preferred that aircraft's complete protection system. In summary, there is a difference in the design of envelope protection systems between the major aircraft manufacturers, this difference is significant, this difference is perceived by users, and this difference points to uncertainty as to the optimal approach to sharing between human and machine. Uncertainty is centred on what is required from humans in non-routine operations, and how humans should share tasks with machines under these conditions.

10.4.2 System feedback

Another area of uncertainty concerning the sharing between humans and machines relates to the feedback that the aircraft gives the human about what it is doing. There are many systems in modern aircraft which operate autonomously and their activity is not signalled. For example, dampers are required by swept wing jet aircraft during banked turns to counter adverse yaw and these operate autonomously without their activity being signalled to the flightdeck. Similarly, there are pitch trim compensators and spoiler control systems whose states of deployment are not signalled in the cockpit. The approach of all manufacturers to feeding back information about these sub-systems follows the 'need-to-know' principle, most sub-systems functioning unseen until a problem occurs. Then, pictorial or alphanumeric displays highlight the failure type, with either the pilots or the machine being tasked with handling the faults.

There are other sub-systems where autonomous automation is present, but where there is continuous signalling of status. Hence, wing lift devices like flaps and leading edge systems have their current position signalled, as are the levels of thrust from engines. These allow pilots to appreciate the performance of these systems during automated flight sequences such as descent or climb. This feedback is seen as an essential element in helping the pilot appreciate the situation of the aircraft. When mixed with all the other information on aircraft attitude and its position in space, this feedback helps the pilot continuously create and refresh a mental picture of the aircraft' progress (9.1). However, there are significant differences in aircraft design related to the degree to which pilots are informed about the progress of a shared task.

A simple example is the position of engine thrust levers. In most aircraft, the engine thrust levers move pari-passu with the thrust delivered by the autothrust system. At a glance, flightdeck personnel know what the thrust settings are by seeing the lever positions, this providing yet another piece of information about aircraft state. During programmed descent and climb, the levers move without human input and engine performance is indicated on visual display units. This is the system in current McDonald Douglas and Boeing aircraft. In the Airbus A-320, the levers do not move when power is applied or withdrawn by the autothrust system, though the power commanded and delivered is displayed (Billings, 1991).

The 'motionless' levers and their inability to provide visual or tactile feedback has produced concern[27], but this has not been shared by airlines who operate this aircraft, nor is it reflected in the pilot ratings of A-320 automation. Indeed, the converse is true. In one survey, the A-320 providing the greatest satisfaction from its automation for both different flight conditions and different flight phases (Tenny et al., 1995). This result might suggest that the 'motionless' state of the thrust levers is not that important. However, other evidence and the known deficiencies in surveys creates doubt. There have been a number of incidents and accidents with the A-320 (*Example 11*) where the aircraft has been technically faultless and yet abnormal flight modes have been selected[28]. Discussion and consequent design recommendations have centred on the mode selection system, but what has not been addressed has been the general lack of involvement of aircrew when the aircraft has been in the wrong mode (*Example 11*). This lack of involvement has occurred, despite clear indications on flightdeck display systems of the consequences of an incorrect mode. When complete envelope protection is coupled with motionless thrust levers, it is reasonable to speculate that isolation of the pilots from the machine might on some occasions become part of some more generalised behavioural phenomenon (see 'cocooning' in 9.3). That this has occurred in the first fly-by-wire, commercial, passenger aircraft has been tragic, but it suggests that there may be factors in the automation process that are not understood, despite the experience and knowledge base of the world's best designers.

Further evidence that this is an area of uncertainty comes from the measures that Boeing has gone to in providing feedback about engine thrust in their latest aircraft, the Boeing 777. Although this is a fly-by-wire aircraft and has come into service nearly 10 years later than the A-320, the thrust levers for its two massive turbofans are back-driven by the autothrust management system so as to move the thrust levers in a manner similar to those in aircraft with traditional thrust control systems. Boeing has gone to a lot of trouble to provide as much feedback as possible, even though in a fly-by-wire aircraft there is no direct control between the thrust levers and the engines, and back-driving the thrust levers adds complexity and weight. The motionless thrust levers of Airbus aircraft are in stark contrast and this difference is powerful and direct evidence of the uncertainty surrounding the optimal way to provide feedback. The two major manufacturers have made considerable investments in their respective systems, and if this uncertainty was ever resolved, it would have significant commercial implications.

The key issues underlying the different approaches to feedback are how dissociated do you allow machine activity to become before the human becomes a passive and less useful player, and how do you facilitate sharing by informing humans of machine status, without swamping them with information. The counter issue, which is fulfilling the machines needs of knowing how the human is coping with the processing of joint vital information has arisen (7.4.4), but machines are too unsophisticated to have made much progress in this area. Together, the issues of protective automation and feedback on flight decks suggest that human-machine sharing is incompletely understood and may not have an adequate approach.

10.4.3 Importance of current uncertainties for human machine sharing

The previous sections have provided two examples of the current uncertainty as to how humans and machines should share. One uncertainty to authority and control, while the other relates to feedback and comprehensibility. These are fundamental areas of sharing, for the first reflects doubt about the alignment of purpose between the human and the machine, while the second reflects doubt about one aspect of bringing about trust. Purpose and trust for human-machine sharing are considered in the next three chapters.

Aircraft from different manufacturers look remarkably similar, many of the visible differences being cosmetic. There are real differences which are the manufacturers' way of tailoring their product to specific market needs. Creating a particular capability in a product usually requires some 'trade off', the whole ensemble suiting the needs of particular market segments. Thus, one possibility for explaining differences in flightdecks, and the perception of design uncertainty, is that the differences are of lesser importance, and that what occurs on flightdecks is lumped into a 'trade-off' area. This proposition would have aircraft purchasers seeing flightdeck design differences as idiosyncrasies, which are of lesser importance compared with aerofoil and engine features which continuously affect range, load, speed, reliability and cost per seat kilometre.

10.5 Collective disquiet about current sharing with machines

There are numerous accounts of aircraft incidents and accidents which have been collected together to demonstrate disquiet about human performance in flightdecks (Billings and Reynards, 1984; Billings, 1996). Analysis of accidents and incidents has suggested that crew coordination and standardised management have been only part of the issue, and that the flightdeck environment has not been blameless (Degani and Wiener, 1991; 1994). Some have gone further, and collected incidents and accidents, attempting to cluster them such that the destructive processes underlying dysfunction of the human-machine interface might be perceived (Billings, 1991, 1996; Satchell, 1993; FAA 1966).

Others have been expressing disquiet about the whole approach to automation, particularly of flightdecks. Thus the Air Transport Association of America has created an initiative which seeks to achieve clarity in the allocation of tasks to machine and the pilot, while NASA has initiated a program which seeks to develop a flightdeck automation philosophy. Recently the Federal Aviation Authority, working with NASA, United States Universities and the European Joint Aviation Authorities has released a report which was critical of the progress made with the understanding of human factors issues in automation. This document lists 24 incidents and accidents as evidence of an underlying lack of a rigorous approach to automation of flightdecks (FAA, 1966). While other industries are less currently affected by failure of automated systems, it can be assumed that their need is at least as great, if unrealised. Many industries fail to realise significant benefits from new technology (Landauer, 1995), with only those that are technology-dependent service providers being spared poor returns. This suggests that poor understanding of human factors at the human-machine interface will be widespread.

10.6 Sharing with machines - a background

Humans and machines have coexisted beneficially for a considerable period of time. Once machines became capable of replacing humans, or being better at many tasks than humans, task allocation became necessary. Fitts (1951) put forward a set of rules for task allocation which are still used. The core of his approach was to allocate tasks that the human excelled at to humans, and to allocate tasks that the machine excelled at to machines. Thus, machines and humans competed for the various functions within the overall system, each being rewarded with those functions that they could perform better than the other. Once tasks had been allocated, some shifting of marginal allocations could occur to ensure that either the human or the machine was not overloaded (Kantowitz and Sorkin, 1987).

Fitts' approach influences task allocation today despite practical difficulties in applying allocation tables. Thus, allocation of tasks between humans and machines is still viewed competitively. Further, the competitive component has been enhanced by differences between designers as to who has overall control of a system. Reallocation of tasks by shifting marginal allocations still occurs for humans, but not machines, because only humans have to be unloaded by workload reduction programs.

There are a number of criticisms of Fitts' approach. These criticisms are not about the methods used to do the comparisons between humans and machines, for the mathematical terms are accurate. Jordan (1963) suggested that the failure of Fitts' approach to achieve satisfactory allocation depended upon the central process being one of comparison. The issue is not one of whether machines and humans could be compared, but whether they should be compared because they are so different.

An inevitable result of the competitive approach is that humans end up with no tasks, if the framework for comparison is competitive and done on machine terms (Jordan, 1963; Rouse, 1977; Kantowitz and Sorkin, 1987). Machine based comparisons must remove humans, because the design of a machine can be altered to improve its performance relative to that of the human, while the human design is unalterable. The continual shifting of tasks from humans to machines and never in the reverse direction is occurring (Jordan, 1963; Kantowitz and Sorkin, 1987). The paradox of saying that there is no place for humans in situations where human-machine sharing occurs, while knowing that complex, autonomous machines are incapable of operating alone (10.1.6), has been realised for a long time (Birmingham and Taylor, 1954; Jordan, 1963, Rouse, 1977; Kantowitz and Sorkin, 1987, Billings, 1991).

Jordan (1963) suggested that changing the context of the comparison might be beneficial. Thus, instead of viewing humans and machines competitively, by relying on comparisons based on machine terms, they should be viewed in terms of their complementarity. Despite this being written thirty years ago, it is only recently that some complementarity has crept in with the approach (7.4) called human-centred automation (Billings, 1991). Until the advent of human-centred automation, technology-centred automation dominated aviation, and it continues to dominate in many non-aviation forms of automation. Despite human-centred automation being accepted in principle in aviation, the competitive allocation of tasks is still present, and the interchangeability of the human and the machine at various tasks still dominates thinking. Inevitably this has had undesired consequences (Chapter 8 & 9). Unfortunately, the antidote of human-centred automation does not clearly grapple with the complementarity approach to meeting task requirements. Human-centred automation still uses machine parameters for assessing a machine's capacity to be a complementary partner and has been unable to be impartial about the issue of human control (7.4.1).

10.7 Summary

Current sharing between machines and humans occurs in many forms, in part related to the level of automation, and in part related to the individual's approach to sharing tasks with machines. This sharing has been very successful, but is not trouble free, with the most evolved forms of human-machine sharing causing specific concerns to even the most committed of users. This book considers that the difficulties that have been occurring at the human-machine interface (Chapters 8 & 9) have not arisen because of a limited capability with machines, which has tethered development into some intermediate stage where humans and machines are forced to share. An implication of this line of thinking is that machine power will resolve it, often by further displacement of the human. This book has no place for this approach, for it is human replacement, or distancing rather than involvement, that is at the heart of current difficulties. The key issue is our limited understanding of how humans and machines should share, and this chapter provides evidence of the uncertainty surrounding this type of sharing, and the need for a different approach

In the current section (Chapters 7-10), the uncertainty of how sharing should occur has been treated generally with little attention being paid to the end point of the first section (Chapters 2-6), which focussed on organisational factors and their interference with the translation of creativity into innovatory behaviour. One major organisational factor not considered in the first section was the effect of technology on current organisational environments. The capacity of the technologically complex organisational environment to harness creativity is considered in the next section.

The chapters in this section have focussed strongly on the aviation industry. Some might see the material presented as being excessively critical. This is not the intention, because the development of the modern flightdeck and the machine of which it is a part, is one of the great human creations, and it is only because it is so evolved that it is possible to see current and future challenges for all work places. There is little doubt that what flightdeck designers are struggling with at present is either a battleground for humans in future work places, or, if there was a little more reflection and understanding of what is being learned, the way to affirm a key place for humans in future work.

Notes

1   See 6.4, 6.7.1 and Goffman (1967).
2   Modern aircraft have hydraulic or electrical amplification of control inputs. These are designed to work full-time with no real intention that they would be turned off under normal operating conditions. See pp. 103, Billings (1996).
3   Early versions of electronic prescribing systems did not have these. It is possible to disable them, but most practitioners find this assistance vital and instructive.
4   The electronic audit system is not universal and a feature of some military medical systems. Its presence reflects larger organisational and health system issues.
5   See pp. 104 of Billings (1996). There are no real analogies in clinical practice.
6   See pp. 105 of Billings (1996).
7   The reveille system in the Boeing 747-400, the human controller interface on the SNCF railway system, and the SIFA system on the German Federal Railway have a continuous 'consent' approach. See pp. 108-109, Satchell (1993).
8   See pp. 103, Billings (1996).
9   See Barrie (1997) where the use of Unmanned Air Vehicles (UAV) is considered in the light of the trouble they have caused in military exercises and their potential use in digitised battlefields of the future.
10 Other systems include NASA's X-33 single stage-to-orbit, reusable, launch vehicle, and its predecessor, the DC-X
11 See Flight International of 7th August (1996) pp. 11 'NTSB urges increase in inspection of JT8D fan-hubs'. The NTSB stated that the fan hub fractured during take-off because of a fatigue crack caused by 'abusive machining'. Debris from the engine penetrated the passenger cabin with fatal results.
12 See pp. 35-49, Kingsley-Jones (1996).
13 See pp. 99-100, Billings (1991). In the Flight 232 incident (ref 25.), an uncontained engine failure led to loss of all hydraulics and flight control systems in a DC-10-10. See also the structural failure of the fuselage of a 737-200 (ref.27) and the loss of 18ft of cabin. Both incidents requiring consummate skill on the flightdeck which saved significant numbers of lives.
14 See Figure 8.1, Billings (1996).
15 See Fig. 4a, pp. 25 of Tenny et al. (1995).
16 See Fig. 5b, pp. 29, ibid.
17 See survey result No. 5, pp. 59, Wiener et al. (1991).
18 See pp. 13-18, Tenny et al. (1995). 'Full automation' means automation which commands rather than recommends, provides one alternative rather than many, automatically executes plans rather than evaluates and advises, etc.
19 See individual items and scores for Fig. 5b, pp. 29, ibid.
20 See pp. 24, ibid.
21 Industrial relations can be a much more powerful orchestrating force for flexible work arrangements than any machine design philosophy.
22 See No.11, pp. 60, Wiener et al. (1991).
23 See Table 5b, Tenny et al. (1995).
24 At the time of writing this book, McDonald Douglas and Boeing are merging.
25 Fly-by-wire systems make flight possible in aircraft which have neutral stability, a state which normally precludes human control, but provides significant reductions in drag. The MD-11 has reduced longitudinal stability which is compensated by a stability augmentation system. See pp. 23, Billings (1996).
26 It has been argued that designers and manufacturers should make it possible for crew to make demands upon the structural reserves of a machine, even if this type of use leads to a shortened life for some machine components. This may allow for machine survival, with the early replacement of some parts, which is preferable to the destruction of the machine and a very shortened life for all components. See pp. 29-30 under 'autonomous operation' in Billings (1991), or pp. 109-110 in Billings (1996).
27 See 'Issues raised by advanced flight control systems' pp. 25-26, Billings (1996).
28 See note 10 & 11 of Chapter 8.

Part C

Sharing Automation
and
Innovative Behaviour

11 Current technology, creativity and rituals

Current technology is being used creatively. Whether it is on the flightdeck when the unexpected occurs, the production line when improvement is called for, or health care when care is tailored for the individual, the human and the machine have been sharing in creative tasks. Machines are being used in novel and unexpected ways as part of creative processes, but this largely reflects the human capacity to be creative, despite restrictions imposed by machines.

The present chapter brings together two previous areas, merging the stream of thought pertaining to creativity and ritual in organisations (Chapter 5 & 6), with views on the current approaches to automation and sharing with machines (Chapter 7 to 10). The chapter starts by describing automation's capacity to produce difficulties for those involved in both routine and unexpected tasks. These difficulties are related to those features of the technology-centred approach to automation (7.3, 9.1.4) which modulate creativity. Some features of this approach make it prone to ritualised behaviours, and these are amplified by other ritual promoting factors, namely the lack of clarity in defining roles at the human-machine interface, and the effects of current technology on the locus of control. Some of the current responses, such as the use of policies and procedures further ritualise work places in ways that impair creativity.

11.1 Routine and non-routine human-machine interactions

When automation has been applied to shared tasks, it has been difficult to amplify human cognitive capabilities. Automation has been very successful in improving task repetition or multiplying force, but has had a much smaller effect on promoting creativity and decision making[1]. Technology designed for shared tasks has not been designed to assist creativity, nor for promoting innovatory behaviour, and these design issues are often only considered after an incident or accident[2]. Some of the effects of automation on human creativity have already been described (*Example 8-13*). Two further examples follow, the first illustrating the anti-creative effect of current technology on routine creative work, and the second showing the lack of attention that has been given to the use of technology in the unexpected situation where creativity can be vital.

11.1.1 Continuous innovative behaviour

In the following example, it is necessary to accept that the doctor is working in a relatively creative way as part of her routine work.

Example 14. Tailoring treatment[3]

Virginia swore under her breath. At times she wondered whether her office technology was working with her or against her, for her frustration with her medical computing system was increasing. Three years ago she had bought a practice in the heart of the business district. On surveying her patients, who generally were well-off business people, she realised that they wanted their care to be 'right', with little compromise. In exchange for a fee which was several times the standard in the community, Virginia offered her business men and women 'personalised' care.

Virginia's approach started with the best of the non-drug treatments, tailored to the individual. The 'personalised' component really came to the fore when drug therapy was necessary, for here Virginia used a wide range of agents, titrating dose for maximum effect and minimum risk. This involved trialing a number of different agents, punctuated by periods of no therapy when that was possible. Once she had established which was the best agent for an individual, the correct dose and continuing efficacy of the drug was checked by brief periods of withdrawal or dose change, all changes being tracked by repeated measurement. This 'personalised' approach to care had met with an overwhelmingly positive response from her hard-nosed clients and her commitment to a treatment partnership had become the talk of boardrooms and senior executives' offices.

The 'personalised' approach produced much greater demands for machine assistance than required in normal medical practices. Virginia had used computers in her practice ever since she graduated and her practice had been a trial site for new technology. Her current system was state of the art in many respects. It was modular, with the key functions of disease management, prescribing, information retrieval, investigation, care plans, and referral being supported by electronic guidelines. These guidelines were sophisticated, in that their content had been created by the joint efforts of many health system players, while the process for using them was partly user-defined[4]. In Virginia's system, the user-centred guideline module was fully functional, as was its associated system for capturing variation.

Virginia's swearing was due to her frustration. She was often faced with a trade-off when she worked with her machine, in which the variation demanded by personalising treatment came up against constraints dictated by best practice for large populations. Her computerised disease management system made it easy for her to personalise treatment, but all the while reminded her how far she was straying from the orthodox. Virginia was in awe of her systems capacity to review an individual's care plan, display it in a way that made it as vibrant as when it was created, and then focus on the current treatment issue. However, the guideline and prescribing systems, user-centred though they were, kept getting in the way. Turning these constraining options off was possible. However, her marketing promoted these features, her practice accreditation required them, and their presence made her eligible for government payments that her business needed.

Some of her treatment options were unorthodox at face value. The machine treated these with disdain, a sort of machine 'contempt', which would have been deserved if they had been unconsidered or a random choice. Her system was unable to appreciate the long-term purpose behind some of her treatment choices. Even simple options like sub-therapeutic doses were flagged as variations, despite her ability to show effectiveness in an individual's cases. Similarly, her own trials in an individual of different brands of the one type of drug were judged to be pointless, because brand differences were not demonstrable in populations. Virginia's approach of occasionally ceasing therapy to demonstrate to a patient the continuing need for treatment was always classified by her system as a treatment failure. Together, these machine interpretations introduced additional tasks and unnecessary complexity to Virginia's job.

Virginia was convinced of the benefit of her approach, for she had realised that successful treatment transcended that possible with an approach driven purely by medical science, particularly in situations where individuals had to cope with the onerous task of life long medication. Treatment of the individual that was based on good science, but which was also individualised as a part of the 'art' of medicine, was Virginia's strategy. This appeared to be a very successful approach, both financially and for her patient's health, though Virginia was aware that there were threats. Last year she had been asked to appear in front of a Government sponsored drug use committee., a group that reviewed drug use as a means of creating medicinal policy. Her drug use had been selected, because it had so much variety and so many non-standard doses. Although not required to, she had managed to justify her innovative approaches, but the spectre of a more sinister review process disturbed her. The larger health system seemed to be ready to reinforce the checks that her own technology was making on her. At times she wondered if her 'personalised' approach was worth it.

Flexibility is a feature of technology-centred automation (7.3.2). Some people use this flexibility in being innovative about the way they work (*Example 1-4, 9, 10, 14*). However, the system in which individuals work, whether it be the transport, health or some other system, can corral innovative approaches. This can be appropriate, because the capacity for technology to enhance innovative behaviour is large[5]. In attempting to control this variation, these systems first used people for inspection and audit purposes. With the advent of widespread, complex technology, control via people has become inefficient and ineffective, and the control task is being passed onto the machine. In the example, there is coupling between the capacity of the system to give flexibility in an approach to treatment and the capacity to restrict variation in treatment. Indeed, a health system can become 'anxious' when a technological development results in the passing on of a level of freedom without a coexistent level of constraint[6]. The ambiguities arising from the juxta-position of machine-mediated constraint and flexibility makes 'creative' interactions problematic (5.4.2). The solution for optimising creativity in the above example is to make the machine share in the 'purpose' of its contribution (12.2).

11.1.2 Acute innovative behaviour

The following example illustrates how difficult it can be in an unexpected situation to convert creativity into innovatory behaviour in the technologically complex work place.

Example 15 Innovation brings survival[7]

The take off was on time, despite the heavy rain and gusty winds, and the climb out was normal. Because of the duration of the flight, a second crew was on board. All was routine during the ascent until the aircraft passed 24000ft, when numerous caution and warning messages commenced, concerning the mechanical state of the four engined aircraft. The first message warned of overheating in the cowling of No.1 engine, closely followed by warnings related to engine air leakages, low oil pressure and trouble with the engine starting system. At the same time warnings related to the flaps and one of the flight management computers appeared. As more warning messages appeared, mechanical malfunction appeared to begin, as the electrical generator of No.1 engine stopped working and the air pressure in the passenger cabin began to drop. The display of speed reference information on the primary flight display became abnormal and a stall protection system activated, although the aircraft was not flying slowly. A warning light appeared indicating that No.1 engine's reversing system was no longer in the stowed position, although there was no evidence of asymmetric thrust. The air pressure in the passenger cabin continued to drop and was not controlled.

The two man crew initiated an emergency descent back to the departure airport, while declaring their problem, and starting the emergency procedures. The emergency descent was a non standard one, as from 26000ft to 20000ft the stall warning system activated a number of times, and the abnormal flap indication and the No.1 engine reversing condition remained. This necessitated a modification of the standard emergency decent procedure.

At this point the captain called upon both members of the second crew to assist. The problem with the aircraft was unclear and required diagnosis, the flying tasks were complex and would get much more so with landing a 'heavy' aircraft in difficult flying conditions, and there was need to communicate with the cabin and the company. While the captain maintained control of the aircraft, he assigned the problem and its management to the first pilot and the additional first officer. Other tasks were distributed amongst the expanded team. While the crew suspected that there were problems with No.1 engine, the plethora of messages from the engine indication and crew alerting system (EICAS) suggested that this was not a standard problem, and working their way through it required more resources than normally available.

In addition, numerous standard tasks had to be completed before landing, and because of the uncertainty surrounding the problem, some of these required non-standard approaches. The routine task of dumping just over 70tons of fuel to make the plane light enough to land was non-standard, as one of the dump nozzles appeared to be inoperative. The flaps on the aircraft had to be configured for landing using alternate procedures, because of warning messages related to their deployment. The approach configuration, landing speed, braking manoeuvre and use of reverse thrust all required compromise solutions, given the uncertainty as to system function.

After touchdown in difficult weather conditions with a deliberately high landing speed, the braking manoeuvre was commenced using reverse thrust maximally on No.2 and No.3 engine and partially on No.4 engine. At this point, the control tower advised the crew that a fire was observable on the left side of the aircraft. The aircraft was stopped on a taxiway. Assisted by the spare captain, a difficult but successful evacuation followed.

This example highlights a human 'tour de force', an adroit, innovative effort by skilled people, who, by working together, created a sequence of 'correct' choices within a maze of potentially disastrous options. Recent accidents, where incomplete and inaccurate information has been present on the flightdeck[8], attest to the acute danger that this aircraft was in. These people never knew what was wrong, yet despite this hideous uncertainty, the human and the machine survived. This example illustrates the vital contribution of a number of unique human capabilities, namely the ability to make decisions with incomplete information, the selection of those issues that matter out of a myriad of others which attract attention, and above all, the capacity to create an operating approach which was a workable compromise and which could be continually tailored to the changing circumstances. It is the last, the creation, the 'new' way of doing something, that stands out as the triumphant contribution .

It is legitimate to ask how much the machine helped. The crew recognised that many of the machine's warnings were conflicting. Indeed, they may have been diverting, as the crews working formulation centred around problems with No.1 engine, when it in fact was operating normally. The crew had to cope with 42 engine indication and crew warning system messages, 12 caution or warning indications, activation of the stall warning system and abnormal speed reference information. Outwardly, it appears as if the machine was not particularly sympathetic to its human partners in helping them find a working solution.

An alternative view is that in this aircraft it was possible to introduce humans into the control loops, such that they were involved, rather than excluded. Further, systems were designed such that they could be unravelled and a different operating state created. It is not clear that other aircraft designs would have allowed as much human creativity to be brought to bear. The circumstances which allowed the crew to increase their number, and hence expand the human problem solving resource, were fortunate. It is not apparent that flightdecks are designed such that the contribution of additional humans can be easily harnessed in the type of circumstances described in the above example.

11.1.3 Automation unsuited for creatives

Perhaps it is unfair to criticise current human-machine interfaces for their failure to enhance creativity. After all, most machines were not designed to modulate creativity specifically. However, machines like the word processor are designed to enhance cognitive activities. Thus, if there was to be criticism, it is that machine designers have tried to assist creativity, with the underlying processes being unknown or argued about[9].

The word processor has altered creative writing. This technology also makes accessible the domains (5.4.2) that contain our art, our law, our science and many other features of our cultures. Yet, the technology that immerses humans in these domains was not designed to aid creativity. It was designed to give access to the domains, without consideration of the other parts of the creativity process that would inevitably come into play. For some, the means of access impinge harmfully on their creativity, possibly because of procedural issues due to operating systems and keyboards. For others, display issues are the problem, from limited text display, vertical scrolling, or the vertical screen. None of these effects need be present[10]. It is likely that the affect of current human-machine sharing on creatives has been little considered.

11.1.4 Summary

It is safe to conclude that modulating human creativity has not rated highly as a goal in the design of that technology which shares tasks with humans. The costs of this oversight, financial and otherwise, are unknown, but are likely to be large. Even in those human-machine situations which are dominated by routine, procedural work, as on the modern flightdeck, the inability to convert creativity into innovatory behaviour can be disastrous. In less procedural areas, modulating innovatory behaviour via technology can be important, but it remains a little considered 'art' at this point in time. Organisations will have to be able to entrain creativity in the strategy development, their customer interface, and the design of production and management processes, if they are to be innovative and competitive.

11.2 Technology-centred automation and creativity

Technology-centred automation is intolerant of its human partners using creative approaches to achieving tasks. In part, this reflects limitations in the capacities of current machines, and in part, it reflects the 'narrowness' of the technology-centred approach in viewing human potential. This has already been considered in a preliminary way (7.3, 9.1.4).

11.2.1 Creativity, enviromental interaction and technology-centred automation

Creativity involves a two way interaction with the environment, where humans respond to their surroundings and the surroundings respond to the human (5.4.2). The interactive relationship with the environment is a key feature of the creative process and technology has the potential to increase this interactivity[11], but most human-machine situations limit it. This limitation comes in two forms, either as an issue of access to information, or as an issue of comprehensibility (Fig. 11.1).

Access to information Restrictions on access to useful information about the surroundings abound with technology-centred automation. The key restriction at present is feedback, which is fundamental to interactions with the environment. The importance of feedback for creativity cannot be understated, for the subliminal testing of possibilities requires continuous appreciation of effects and trends. In terms of 'domain' and 'field' (5.4.2), inadequate feedback damages the domain of which the machine is a part. Feedback is a difficult area for the technology-centred approach to automation, as its development has lagged behind the development of authority and autonomy (7.3.1), with consequences on vital processes like situation awareness (9.1.4). Even more perturbing is the current uncertainty as to what is the most appropriate way to provide feedback in technologically complex environments (10.4.2).

A closely related issue which limits interactivity with the environment is technology's interference with the conversion of information into knowledge. The technology-centred approach to automation is not solely responsible. Knowledge's importance for creativity and innovatory behaviour is widely accepted (3.4, 4.6.3, 4.6.4, 5.6), but in situations where innovatory behaviour has been required, there have been technology-dependent barriers to the assimilation of knowledge, which have had significant consequences[12]. There are other barriers which reflect uncertainties as to the practical form which information provision should take. Thus, on the flightdeck, one aircraft manufacturer has gone to considerable trouble to address the issue by providing the option of an electronic library, only to find that airlines have been unwilling to pay for it[13]. Information provision in health systems abound, yet only a minority of health care professionals access these systems[14]. In corporate settings, libraries are disappointing and systems that provide information electronically remain poorly utilised[15].

Comprehensibility Comprehensibility also limits the conversion of information into knowledge and is acknowledged to be another difficult area for the technology-centred approach to automation (7.3.2). As with feedback, poor comprehensibility currently diverts cognitive resource, including significant amounts of creativity, and this has been considered previously (9.1.4). The comprehensibility issue forces the human to work in the wrong domain, namely the little piece of the environment that encompasses the processes of the human-machine interface, rather than the larger environment beyond it.

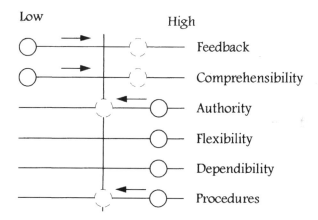

Figure 11.1 Features of the technology-centred approach to automation which impact creativity. The current position (complete circle) and a preferred position (dashed circle) are shown. Human-centred automation will produce some of these changes when the 'how to' is determined.

11.2.2 Creativity, control and technology-centred automation

Creativity depends upon motivation (5.3.2), and work places where humans feel controlled are known to be less creative. The technology-centred approach has produced technology which directly controls behaviour, or plays a key part in the translation of other controlling influences (*Example 9, 14, 17*). This is a natural expression of this approach's prowess with respect to authority and autonomy (7.3.1), and its inability to have machines perform as 'perfect' agents. The contradiction about control, of humans wanting more automation, with its attendant autonomy and authority, but also wanting to have complete control of it, remains unresolved. These uncertainties and contradictions are able to sap creativity under some circumstances.

11.2.3 Summary

There are a number of features of the technology-centred approach to automation which are powerful positive factors for enhancing innovatory behaviour (Fig. 11.1). Flexibility and dependability can enrich the domain in which creativity might be required (7.3.2). They can also enhance access to the domain. These positive effects are offset by factors like poor feedback and uncertain comprehensibility. The restrictions produced by controlling behaviour (7.3.3) are considered later (11.4.2).

11.3 Current automation, roles and rituals

The ubiquitous nature of rites and rituals (Chapter 6) makes it inevitable that many are associated with the use of technology. Technology which is autonomous, or not automated at all, has numerous well entrenched rites, many being beneficial[16]. The same applies to technology which involves humans and machines sharing tasks[17]. However, not all the behavioural consequences of technology are beneficial (Chapter 9 & 10). Automation designed to have minimal cognitive impact may do so, but there are exceptions. Automation can assist cognitive activities, but can also produce many other effects, including rituals (Chapter 6). Factors which contribute to these rituals include poor clarity in role definition, failure to recognise the cognitive components of roles, a suboptimal organisational context, and the presence of ritualising forces like 'face work' (6.7.1). These can combine to produce a potpourri of rituals, some of which underlie the destructive behaviours that have been observed in highly automated environments (Chapter 9).

11.3.1 Current automation, behavioural states and rituals

There are a number of dysfunctional behavioural states that are being associated with highly automated work places. The best known is impaired situation awareness (9.1), but complacency should also be included (9.2.1). Recent incidents and accidents suggest there may be others (9.3). It is likely that some of these states can be classed as rituals as they are complex behavioural states that affect creativity (6.5, 6.6). It is also likely that there are 'ritualising' components inside these behavioural states. For example, mature machine systems require tailored activities, which encourage their human partners develop stereotyped, highly practiced routines (Cook and Woods, 1995). The stereotyped nature of these highly practiced routines causes knowledge to become detached and behaviour to become sequenced[18]. In this form, these behavioural states have many of the features of a millstone ritual (Fig. 6.1, 6.2). These may be useful in routine circumstances, but once knowledge and context become detached, as in an emergency or other non-routine situation, creativity is likely to be suppressed and impossible to convert into innovatory behaviour.

11.3.2 Roles and the need for creativity

The examples provided in this book come predominantly from the health care and aviation industries and from two particular situations, the medical consulting room when doctor and consumer first meet, and the flightdeck of the modern, long-distance, passenger aircraft. In both work situations, human-machine sharing is likely to always be required (10.1.6) and neither requires a 'creative' (*Example 16, 17*). Thus, the flightdeck is not a place for non-standard approaches to tasks and a great deal of effort goes into optimising standard operating procedures. Similarly, health care consumers do not want their doctor to be 'creative' with their own therapy, though they do want to be treated as individuals. These two work situations have been chosen deliberately, because they both have an 'aversion' to creativity, but both share a need for it which is not appreciated. This uncertainty reflects a lack of clarity with role definition, particularly with respect to the place of creativity and innovatory behaviour. This leads to creativity inhibiting rituals in these and other work places.

Flight deck On flightdecks, humans are the only source of creativity and this capability is one of the key reasons for retaining humans in this work place. The roles of diagnostician, solution provider and resource of last resort (10.1.6) are not aided by the technology-centred approach to automation, yet these are the key roles that justify a human presence on a flightdeck. Whether the need for creativity is intense and immediate (*Example 15*), or minimal but continuous (*Example 16*), the human is the sole source. Some acknowledge that the 'creative' contributor is part of the human's role on the flightdeck, and making this role viable has led to approaches like adaptive automation (12.4.3). Currently, the uncertainty surrounding human and machine contributions to creativity on flightdecks is a driver for creativity inhibiting rituals.

Clinical practice In clinical practice, consumers are better off with a 'recipe' approach to care rather than no care, as it ensures that a minimum standard is achieved. There is uncertainty in clinical practice with what is considered to be a suitable 'recipe', or what constitutes best practice, or even what best practice can be practically translated into (*Example 14*). This is coupled with the medical profession's propensity to try unproven therapeutic approaches, partly driven by desperation[19] and partly driven by fashion[20]. In addition, many consumers are rightfully dissatisfied with a minimum standard and want much more. Thus, individualised therapy represents an ideal for consumer and provider, and effective tailoring requires creativity. However, there is little acknowledgment that creativity is required, whether it be in how a person heals others by using themselves as the therapy, or by variably merging themselves with other therapeutic agents. Current clinical-practice automation does not acknowledge that there is a creative component in caring for people (*Example 17*). Creativity is needed continuously, and if appropriately entrained by humans and machines in shared tasks, can provide efficient, effective and satisfying health delivery (*Example 14*). The failure to acknowledge the creative component in a doctor's role, when it is part of every consumer contact, is a feature of the technology-centred approach, and much health system structure and policy is about producing creativity-dampening rituals in practitioners.

These two work environments require humans be continuously creative, minimally on a flightdeck and somewhat more in medical practice. These environments are variably dominated by machines, which are designed for tasks where creative contribution is not sought from the human. Indeed, it is not that technology centred-automation cannot contribute to the creative parts of a role, but more that it has been optimised by designers who have seen no need for creativity. Many other work places provide even more flamboyant examples of work roles with poorly defined creative components.

Offices   The office environment is not as procedurally dominated as are the consulting room and the flightdeck. Even here, where creativity is recognised as an essential component of many organisational roles, designers of task-sharing technology make next to know allowance for it. The purchase of office automation is not tied to specific goals or roles. Office automation remains a piece of infrastructure, whose capacity and capability is driven by suppliers, outsourcing agencies, the half-life of technology and fashion. For many of the tasks that it is engaged in, roles are not considered and the need for helping individuals be creative is never entertained. Only recently has quality, efficiency and return on assets and investment become of interest (Landauer, 1995), but there is still little concern about technology's ability to contribute to creative roles. Indeed, there is much in this automation which channels and sterilises, even when it is working well, and its own operations do not interfere with the user-interface. Often it does not work that well, with even the best office automation interposing its own machinations between the individual and their task, diverting creative resource to the trivial and leading to role uncertainty and creativity dampening rituals of dissociation and resignation. At best, current office machines provide small benefits in some aspects of routine work, but in any type of creative activity, these machines have the power to remove the novel and interesting, and convert it into a stereotyped offering with negligible impact. Current machines need not be so dampening on creativity, as they could be partly tailored for individual users, though this is cumbersome, complex and costly[21]. Tailoring the useability of current machines to a role is far from ideal, as this currently could only reduce, rather than remove, the diversion of creative resource by the human-machine interface.

Other organisational areas   Manufacturing automation is similar in many respects, with technology appropriately attuned to quality, efficiency and return on investment, but dissociated from helping individuals make unique contributions. Yet, manufacturing almost universally wants to see continuous improvement as part of routine activities. While the approach for continuous improvement is quite distinct from that for innovation (4.4), both require human creativity. Again, roles which require continuous improvement fail to have defined creative components, and end up lamely dictating a need for change in unconducive, technology-complex environments. Current manufacturing automation is often resistant to user-generated improvement initiatives, and this type of overt dissociation makes rituals likely. This dissociation may underlie much of the 'automaton' behaviour[22] of many of those involved in improvement activities. Similarly, the customer interface could be a place where unique solutions were sought and resourced, but current technology-centred automation and associated management practices often constrain roles and produce millstone rituals.

In summary, organisations have failed to be clear about the need for creativity in individual roles. This contrasts with organisations acknowledging the importance of innovation (Chapter 3 & 4) and accepting the need to enhance organisational creativity (Chapter 5 & 6). This paradox is partly due to organisations being threatened by creativity (6.4) with the result that many roles also reflect the need to keep creativity in check (6.6). This ambiguity translates into a lack of clarity in role definition which bedevils interactions at the human-machine interface and contributes to behavioural sets which suppress creativity.

11.4 Technology, rituals and other contributing factors

The technologically complex work environment of today has a number of other factors which promote creativity regulating rituals. These are contained in technology's capacity to induce an external locus of control (Fig. 11.2), and from the translation of an organisation's automation philosophy into policies, procedures and practices (Degani and Wiener, 1994).

11.4.1 External locus-of-control

In flightdecks, high levels of automation with low human involvement (10.1), modes (10.3.1) and protective automation systems (10.4.1), externalise the locus-of-control. The design of current machines gives very limited freedom to crews to be creative in threatening circumstances (10.4.1). Medical consulting room technology has a variable locus, largely depending upon health system structure. Thus, in the highly audited systems of some military medical systems, auditing modules exist alongside consultation modules and powerfully externalise the locus-of-control. These systems are designed by suppliers rather than users, and are a significant contrast with the relatively neutral locus-of-control of systems designed by non-military, community-based practitioners[23]. Electronic territory management systems for sales forces are in early stages of development, but already have an external locus-of-control. Current office automation is very variable in its locus, principally because the machine's contribution to sharing cognitive tasks is not defined. The locus-of-control in manufacturing reflects an organisation's underlying approach to empowerment. Thus, some organisations have deliberately chosen technology which induces a neutral locus as a means to helping staff engage in improvement activities[24].

11.4.2 Automation policies and procedures

The technological context for roles, the place of creativity in roles, the locus of control in technologically complex environments and technology's contribution to ritualising forces like 'face work' (6.7.1) all reflect the prevailing automation philosophy of an organisation. This is rarely stated but is usually present[25], and it drives polices and procedures. The topic of automation philosophy is considered later (12.6).

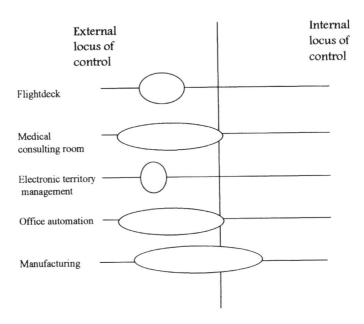

External
locus of
control

Internal
locus of
control

Flightdeck

Medical
consulting room

Electronic territory
management

Office automation

Manufacturing

Figure 11.2   Locus-of-control in various work situations where humans and machines share tasks[26]. The locus-of-control depends on many factors. Thus, the locus for the practitioner in a medical consulting room depends a great deal on the type of health system.

Policies A philosophy, overt or occult, generates policies which are broad specifications of the manner in which management expects tasks to be carried out (Degani and Wiener, 1994). Some policies are not well focussed. Hence in some airlines, owners have used policies which dictate that automation be used to its full extent, rather than encourage approaches which seek efficient and effective use of automation in flightdeck operations. Sometimes policies are not well aligned with one another, with the juxtaposition of contradictory management practices being a powerful source of destructive rituals. Hence, policies related to customer focus and policies related to early closure at the customer interface have the potential to produce paradox and rituals. These are accentuated if the customer interface uses current, cognitive-assisting technology as an intermediary or an adjunct. In contrast, policies that give operators freedom as to how they interact with a machine can be a powerful antidote to the external locus-of-control bias of current technology and thus reduce the potential for dissociating rituals (Fig. 11.3).

172

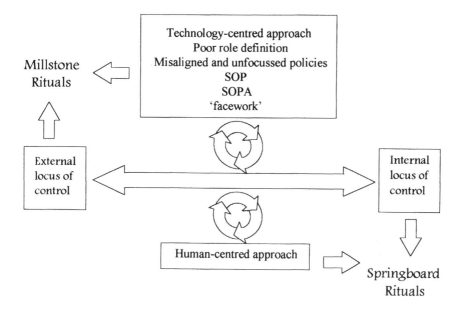

Figure 11.3 Many factors interact to produce rituals in technologically complex environments. SOP(A) is Standard Operating Procedures (Amplified). The relationship between locus of control and ritual has been displayed previously (Fig. 6.2, 6.3). 'Facework' is considered in 11.4.3.

Procedures The envelopment of technology-centred automation by standard operating procedures is very evident in some work places. These do not necessarily emphasise machine dominance, but do emphasise control by other agents, rather than by the human operator. If the procedures are expressions of poorly focussed, or poorly aligned policies, their translation can become ritualised and dysfunctional. On flightdecks there has been a continual struggle to keep automation philosophy, policies and procedures aligned and the deviation between practices and procedures to a minimum (Degani and Wiener, 1994). For some, standard operating procedures have been insufficient, and flight operations groups have migrated to 'standard operating procedures amplified' (SOPA). In these situations, the procedural environment has increasingly taken on an external locus of control. The need for 'tighter' procedures may have arisen from the increased capacity of modern flightdeck technology to translate the creative inclinations of flight crew, but increasing procedural intensity is treating an effect, rather than addressing root causes. The move to electronic checklists further externalises the locus of control. Some aircraft even have an electronic cursor system to help with electronic checklists. The danger of procedures becoming ineffective has been acknowledged for a long time, and the advent of machine assistance makes ritualised, non-useful dampening of creativity more likely.

11.4.3 'Facework' of automation, fashion and ritual

Technology-centred automation has already acquired a 'facework' component (6.7.1), where automation reinforces the plausibility and legitimacy of the organisation, without it having to demonstrate value, or be aligned clearly with purpose. The need to automate has been driven by suppliers, and the 'facework' effect has been submerged in marketing and promotional messages which emphasise the acquisition of technology as an end in itself. Not all industries are equally afflicted by this 'facework' aspect of technology.

11.5 Current antidotes to technology related rituals

There are many factors which have combined to produce millstone rituals (6.5). In many work places, millstone rituals are exactly what have been wanted. In recent times, routine tasks have become increasingly automated, and there has been the expectation that humans will shift to more innovatory tasks. This expectation is increasing, despite the achievement of routine objectives being the unstated goal. Along with all the other factors covered in previous parts of this book, this ambiguity reinforces the power of current technology to inhibit innovatory behaviour.

It is possible that the human-centred approach to automation (7.4) contains some elements that will help reduce the number of millstone rituals that currently feature in most work places. Human-centred automation by its 'name' suggests that creativity is either more likely to be directly promoted or less likely to be dampened. While it is not apparent that human-centred automation has ever seriously addressed the issue of creativity (7.4), many of the changes that it promotes are central to promoting creativity (Fig. 11.1). At present, the human-centred approach is not able to define how some of its changes should be brought about and in isolation is unlikely to be effective. Policies, procedures, uncertainty as to the human role, and 'facework' issues will all have to be addressed.

Other general issues related to control also require attention if millstone rituals are to be nullified. In organisation, empowerment commonly has a significant element of 'window dressing', reinforcing control, restriction and authority under a guise of restricting it. Similarly, there are many aspects of the quality movement which have other agendas related to control, apart from the primary one of reducing variation. Other business change agendas also play forcefully in the area of locus-of-control. In many systems, health, telecommunication, transport, tourism, the need to corral and control has never been greater. Indeed, there is almost a type of conflict occurring at present between automation's capability to increase flexibility in making decisions at the point of product and service delivery and the need to control this flexibility via technology and behavioural modification. Other control forces which fetter and limit are being upgraded via the accreditation of work places and certification of individuals. Individually many of these initiatives can be justified, but together, and in concert with automation designed with a technology-centred approach, they produce a lethal cocktail for an organisation which wants to convert creativity into innovative behaviour.

Many solutions are required to alter work places such that innovatory behaviour is the norm. With respect to altering the contribution of automation, the starting point is the review and recasting of current automation philosophies. In the next chapter, this is attempted by refashioning the human-centred approach to automation such that it becomes an approach that is a complete expression of the complementary potential of humans and machines.

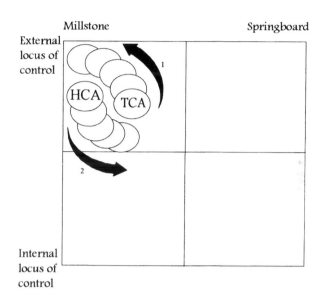

Figure 11.4 Technology-centred automation (TCA), by its own approach and other factors (see Fig. 11.3), is associated with rituals that increasingly dampen creativity (arrow 1). Human-centred automation (HCA) can undo some of this effect, once it is determined how to put its principles (arrow 2) into practice. Note that even then, the latter approach to automation is unlikely to be associated with springboard rituals. See Fig. 6.2 for the basis of the diagram.

11.6 Summary

The complex interplay between machines and humans threatens many in work and non-work roles. Even if one ignores the implications of humans no longer being required for their strength, or their capacity to do repetitive tasks, the increasing need for cognitive contributions complicates human-machine interactions immensely and is producing daunting behavioural consequences. The ability to be creative and to translate this into innovatory behaviour is particularly vulnerable to the current interplay between humans and complex machines. Current approaches to automation are altering the human capacity to be creative in a variety of ways, but there are related factors which go beyond the design of the machine. Many reflect an organisation's approach to using technology and its capacity to cope with human creativity. Together these produce creativity-dampening, ritualised behaviours. There is significant potential with current technology to provide means for creative expression, but the creativity that is likely to appear at present is that which is not aligned with purpose. The behavioural control antics that are induced by current technology make it very difficult for there to be innovatory behaviour and most current antidotes are likely to be ineffective.

Notes

1 See introductory section of Chapter 7.
2 See the interest in using selective engine thrust as a means of controlling aircraft in situations where primary flight controls have been lost. This arose after the Flight 232 accident at Sioux City where an expanded crew managed to crash land an aircraft using engine thrust as the only means of altering direction and height. See (Gerren, 1995).
3 This example is fictitious with respect to the person and the practice. It is set in a country where fee-for-service is how doctors are remunerated and where consumers can choose between health providers. It is possible to transpose its technology/creativity issues into other types of health system, although the capacity of those systems that have payor/purchaser systems (Health Management Organisations and Pharmaceutical Benefit Management Organisations) to cope with this individualised model would be limited. It can be applied to current fundholding models. Note the following:
      a.) The use of the n=1 experiment for treatment is a feature of specialist medical practice.
      b.) Modularised medical care systems are one approach to the computerisation of primary care.
      c.) The use of sub-therapeutic doses can be effective in individuals, particularly if multiple drugs are used.
      d.) The realisation that primary care is an 'art', and only partly science based, comes to many practitioners in time. It is not often part of the thinking of those in medical education and training, and is rarely countenanced by those supplying technology to health systems.
4 The ineffectiveness of guidelines in health systems had lead to the realisation that the user should have a role in their creation.
5 Current non-work uses of personal computing technology, the different applications of Ground Positioning Systems (GPS), the approaches to teleworking in organisations.
6 The anxiety produced by GPS use in the hands of General Aviation pilots, where the technology allows pilots to carry out flying beyond their capability. The flexibility afforded by GPS is considerable, but the vulnerability (a flat GPS receiver battery) is also significant.
7 This example has been modified to make it readable for those without an aviation background. See Billings and Dekker (1996).
8 See following examples: Tahiti, 13/9/93 ~ pp. D-4, Paris-Orly, 24/9/94 ~ pp. D-7, Puerto Plata, 6/2/96 ~ pp. D-9 in FAA (1996).
9 See the various theories surrounding situation awareness (9.1).
10 See section on the superbook, pp. 247-275, Landauer (1995).
11 See pp. 11-12 of Warwick (1997). Also see pp. 77-78 on the value of predictive displays in Wickens (1987).
12 See the issue of automation modes and their role in the trade-off with depth of knowledge in any one mode (Sarter and Woods, 1992; 1995)
13 See pp. 57-58, Billings (1996).
14 Very few doctors currently access either CD-ROM or Internet based material during consultations and a minority search these systems in the spare time between consumers or at other times.
15 There are numerous information providers to organisations yet many senior people do not search for information, and are much more attuned to reading what has to be read, and listening to the synthesis of the information searches of others. This approach is vulnerable because translation and assimilation has occurred so many times that the original data and/or information can lose much of its potential for fuelling innovatory thinking.
16 The automated channel tracking capability and timer functions of the modern radio means that many people wake to similar sounds and start their day with a rite.
17 The use of the car abounds in rites.
18 See pp. 610, Cook and Woods (1995).

19 Oncology currently has multiple therapeutic approaches to many malignant conditions. The first line therapy may be supported by evidence or itself be part of a multi-centre trail. From this point on therapy is usually creative. Unfortunately, the medical profession often fails to offer 'no therapy' as an option as viable as a 'creative' therapy.

20 'Fashionable' therapeutics is the same as that used by 'early adopters'. It is often initiated by a practitioner reporting a positive drug effect in the letters of a medical publication. 'Early adopters' mimic the occurrence of the first letter on no extra other evidence and correspondence can last for several months.

21 The 'roving tutor' model works well for user modification of office technology but is costly. It is likely that this model can be made more efficient and effective with software that tracks the use of software.

22 Some organisations produce almost slavish, 'automaton' behaviour amongst people involved in improvement teams. When assessing organisations these people stand out like beacons compared with the unobtrusive, rare, flexible, adaptive and pragmatic individual who can make improvement and innovation work (*Example 6*).

23 Observations from interactions with Australian General Practitioners.

24 Already mentioned in Chapter 3, re Toyota's approach to automation.

25 Personal observation, and see pp. 6, Degani and Wiener (1994).

26 This diagram is not supported by data. It reflects the authors' estimate from exposure to a number of industries

12 A new approach to human-machine sharing

Automation currently subdues and inhibits creativity. Automation's inability to facilitate innovatory behaviour is only part of a larger problem, which is a more general inability to facilitate cognitive tasks. This chapter suggests a way to approach the sharing of cognitive tasks by humans and machines. Without this general approach, there is little point in considering the more specific changes required to foster innovatory behaviour in machine dominated environments.

Current approaches to human-machine sharing have advanced as far as human-centred automation (7.4). Admirable as this is, it is currently a set of principles about some human-machine issues which require greater definition. It does not significantly tap the unique capabilities of humans, though it does recognise them. In human-centred automation, humans still 'compete' with machines, comparability reigning supreme and complimentarity being limited.

What has not been apparent, even in the thinking of those responsible for the complimentarity approach to human-machine sharing (Jordan, 1963, Weiner and Curry, 1980; Roth, Bennett and Woods, 1988; Billings, 1991), is the path necessary to make complimentarity a feature of the process of sharing as well as the endpoint of sharing. When humans share, what is shared matters, but how sharing occurs is also important. The emphasis on product or process varies, with process being more evident in adult sharing and being very dependent upon shaping by participants.

It is only under relatively constrained conditions that a third party controls how other humans share, and often only transiently. Yet this is the endpoint of current approaches to human-machine sharing. Between humans and machines, sharing should not depend upon some third-party, mixing, in a detached way, task-achieving capabilities which are uniquely human-based and uniquely machine-based. Designers or owners have their place in the process, but not to the extent of the total orchestration of how humans and machines should complement each other[1].

This book takes the view that the iterative, individualised way humans share with each other should also be the way humans share with machines. This chapter starts from this premise, using a simple model for elaborating the attributes of human sharing (Fig. 12.1). The implications of these attributes on sharing between humans and machines will be considered where possible, and this approach to an automation philosophy contrasted with others and put into a context for the work place.

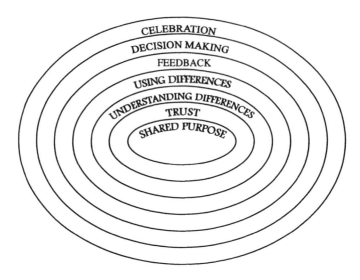

**Figure 12.1 A schematic view of human to human sharing[2]. Sharing starts
with the sharing of purpose. It becomes more evolved as the
behaviour in each successive ring is trialed and is incorporated
into the sharing repertoire.**

12.1 The sharing process between humans

The way humans share is variable, but a number of common elements have been
observed. In situations where sharing is to be promoted, it has been found useful to
bring about progressive engagement[3] of these elements (Fig. 12.1). In such a situation,
the starting point to successful sharing is the sharing of purpose. The levels of purpose
revolve around tactical and strategic objectives[4]. The next layer required for
successful sharing is trust. As the sharing of purpose becomes entrenched, trust
spreads from the mutual achievement of objectives, to a tolerance and appreciation of
the individual differences between those sharing. Sharing that can take advantage of
those differences is a more advanced form, and eventually very different individuals
are able to give feedback to each other. The most successful sharing is characterised
by the presence of processes which facilitate mutual decision making (Fig. 12.1), and
sharing in celebration or commiseration.

The context for human sharing is largely, though not exclusively, with other
humans[5], and its variation may have inhibited machine designers from considering the
process of human sharing as a template for human-machine sharing. It is possible that
there are more ways of sharing than there are people, as sharing is contextually
dependent. While this looks daunting, the elements that have been described (Fig.

12.1) provide starting points. Thus, much sharing between humans is at the level of purpose only, and there are many situations where this is sufficient. Longer term sharing between humans inevitably develops some form of trust. In organisations, the need for sharing is so great that formalising the process[6] of sharing (Fig. 12.1) is thought to have distinct benefits.

In the following sections, the elements of human sharing, such as the sharing of purpose, trust, understanding differences, using differences and feedback will be reviewed with respect to what is known in the field of human-machine sharing. Other layers like sharing decision making and celebration or commiseration provide further advantages, but also require that the initial elements are present. After exploring what is known in each of these areas, each section finishes with some comments on what is necessary for progress in advancing the sharing approach to automation.

12.2 Sharing purpose

The sharing of purpose is the starting point for much sharing between humans, particularly in the work place. Purpose involves the understanding of something to be done or attained[7]. It is both a statement mixing intention and action, and a statement about a future state of affairs which it will help bring about[8]. A purpose is not an independent entity, being hierarchically related to other purposes. The hierarchy articulates values and their translation into actions.

Values are produced by valuing something and originate purpose[9]. Values and valuing something depends upon many particularly human attributes mixed with human experience, and their embodiment within purposes effectively excludes machines from having purpose. Machines do not have values, although aspects of their design might reflect their designers' values. A machine might be made to appear to value something, but it would require either transposing a designer's experience, or, if capable of accumulating experience, it would need the machine to aggregate it in a way which varies with time and recent events. At best, machines will appear to share purposes, without a values framework.

In Kinston's (1995) approach to unravelling purpose[10], there are five levels which are concerned with deliberate action, two of which machines can share in a limited way. Thus, machines can share in strategic objectives, which are purposes which specify desired, feasible outcomes which maximise impact[11]. In addition, machines can share in tactical objectives, which are purposes which specify precise, tangible results which are produced to a time deadline as a step to a desired outcome[12]. In both levels of purpose, specification of purpose requires explicit communication of intentions, both the what, and sometimes the why, by both the machine and the human (Roth et al., 1988; Billings, 1996).

12.2.1 Current sharing of purpose in aviation

Many of the shared levels of automation can be seen as means whereby both machine and human share purpose. Hence, management by delegation (10.1.3) and management by consent (10.1.4) can have sharing of purpose at a strategic level, their common intention being communicated to a variable degree. The interrelationships between the air traffic control machine, the aircraft machine, and both groups of associated humans, have a number of procedures which ensure that there is a sharing of purpose at both a strategic and tactical level between all parties[13]. The same applies to the use of collision avoidance technology within and between aircraft[14].

Machines and humans share purpose imperfectly. When economic imperatives within flight management software clash with a pilot's perception of passenger comfort or traffic issues (*Example 9*), sharing of purpose can be impaired. There have also been multiple incidents and some accidents where purposes as tactical objectives (*Example 11, 12, 15*) have been at odds with one another. In all of these, the purposes of the human and the machine have not been transmitted to each other. The failure to share purpose can be even more dramatic than this. The spectre of machine and human being at such cross purposes (*Example 15*) that the human struggles to do one thing as the machine struggles to do another is no longer academic or fictional. There have been multiple examples of this[15], with training, operations and design contributing to these tragedies.

12.2.2. Other current sharing of purpose

Although not nearly as sophisticated as that on the flightdeck, the information management and decision support system in some primary care consulting rooms is also capable of sharing purpose. The selection of a diagnosis is the signal in some systems that the care giver now wants to share the management of that diagnosis with the machine. This sharing is limited to strategic and tactical levels of purpose. Hence, the strategic level of purpose is about achieving health outcomes which have specified levels of quality tied with specified levels of cost effectiveness. Tactical levels of purpose manifest as guidelines which detail tasks that the human and machine will share . They are quite specific as to what should be achieved, when, and by whom. It is unknown how successful such human-machine sharing can be, though the likelihood is that it will be low, because larger health system issues induce contradictory purposes.

Choice in being able to modify guidelines is a feature of some systems. But, choice which rations a limited amount of health care resources, necessary as this may be, can be at odds with choice which allows a practitioner to humanise and give 'art' to health care. Their are different hierarchies of purpose in these two arenas of choice (*Example 14*), and these can make a human or a human-machine combination dysfunctional under some circumstances. Different national approaches to health delivery complicate human-machine sharing of purpose[16].

There are many examples in industry of rudimentary sharing of strategic and tactical purpose, with this occurring more in manufacturing than in the office. The latter remains remarkably free of definition of purpose, with little to no communication of intention by humans or machines. The technology surrounding the activity of leaderships groups is also relatively dissociated from leadership purpose (*Example 18*).

12.2.3 Sharing purpose and future automation

The fundamental importance of sharing purpose has already been acknowledged (7.4.5) and the significant benefits that can accrue from improving this sharing suggest that weeding out purpose misalignments should improve the cognitive-sharing capacity of human-machine combinations. Ideally, design should make conflict of purpose impossible for any human-machine interface, but given the uncertainty as to how to systematically align purpose, a piecemeal approach is inevitable and probably beneficial. In addition to weeding out errors, explicit communication of intentions by humans and machines (Billings, 1996) would significantly help in the sharing of purpose, as well as the detection of misaligned purpose. Owners have a responsibility to allow greater freedom for operators to choose those capacities of the machine which they perceive share purpose. This means giving operators the freedom to turn off machine functions where there is uncertainty[17] as to the sharing of purpose.

12.3 Trust

Trust is probably an 'intervening' variable. Intervening variables exist in the mind and mediate responses to environmental stimuli[18], but cannot be accessed, observed or measured (Muir, 1994).

12.3.1 Trust between people

There are a variety of definitions for the trust that occurs between people (Deutsch, 1958; Barber, 1983; Muir, 1994). One common element in these definitions is predictability and the expectation of persistence. Another is an expectation of a competent performance, or confidence in and reliance on, some attributes of a referent, or on the complete referent. Some add an expectation of fulfilling fiduciary obligations and responsibilities (Barber, 1983).

Trust is not a static entity but is variable, with both evolving and fluctuating components. Rempel, Holmes and Zanna (1985) have proposed that the evolution of trust between people has a developmental sequence which depends upon a hierarchy of outcomes. Thus, evidence of predictability dominates early, followed by evidence of dependability, with manifestations of faith appearing eventually. Predictability refers to the pattern of behaviours of the person. This earliest stage of trust is enhanced by the consistency and desirability of recurrent behaviours. Later stages of trust rely on evidence of dependability. This is more the aggregation of behavioural evidence which points to predictability, particularly with respect to risk and personal vulnerability. Faith is where an individual goes beyond evidence in believing that another will continue to behave as they have. Behaviours which signal the motives for sharing are those that orchestrate this most emotive and evolved form of trust (Rempel et al., 1985). As trust evolves and an emotive component appears, fluctuations in behaviour have less impact on the level of trust.

12.3.2 Trust in machines

Some have attempted to create models for trust in machines, based upon the limited understanding of the development of trust in people (Riley, 1989; Muir, 1994). Previous thinking has a rather piecemeal character. In this section, it is loosely clustered around behavioural links, the demand and supply of trust, and complacency. Trust reciprocity, expressed as machines trusting humans, is considered as well.

Behavioural links Trust between humans and machines has been described as a multi-dimensional construct with both cognitive and emotive components (Riley, 1989). Trust in machines has been linked to behaviour (Taylor, 1990). It has been suggested that this overlap has an interdependence to it, in that the allocation of internal resources to behaviours on the basis of trust will lead to some behavioural success which in turn affects the stability of related trust.

The behavioural link is a key element in the development of trust between humans (12.3.1). If it is assumed that there is only one process whereby humans develop trust, and that this process is used with animate and inanimate objects, then it is probable that the behavioural link is also fundamental to the development of trust in machines. Machine 'behaviour', like human behaviour, will be a key determinant. When this has been modelled (Riley, 1989), machine 'behaviour' has been equated with performance, and the performance parameter of interest has been reliability. For the operator, this has been translated into the perception of reliability, and this perception interacts with self confidence and the perception of risk, own workload, skill level and own performance level. There is experimental evidence which suggests that machine performance, and the capacity of the machine to fulfil the expectation of competence, has a key role in the development of trust in machines (Muir and Moray, 1996). Trust and the perception of reliability are also probably influenced by current approaches to automation, with the technology-centred approach's focus on dependability (7.3.2) being a factor which cannot be ignored[19]. That predictability and dependability, and hence their behavioural links, are vital items in human-machine trust has been demonstrated in a survey of pilot opinions on high-level, flightdeck automation (Tenny et al., 1995).

Another way of thinking about the behavioural link is to consider trust in terms of how likely the current use of the machine will be retained, versus it being discarded and a new way of use adopted. This approach assumes that the capacity of a machine to achieve constancy of use is equated to it being perceived as trustworthy. The capacity of a machine to reinforce existing use depends upon those factors known to sustain an existing behaviour, such as success or reward, feedback and participation[20]. Conversely, failure or punishment, lack of feedback and inadequate participation will enhance the possibility of the pattern of use being changed, because the machine is perceived as being untrustworthy. Other behavioural linkages seem plausible. Thus, relatively little evidence is required to develop mistrust in a 'new' behaviour, compared with that required to mistrust an established behaviour. This emphasises the initial fragility of trust and the importance of having as few untoward events as possible when humans and machines first start working together. There are some people for who there is virtually no machine behaviour which would lead to mistrust.

Behavioural linkages probably underlie other temporal characteristics of the trust between humans and machines. Thus, there is an asymmetry between the rapidity with which trust can be lost, and the much slower time course of its restoration (Rempel et al., 1985). This has been modelled for the trust between humans and machines (Riley, 1989), although it is not understood. Trust and reliance wane immediately after an incident where trust is abrogated, successive episodes of broken trust extending the duration of each successive period of mistrust.

Demand and supply of trust It has been suggested that the demand for trust exceeds the supply of trust (Taylor, 1990). The key determinant of the demand for trust is the perception of risk, while the key determinants of the supply of trust are the level of judgement, awareness, uncertainty and doubt (Taylor, 1990). Judgement and awareness appear to be dependent upon the perception of the competence of the machine (Muir and Morey, 1996). The need for certainty for the supply of trust is well known[21].

Complacency Riley (1989) has suggested that trust, reliance and confidence are three cognitive entities that act as mediating variables for human-machine interactions. Confidence in human capacities and intermediate levels of trust in machines can cause a shift to manual control in risky situations, despite other variables being present. Increased workload can raise the threshold for shifting to manual control, such that the confidence-trust interrelationship shifts to trusting automation, more than may be justified. This has been proposed as one way of understanding the development of complacency.

Trust reciprocity If it is accepted that trust is an intervening variable, then it is unlikely that humans will ever design machines that trust humans as humans trust humans or machines. It may be that machines will appear to trust humans by how much they allow humans to contribute. Hence, the different styles of protective automation (10.4.1) point to machines having different levels of trust in the predictability and dependability of humans.

12.3.3 A scheme for linking automation, trust and complacency

The interrelationship between trust and complacency has already been considered and some brief observations have been made on complacency, trust and automation in aviation and health (9.2.1). The relationship between trust and complacency for humans and machines can be viewed diagrammatically (Fig. 12.2), if the evolving and fluctuating model of Rempel et al. (1985) is accepted (12.3.1). Thus, there is increasing advantage in providing more trust through the stages of predictability and dependability, until trust moves into the area of faith, where complacency appears and blunts benefit.

Currently, pilots trust their aircraft on the grounds of extraordinary predictability and dependability. Their faith in their machine is tempered by training and professionalism in most circumstances. Comments made by pilots about highly automated flightdecks and their machine's apparent autonomy (9.2.1, 10.2, 10.3) may only be a means of experienced crew keeping their faith in check., and stopping complacency. However, trust's behavioural linkages suggest that fluctuation is a feature[22] and that intermittent complacency on flightdecks must almost be inevitable (Fig. 12.2).

185

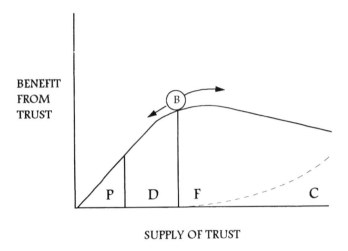

BENEFIT
FROM
TRUST

SUPPLY OF TRUST

Figure 12.2 The relationship between behaviours of different types and the supply of trust. 'P' is zone of predictable behaviour, 'D' is zone of dependable behaviour, 'F' is where there is faith in future behaviour. Lower dotted line represents the onset of complacent 'C' behaviour (9.2). 'B' shows an 'optimal' behavioural range which fluctuates, from being able to benefit from more trust, which manifests as greater dependability, to being unable to increase benefit further because of the consequences of complacent behaviour.

12.3.4 Paradoxes

Some machines legitimately produce trust because they are dependable, but the faith that humans have in them is excessive. The car and the mobile phone are both trusted in a whole hearted and unquestioning manner, yet this trust has irrational and complacent components.

Many cars trap their occupants into being immobile rather than mobile, the key cause being the car itself. In many cities, the car is no longer a machine that provides transport and mobility, yet it is highly trusted to do this task. There is a paradox in our excessive trust of cars, for our trust no longer reflects a rational evaluation of alternatives in terms of utility, safety and cost effectiveness[23]. Our trust stems from the cars extraordinary reliability, but there are many other behaviour-linked factors. These include the level of risk, the absence of untoward events, the participative nature of driving, the apparent choice when buying a vehicle, the opportunity to use machines without training, the opportunity to use a machine without preparation, and the absence of incremental effort or expense. Some would propose that this shows the success of marketing, but the sustained and often excessive levels of trust go far beyond what could be achieved by any loyalty or branding initiative.

Compared with stationary phones, mobile phones do not currently match their quality of communication, security, or anonymity of use. There are dangers with use which include both inattention to a concurrent task[24], as well as concurrent tasks distracting individuals from communication tasks. There are instances where mobile phones have been used to track movements of individuals and worse[25]. Yet, the level of trust in mobile phones is universally high. Again there is a paradox, for the trust exceeds that which would reflect their comparative utility, risk, safety and cost effectiveness.

12.3.5 Trust and future automation

Optimising the levels of trust between human and machine for critical human-machine situations is vital, but difficult. Whereas weeding out purpose misalignment (12.2.3) is possible, the fluctuating state of trust, its behavioural linkage, its emotive component and the extraordinary predictability and dependability of modern machines complicate the manipulation of trust. Given that purpose between human and machine will become even better aligned, and given that extreme predictability and dependability are behavioural outcomes not to be tampered with, the importance of developing trust to the point where faith is present but complacency is not, cannot be overstated. Whether trust can be manipulated as faith develops is unclear[26]. The emotive component to trust and the likelihood of significant individual differences suggests that trust cannot be easily reigned in once faith is present. This is one of the major current and future design challenges of the human-machine interface. This is only part of the issue, for an area of trust that machine designers do not agree on, is how much machines should trust humans (10.4.1). In the future, the degree to which machines trust humans, and how they will appear to do it, will be a key to successful human-machine sharing.

12.4 Understanding and using differences

Trust tends to develop between humans when they share in an activity for an extended period of time. Similarly, appreciation of how individuals differ, and how these differences contribute to shared endeavours, also evolves with time (Fig. 12.1).

12.4.1 Identifying and using differences between humans

It is uncommon outside work places for individual differences to be formally identified and for these differences to be then utilised. Long-term relationships, counselling, family therapy, and infertility clinics can explore sharing and individual differences, as can psychologists, psychiatrists and medical practitioners. In organisations, the identification of differences in individuals is thought to be useful and occasionally vital, and many approaches, both trivial and thorough, are currently employed. Understanding differences has become part of selection, training, and team building and there is a large investment in this activity in some organisations. Not withstanding all this activity, the exploration of individual differences in the absence of trust can be quite ineffective[27].

In organisations, the idealised goal for exploring individual differences is to improve job definitions such that they better match all the capabilities of individuals, and to better mix capabilities across a number of individuals when people work together on tasks. In reality, this is diffused by those who prefer to define the job first and who have little concern for tapping into an individual's broader set of capabilities. Currently, exploring differences appears to provide benefits via some improvements in team function, a better selection process, and more tolerance by individuals of others' management and leadership styles. The best organisations appear to use the process of exploring differences to increase the capacity of their leadership group in taking advantage of variation in the business environment[27].

12.4.2 Identifying differences between humans and machines

The technology-centred approach to automation relies on comparability between machines and humans (10.6), and the unique contributions that humans offer to shared tasks tend to be forgotten. Machines are potent controllers, sensors and decision makers, as well as being flexible, predictable and fatigue-free. In contrast, humans are excellent detectors of signals in the midst of noise, they have the capacity to reason effectively in the face of uncertainty, and they have the ability to carry out abstraction and conceptual organisation (Billings, 1991). Other key attributes are their intelligence and their capacity to learn quickly and efficiently from experience. The ability to produce quick and successful solutions to new situations is a manifestation of their creativity, which is another key distinguishing feature. This can often be done on relatively incomplete information.

12.4.3 Using the differences between humans and machines

The overwhelming presence of technology-centred automation (7.3), and its ethos of comparability, has meant that many of the unique capabilities of humans have been ignored or deemed too difficult to engage. Technology-centred automation is constraining or intolerant of much that is human (7.3.1, 7.3.2., 7.3.3). In addition, automation now orchestrates behaviour in various ways (7.2.2, Fig. 7.1) as a necessary adjunct to implementing the technology-centred approach. This has made it less likely that many of the unique human contributions to human-machine task sharing (12.4.2) can be used. There are alternatives which focus on the potential for complimentarity between humans and machines and these are considered briefly below. They include the discipline of human factors, the approach to automation design called adaptive automation, and the concept of the electronic assistant.

Human factors The discipline of human factors has made its presence felt in some areas of human-machine sharing such that some humans capabilities have influenced the design of human-machine interfaces. This applies particularly to flightdecks, where human factors have been an influence. It is fair to say that human factors have been more used to awaken designers, owners and operators to the extensive range of human limitations, rather than to entice them to use unique human capabilities.

Adaptive automation Adaptive automation is an approach to automation which is still predominantly at the concept stage. Its key tenet, that automation be implemented in an adaptive manner, rather than an all-or-none fashion allows for a non-stereotyped engagement of human and machine capabilities. Thus, adaptive automation might have the capacity to degrade slowly when a problem occurred so that the human had time to build up situation awareness and engage with current issues. Adaptive automation could help allocate tasks between human and machine on the grounds of whether they compete for the same human information processing resource. Adaptive task allocation appears to be beneficial in experimental studies (Parasuraman, Mouloua, Molloy and Hilburn, 1993).

While the intent of adaptive automation has humans working with, rather than for, machines (Parasuraman et al., 1990), it does appear that human limitations, rather than human capabilities, are the driving force for this approach.

Electronic assistant The electronic assistant is a device that knows enough about each individual, such that the machine is configured to take advantage of the individual's strengths and buffer weaknesses. Whether this has progressed far beyond the concept stage is unknown, and its application in civil aviation is not contemplated for the foreseeable future. The concept of an electronic assistant is being contemplated in a variety of other work place[28].

In summary, there is little evidence of any concerted effort to take advantage of those unique human attributes that machines can never have. The inability to acknowledge the unique capacities and deficiencies of humans and the propensity to paper-over the differences between human and machines underlies many current problems with automation. Too often this has resulted from the legacy of the 'existing job', and the reluctance that exists to changing this when technology has all but extinguished the original reason for human contribution. It is possible for humans to work with machines in much more productive and fulfilling ways, if there is a clearer demarcation and utilisation of differences[29]. This requires a much clearer approach to defining roles (11.3.2, *Examples 16, 17, 18*[30]).

12.5 Feedback

Spontaneous, constructive feedback is a rare feature of human to human sharing within organisations, although it is common in long term relationships and families. Many organisational activities formalise feedback, more to enforce it than to make it constructive. Feedback is already a key issue in human machine sharing (7.3.1, 7.4.3, 7.4.4, 10.4.2, 11.2.1, Fig. 11.1), and its unsatisfactory nature has been discussed and illustrated (*Example 11, 12, 15*).

The human to human model of sharing (Fig. 12.1) has feedback as a feature of relatively evolved levels of sharing, yet it is already acknowledged to be a key issue for humans and machines. This should not surprise, as good feedback in the absence of sharing of purpose, sufficient trust, and effective use of differences would seriously question the relevance of the model of sharing (Fig. 12.1). It may be that some of the problems currently experienced with feedback would be better approached by improving the other elements of good sharing, rather than concentrating on the niceties of displays and the monitoring abilities of humans. Thus, resolution of human-machine issues like the misalignment of purpose, inappropriate levels of trust, and the inappropriate allocation of tasks with respect to complementary capabilities may be a more fruitful approach[31] for solving feedback problems.

Up to now, thoughts about feedback have been limited to feedback from the machine to the human, but feedback from the human to the machine may have a place in a shared approach to automation. This sounds fanciful at first, but it is far from that, for machines are highly attuned to receiving human input and, lacking the emotive faculty of humans, are much more likely to deal with feedback rationally. Iterative, learning machines are no longer fanciful, and feedback from the human is likely to have a place in future, shared automation systems.

12.6 Sharing-centred automation as an automation philosophy

Sharing-centred automation moves automation philosophy away from items such as technology and humans to a process. Thus, it differs considerably from its predecessors, technology-centred automation and human-centred automation. Both of these have been difficult to express in any form that is useful in the work place, the only visible expression being the statement of automation principles by Delta Airlines which draws on both philosophies[32]. It is not apparent that the statement has provided benefit.

One of the dilemmas with prior approaches to developing an automation philosophy is that there are multiple elements which are not unified. They are a piece-meal collection of preferred practice which lack that underlying thread or structure that would make them a cohesive entity that could be operationalised. In this respect, sharing-centred automation differs significantly from its predecessors. It has an underlying thread, centred on the way humans share with each other. Upon this are placed unique human capabilities, rather than a set of accommodations imposed by others' preferences to meet machine needs first. A translation of its parts is as follows

- *Purpose* in human terms must be translated into purposeful logic with respect to task, implying that tasks in isolation have no meaning. The purposes of the human and the machine must be aligned to an overall goal that occasionally has to be explicit, but always must be implicit. Where there is disagreement about purpose, feedback from both human and machine must be clear, concise and sufficient.
- *Trust* manifests as either the machine or the human orchestrating the shared task. Locus of control shifts are possible and indeed likely. Trust between human and machine is tolerant of an occasional failure, providing there is warning that a goal is not going to be met, but is very intolerant of achieving something unexpected. Cyclical fluctuation in faith may be the marker that the trust is at an appropriate level between human and machine.

- *Recognition of differences* requires much greater precision and ruthlessness. Humans are unique and irreplaceable, but poor role definition makes them ordinary and dispensable. Current 'wishy-washy' approaches to sharing between humans and machines reflects the desire of some to keep a human presence for the wrong reasons. Machines will never be able to have situation awareness. Humans do not need to worry about authority when they are the only ones which can appreciate the overall state of a task and the progression of that state. Machines can have a form of it, but never that form which encompasses experience and being able to juggle weightings of progress on incomplete evidence. This is a quintessential human capability and is the human contribution.

- *Understanding and using differences* is amongst the most evolved forms of sharing whether it be between humans or humans and machines. Whether there is a place for machines to help in the variable allocation of tasks as part of adaptive automation is unknown, but may be useful. What is clear, is that unless the other elements of sharing (purpose, trust and the recognition of differences) are in place, the more evolved sharing processes have little chance of improving the human-machine interface.

Notes

1 See comments on the 'detached omniscient observer' in Woods and Sarter (1995).
2 From a scheme used by B Thomas of Thomas and Associates.
3 See Fig. 3.5 pp. 45, Mink, Mink and Owen (1987).
4 See pp. 322-327, Kinston (1995).
5 Humans and animals can share purpose to varying degrees in work situations - sheepdogs and guide dogs.
6 Many organisations are using teams as a means of doing work. There are a number of ways to engender purpose, trust and an appreciation of the differences between people.
7 The Shorter Oxford English Dictionary.
8 See pp. 25, Kinston (1995).
9 See pp. 27, Kinston (1995).
10 Chapter 3, Kinston (1995).
11 See L-2, Strategic Objectives, pp. 29, Kinston (1995).
12 See L-1, Tactical Objectives, pp. 29, Kinston (1995).
13 See pp. 13, Billings (1996).
14 There has been an incident involving two wide body long distance aircraft fitted with collision avoidance systems where systems have activated because the aircraft have been on a collision course. The devices in both cockpits signalling the avoidance manoeuvre to be followed, but only one aircraft was piloted away from the collision course, the other maintaining its original flight path. Both machines and their respective flightdeck personnel did not share purpose, possibly because of low situation awareness on one flightdeck.
15 See example in Billings (1996), pp. 179, concerning China Airlines A-300-600R at Nagoya, Japan. Concerning this accident the NTSB issued a Safety Recommendation stated that 'pilots may not be aware that under some circumstances the autopilot will work against them if they try to manually control the airplane'.
16 The PRODIGY project in the United Kingdom, the PACES system in Singapore and systems that are part of PBM (Pharmaceutical Benefit Management) and HMO (Health Maintenance Organisation) approaches to health in the United States all have features which reflect complex and sometimes conflicting purposes. None of these human-machine combinations is directly transportable from one health system to another.
17 See Sarter (1994), Section 4.2.3 of a survey on automation modes and the results of the subsequent simulation experiment.
18 A much discussed intervening variable is mental workload.
19 See Chapter 6, Hollnagel (1993).
20 See Chapter 5-7, pp. 91-142, Eisenburg (1986).

21 See pp. 17 of Tenny et al. (1995); also the survey on automation surprises in Sarter (1994).

22 See pp. 20-21, Barber (1983) on trust never being wholly realised.

23 See Hancock and Parasuraman (1992) and their proposition about changing vehicles and driving to be part of the intelligent vehicle highway system. The rational position put in this paper almost completely ignores the 'faith' component of trust.

24 See pp. 185, ibid.

25 The position of a mobile phone that is transmitting can be determined, and even a phone that is on but not transmitting can be detected. A mobile phone has been used to assassinate an individual.

26 Experimental evidence suggests that trust evolves if humans are allowed to grapple with machine performance, provided that the performance is consistently suboptimal, but not if machine deficiencies are variable (Muir and Morey, 1996).

27 Personal observation

28 Server hubs in distributed primary care systems are capable of having specific user information which tailor the care-person's interaction with the medical system. Some health system information management companies are contemplating an 'electronic assistant' system for individual medical practices. A form of electronic assistant for the flight deck is described in *Example 16*, and one for a leadership group of an organisation is described in *Example 18*.

29 See pp. 117, Woods (1988).

30 See comments on role clarification after each of these examples.

31 Human to human sharing in organisations does not have to be very thorough in any one area, such as shared purpose or trust. As long as some effort is being put into each of the fundamental elements then there are significant benefits at the higher levels of sharing such as feedback and decision making. Personal observation.

32 See pp. 61, Degani and Wiener (1994).

13 Sharing-centred automation and innovation

The technology-centred approach to automation limits creativity (Chapter 11). This limitation, along with other deficiencies in enhancing cognitive activities, underlie the need to find a new approach to automation (Landauer, 1995; Billings, 1996; FAA, 1996). In the last chapter it was proposed that a first step is the adoption of a form of human-machine sharing based on the way humans share with each other (12.6). This chapter first considers what this shared approach to automation might do for work place creativity and its conversion into innovatory behaviour, before moving onto some general observations about organisational innovation. It assumes that principle driven design is possible, and that sometime in the future, the technological environment of the work place will reflect thoughtful choice, rather than just what can practically be built (Woods, 1988).

13.1 Sharing-centred automation and creativity

Sharing-centred automation (12.2-12.5) will focus cognitive resource on the task rather than on interactions between human and machine. Currently, significant cognitive resource is diverted into coping with the human-machine interface.

13.1.1 Environment and knowledge

Creativity depends upon a two-way interaction between the human and the environment (5.4). Sharing-centred automation encourages the human and the machine to tailor the way the environment is presented, reducing the need for translation. In presenting the environment in non-standard ways, there is the risk of altered meaning, but this must be weighed against the loss of cognitive resource from translation of any standardised version. Tailoring of technology-dependent interactions with the environment enriches the domain (5.4.2) and is likely to provide considerable benefit. In a limited way, tailoring has already started. It is a feature of the Boeing F-22 cockpit, where the design encourages the pilot to be a tactician, and not a sensor manager[1], in a role which is that of a 'creative' rather than an implementer. Many of this aircraft's displays and systems are designed to minimise the diversion of the cognitive resources away from tactics, with the pilot's decision-making enhanced by the capacity of multiple systems to collect data about a threat, fuse it and present it.

Knowledge acquisition (5.6) is also vital for creativity and it can also be aided by sharing-centred automation. It too should be tailored so as to minimise the resources diverted to acquisition, translation and assimilation. Already, some approaches to electronic libraries are manipulating the ability to tailor knowledge acquisition[2]. The sharing-centred approach to automation does not address motivation or the temporal attributes of creativity (Fig. 6.5). These are issues for the individual which are indirectly affected by technology, but which organisations can modulate significantly.

13.1.2 Modulation of creativity

Many factors in organisations can modulate creativity and alter the level of innovatory behaviour (Chapter 6). Organisations induce behavioural rituals (6.6), some of which enhance creativity, independent of technology, and some of which inhibit it (11.3, 11.4). Technology is playing an increasingly important part in these rituals, particularly as it becomes more capable of orchestrating behaviour itself (7.2.2).

The sharing-centred approach to automation attempts to blur the boundary between the human and the machine, such that control, autonomy and authority issues (7.3.1) are de-emphasised. This promotes innovatory behaviour (6.3.3). As rituals are inevitable, and as many are beneficial, a key outcome for the sharing-centred approach is giving technology related rituals an internal locus-of-control. Technology which already has an internal locus-of-control, is notable for its idiosyncratic, creative applications, even though these are imperfect in many other respects[3]. In contrast, sharing technology with an external locus-of-control continues to disappoint.

13.1.3 Variable need for innovatory behaviour

Organisations need different levels of innovatory behaviour and how technology facilitates these will be considered using examples. Thus, there are tasks where innovatory behaviour is required at a continuous low level (13.2), others at a continuous but higher level (13.3,) and others where fluctuation in the need for innovatory behaviour dominates (13.4). In the following examples, there is no attempt to give a recipe for organisational change, and the vignettes of automation in work places are projected from now into the next decade. These aim to illustrate how creativity is translated into innovatory behaviour in those work places already considered in this book.

13.2 Situation awareness and innovatory behaviour

The example which illustrates the need for low, continuous levels of creativity revolves around the need for, and provision of, situation awareness (9.1). Any work role which requires tracking of a task and awareness of the state of a system can be substituted. The example is about the future flightdeck, but this can be transposed to other transport systems, electricity grid systems, nuclear and other power generating systems, surveillance, automated manufacturing, financial securities systems and many military applications. The example illustrates how machine and human might share in providing situation awareness[4].

Example 16. Sleep as a benefit of vigilance management

On entering the flightdeck of the Boebus 840-900, Jack and Jill put their personal data discs into the Vigilance Management sub-system of the Pilot's Associate and put on their head sets. Each smiled as they checked the other for electrode contact and pupillary alignment. Jack and Jill had flown for some time together. During their layovers they had often discussed the ritual of head-set checking and how similar it might appear to the preening and caring antics of parrots and other paired birds. Jill checked the transfer of personal data and the flight management system's (FMS) acknowledgment of way points, route conditions and the customer profile. Jill started the preparations for take-off.

While Jill' specialty skills were centred around the take-off and landing phases of flight, she was mindful of the need to keep Jack current in these phases. Jill's specialty skills were not essential for the forthcoming take off, because it was not an ultralong-haul flight. Jill offered the take off to Jack, but Jack declined, electing to review their alertness displays for the take-off and ascent phase of the flight. Jill started the automated take-off sequence. From brake release, she watched over various machine functions and the five engines as their 250tons of thrust forced over 500 tons of aircraft, passengers, fuel and freight into the air. As they climbed smoothly, Jill began reviewing the trend data from various machine measurement systems as they were transmitted to the ground, while Jack started the preparation for entering the cruise phase of flight.

Jack was one of the first pilots in the airline to receive an advanced situation awareness rating and this achievement was one reason which allowed Jack and Jill to fly as a pair and bypass the seniority system with respect to choice of assignment. On this trip, Jack elected to use the vigilance management system throughout the flight, much to Jill's relief. Their airline demanded that flight crew vary the way they managed the cruise phase of flight, which had meant that in their two previous trips, Jack had elected not to use option. On those occasions, Jill had been obliged to rotate into a traditional monitoring role, which she freely admitted was not her strength. Jill felt that she and Jack were better prepared for the untoward when they used the vigilance management system, though this had only been demonstrated in the extended line orientated flight training simulator (ELOFTS) and never in any real situation.

Jack put on the sensing glove and wristband of the system and modified the display of his recent sleep patterns and key events of the last twelve hours. After about ten minutes the display added his vigilance status and even gave a measure of his vigilance reserve. This again showed how useful a person's recent behavioural profile was in assisting the vigilance management subsystem. The display also confirmed that his headset sensors, wristband and glove systems were all functional and stable. Jill also looked at the display and its estimate of Jack's vigilance reserve. Both grinned, as his reserve had been getting larger at this point in recent flights.

Jack had been manipulating his activities in the lead up to each flight as improvements in a pilot's vigilance reserve were now recognised by management with bonuses. Jack used modifications stored on his personal data disc to configure the displays presenting his vigilance level and other parameters. Jack was convinced that this continual modification of the data displays further boosted his capacity to provide situation awareness. Jill tapped in her consent for Jack to be solely responsible for the next phase of the flight, and moved to the rest area in the back of the flightdeck.

Several hours later Jill gradually awoke, her eyes not fully taking in the vigilance displays on the screen above her bunk. She realised that there had not been the normal wake-up call from the flightdeck. As she worked her way through the display she realised with a resigned feeling that she would soon have to return to the flightdeck, because Jack's vigilance reserve was now low. With a start she noticed that the time of her waking was nearly 40 minutes later than normal. Rapidly it dawned upon her that Jack had managed to wring real benefits out of the vigilance management system. Normally Jack needed to nap once in the cockpit before breakfast, which required Jill's presence, but Jack had orchestrated his flight preparation and the use of his vigilance resources such that this had not been necessary. Grinning guiltily, Jill jumped up and moved hungrily to the flightdeck, realising how more enjoyable breakfast would be, and how much better placed they both were for the later phases of the flight.

Not all elements of the sharing-centred approach are addressed in this work place, but enough are engaged (Fig. 13.1) such that cognitive resource is minimally diverted to interface issues[5], and mainly retained for providing situation awareness. There is a sharing of purpose at a tactical and strategic level (12.2), there is recognition of differences between human and machine (12.4) and there is some feedback (12.5) between the two. The management of trust (12.3) is indirectly addressed[6]. It is worth considering a number of other features of this example, which also promote innovatory behaviour and which make the sharing-centred approach more effective.

Clarity in role definition The role of the human in this technologically complex environment has been made clear. Under normal operating conditions the pilot provides situation awareness, a uniquely human contribution. Monitoring as an end in itself is not required, and much of the flightdeck's processing capability is given over to helping the human provide situation awareness. Thus, access to trends in the environment is vital and flight crew are free to configure the machine to suit their own 'externally directed consciousness' (9.1.3). Already some displays on flightdecks have this capability, with displays being configureable[7]. Some individuals are already able to alter current information displays in novel ways to provide trend information[8].

Complementarity between humans and machines In this example, the human and machine work in a complimentary manner. The sharing-centred approach to automation does not rigorously explore complementarity, but assumes that this will occur because of the type of sharing it produces, and because of the clarity achieved in defining roles (11.3.2). In the example, the feedback reinforces complimentarity, even though the feedback is only from machine to human. Thus, the pilot specialised in the take-off and landing phases looked for data trends in the information about the take off. The human's unique capacity to detect signals in 'noisy environments' and project the implications of a change within a flux of many other imprecise variables was being used to improve the long term prospects for the flight. The design of the flightdeck is clever in apportioning machine and human resources.

Procedures and mix of rituals Workplaces where low levels of creativity are continuously required, need to encourage appropriate rituals and incorporate work practices which do not interfere with motivation and the temporal attributes of creativity. In this example, the working environment has been significantly deproceduralised, though some standard operating procedures remain. There are many rituals, with a significant number having an internal locus-of-control. Even the choice as to how technology is used and tailored is ritualised. When aggregated, these approaches maintain the creativity required for situation awareness (9.1.3).

In this example the airline owner has had to invest significantly in additional technology but, in contrast with current approaches, the owner is more likely to obtain benefit. The owner will even have some indirect markers of situation awareness. It is assumed that such an approach will reduce the occurrence of the unexpected[9], although never remove it completely. The next example is different, in that the environment is more unpredictable and higher levels of creativity are continuously required.

13.3 Creativity and primary medical care

The need for creativity in primary medical care is relatively high. The care person at the point of first contact between the consumer and their health system copes frequently with the unknown. The care person must detect and create a construct of the consumer's uniqueness, often discarding it as soon as it is compartmentalised. This need for flexibility and creativity around the point of first contact is not unique to health services, as financial, travel, insurance, and legal-service providers are faced with similar issues. What is unique to the point of first contact in primary care is the intrusion of the larger health system. This already produces some ambiguities (*Example 14*). It has a much greater potential to corrupt a key feature of caring, namely the health promoting properties of relationships, unless tactics like those in the following example are used.

Example 17 Variety in health delivery[10]
Ralph felt himself tiring as he worked on the practice audit. Ralph had been a practice manager for three years and enjoyed his job's flexibility. He had been retrenched twice before taking this position, the last time from a senior strategy development role in a multinational telecommunications organisation. He had

thought of retirement, but given his own robust health and his increasing interest in people, he welcomed the offer to work part-time in his local health network. With his technological knowledge and skills, and his tactical and strategic experience in organisations, he had introduced many useful changes.

His capacity to help was partly due to the way in which he had orchestrated the use of technology. Ralph had developed some principles for using new technology that his doctors initially doubted, but which they now acknowledged were proving very beneficial. He had urged his doctors to only purchase information technology products and services which had received general practitioner input in the design stage. The interface systems of payors, suppliers, and other providers, as well as the equivalent government versions were vetted for how human-centred they were, how much the patient and doctor were given primacy in the rules contained in their software, and how much doctors were able to individualise their use. He had argued that his doctors should modify the use of their technology as they saw fit, and he had tracked the tailorability as a marker of how complementary the technology was. Not surprisingly, these features had made the practice distinctive in their heath area.

Despite the success of their health network, Ralph was still puzzled by many features of primary care and the attempts to obtain benefit out of technology. Ralph saw technology in its broadest sense and because his position was part-time, he had ample opportunity to reflect on its contribution to care. In contrast with the telecommunications industry, where technology made distinct and measurable differences to the ease with which individuals could communicate, technology only appeared useful under some specific circumstances in primary care. At other times it appeared dissociated from care, and sometimes even an intrusion. Ralph knew how his thirty four doctors practiced and knew that their consumers' satisfaction with visiting the various practices in their network was only loosely related to the contribution made by technology. Some reasons for this were obvious.

Much of the technology, be it information management or diagnostic technology, was not directly part of altering health. At best, the cleverness of this technology might end up with another form of technology, that contained within a pharmaceutical product, being employed, but this fusion of technologies did not necessarily alter health, unless it was accompanied by significant behavioural changes in consumers and doctors. The benefits from all these technologies were only significant when the partnerships between doctors, consumers and technology were well developed and meaningful.

Ralph knew that it was not the physical presence of technology that was interfering. Consumers liked to see that the practice was as technologically sophisticated as other places that provided them with services. When consumers required information, they enjoyed the adroitness and interactivity of the electronic material that some payors were willing to provide, though some still felt alienated by a machine acting as an intermediary. However, technology was not clearly helpful in a variety of other processes that were occurring with his doctors during the start of most visits. These processes manifested as directed listening, formulation, the testing of alternatives, and reformulation, all on a background of continuous receptivity and watching. On remarkably incomplete information, and with an abundance of distractions, his doctors were able to often define key issue in a uniquely human way. What was occurring were a continuous stream of little creations, little mental constructions of patient's minor and sometimes major distresses, stemming from a multiplicity of causative factors. To Ralph this looked like a form of 'art'. How technology fitted into this process was not straightforward.

Ralph was sure that one reason for technology's small contribution was that the 'art' of being a primary care practitioner was dependent upon the relationship initiated by the doctor and consumer during the first contact. He had been sampling the information from the practitioner's voice logging and pen pad systems in the various offices across their network for their audit process. This de-identified data convinced Ralph that this technology was unable to help the relationship, or the capacity of the doctor to create little mental constructs of the consumer's presentation. The technology's description of the consumer's presentation gave no measure of the adequacy of the relationship. He suspected that technology's approach to compartmentalising consumers had even altered the way a few of his doctors created relationships with people. Even more disturbing was the capacity of technology, carefully chosen as it was, to occasionally force consumers into inappropriate entry points into the health system.

Another problem for the technology lay in the degree to which his doctors wanted it tailored to their individual needs. Ralph had been amazed at how differently each of his doctors devined what consumers wanted, and how differently they engaged technology in this and other clinical tasks. While he was glad that he had insisted on their technology being modifiable by users, he was still surprised at how much some of his doctors altered their systems. His impression was that his more effective doctors used their partnership with the consumer to individualise issues and responses and used the technology as an adjunct, sometimes like a tool-box, sometimes like a palate. The computational power of their medical management system, with its modular design, its off-line voice and pen-pad processing, its user definable guidelines, its almost infinite access to medical information and other supplier services, remained muted in the hands of the more effective practitioners, where their 'art' dominated the scene of contact. The ability of payor systems to limit how much his doctor's could vary a care plan had been curtailed by his doctors actively manipulating when and how they used technology. Ralph was coming to the view that his doctors and their consumers combined well-being required that doctor and patient spend the amount of time they had always spent on the 'art', without being too diverted by technology and the needs of other players in the health system.

This example of humans and machines sharing in the delivery of primary care is depressing. Something like this example is likely to occur, unless there are major shifts in heath system policies and structures, coupled with a reduction in the degree of political intrusion into health delivery. In this example, few elements of the sharing-centred approach are engaged by the doctors and their technology (Fig. 13.1). The technology that the care-giver uses can share purpose at a tactical level and there are options, via payor systems, to share purpose at the strategic level. However, the purpose of these systems is not well aligned with the purposes of the care giver, for a variety of reasons[11]. In situations where purpose can only be shared at its most basic level (12.2), and where other purposes at higher levels are at odds with one another, a key casualty is trust. In the example, trust is minimal. The technology is trusted with information related to consumers, as intimate information is processed elsewhere with equanimity, but it is not trusted such that doctor and machine share tasks. There are many parts of a consultation, where the capacity of technology to audit, reduce variation, alter behaviour (7.2.2) and carry out another party's purpose, intrude so much as to force practitioners to be distrustful. The lack of trust means that more evolved forms of human-machine sharing, like recognition of differences, using differences, and bringing about improvement from feedback cannot occur.

The need for creativity in primary care is continuous and relatively high, and different from the need for creativity in the rest of the health system[12]. Health systems view the creativity currently exhibited in primary care as a problem, explaining it as poor training and even personal unreliability of both consumers and providers. While competencies and knowledge are as much issues in the medical profession as in any other, health systems have generally shown little interest in their human resource, and have responded reactively to performance variation with overt behavioural change programs. Task-sharing technology struggles in this type of situation, as it can amplify inappropriate behaviour as easily as appropriate behaviour. This example fantasises that the profession is clever enough to distance itself from the electronic, behavioural, 'manacle' imposed by technology.

Clarity in role definition The role ambiguity for the practitioner results from the need to balance the health needs of the individual against the needs of all in health and many other areas. Despite the politicisation of the health arena, there are real and difficult allocation issues within health in developed societies. In a national context, limitation of health expenditure makes great sense, but never to an individual with respect to themselves. In between the system and the individual exists the primary care practitioner, faced on one hand with the logical and emotive needs of individuals, and on the other, with the needs of providers, suppliers and payors, as they try to optimise health across a society, albeit coloured by their own agendas.

It is little wonder that the role of rationer sits ill with the practitioner. Practitioners have not been trained to be rationers, with most current medical curricula being relatively or totally incapable of helping graduates come to terms with this role. In this example, the practitioner group chose to optimise what practitioner's have been traditionally trained to do, and minimise the impact of the larger health system, particularly those parts which have the capacity to be intrusive. They chose to depend upon excellent and creative engagements with consumers, their ability to trade smartly with suppliers and providers, and on the tolerance of payors in accepting some variation in work practices. To the practitioners, their role is clear, but it is at odds with the role desired by the health system. Task-sharing technology struggles to provide benefit if roles are ambiguous, no matter what type of automation philosophy is employed.

Motivation The motivation to create a unique description for each contact between a consumer and the health system is continually under threat, and many of the features of high-creativity work-places need to be preserved (6.3.3). A requirement for partial automation of a high-creativity work environment is that the technology optimises locus-of-control, trust, resourcing, and recognition. Technology must also avoid being party to some consequences like work overload, the intrusion of intra- or extra-organisational politics, excessive criticism of originality, and excessive aversion to risk. In the example, the practitioners' concern about their level of motivation resulted in them partly dissociating themselves from their health system by using a manager to manipulate the intrusiveness of technology.

Rituals, technology and health In this example, decisions have been made to avoid millstone rituals (Fig. 6.1), rather than choose approaches which promote springboard rituals. This is a valid approach to optimising organisational creativity and is the current method adopted by some organisations, acknowledged to be 'innovative'. Technology has been chosen to enhance an internal locus-of-control and hence protect creativity.

In contrast with operators of transport systems, those in health systems tend to have much greater variety in their environment. Care-givers' creativity is required to engage with the variety inherent in each individual, and technology can be a useful adjunct to a continuous creative activity. Technology that unobtrusively removes procedural tasks at the care givers' choice is beneficial, but technology that imposes tasks is problematic. Technology that aids recall, provides past information, interconnects care givers and assists with guidance has a place, but only if it fits a care-giver's approach for engaging with an individual's unique circumstances.

13.4 Leadership innovatory behaviour

One of the key areas where innovatory behaviour is required both continuously, and occasionally in large amounts, is amongst the leadership groups of organisations. Currently their environment is technologically complex, but most individuals are being distanced from technology's benefits by their inability to engage with technology, and the inability of their technology to tap their creativity, knowledge and competencies. While change is occurring in leaders and their processes, the final way that these individuals and future technology will interact is far from straight forward. The following example illustrates several of the potential dilemmas for those that want to enhance the performance of leadership groups.

Example 18 An emotional predator[13]
There was a pause in the chatter among members of the design team as the last seventy two hours performance of the 'predator' system appeared on their in-desk monitors. The 'predator' was a system which detected market expansion associations for leadership groups in large organisations. The design team had conceived, designed and was now trialing it, the total elapsed time of the program

being just under eleven months. The chatter continued in a desultory manner but slowly petered out. What had been suspected at the performance review three days ago, but joked about, had appeared again. It was obvious from the usage and partnership data, that the users, the directors in the subsidiary of a major organisation, were having doubts about their shared machine. The director's trust in the 'predator' appeared unchanged, but their willingness to accept the machine as a useful partner was in decline. It was also obvious that a number of the director group had increased their interactions with each other, out of range of the machine's sensors. When queried, the system was able to infer from voice analysis that the out of range interactions had been heavily laden with emotionally rich material.

The 'predator' had been installed in the subsidiary of a multinational energy provider. This subsidiary was used as a development centre, situated as it was in a country with a stable and developed infrastructure, and a well educated work-force. All information, whether video, electronic, telephone or verbal, that passed through the offices of the CEO and her directors, was captured and processed off-line by a variety of search and inferential software engines. This processing occurred in the evening and sometimes into the early morning, and was orchestrated with rule systems that aligned the machine's associative capability with the strategic purposes of the subsidiary. The rules could be used with various degrees of looseness, and their sensitivity and specificity could be manipulated by users. The installation of the 'predator' had gone particularly well, as apart from area microphones and a body tracking system linked to site access cards, most of the technology tapped into existing systems. The senior group had quickly lost their awe and had been thrilled by the associations that were detected, and how much their decision making had been enriched. All had visited the supplier's site and verified the privacy provisions and the capacity of the system to depersonalise its inputs. The trust that had developed reflected this, and the fact that the associations and issues that the system had initially detected were directly aligned to the organisation's purposes. The partnership measures had gradually increased over the first two months as each director and the CEO sorted out their own way of using the 'predator'.

The design team was quiet. The three engineers looked quizzically at their behaviour change expert, an addiction psychologist. He paused, trying to judge how receptive they would be to his thoughts on the current problem. He had mapped out a diagnostic approach to this issue several weeks ago, when he saw the partnership measures were levelling off and the emotive content of communication was changing. While he was very impressed by his work companions, he was not sure that even they would be able to cope with what he had to say about their machine's deficiencies.

His companions were extraordinary individuals, all being mothers who had returned to work part-time for this project. He knew of their capacity to span disciplines, their fervour, their flexibility, and their extraordinary technical excellence. The psychologist commenced by talking about relationships which were rational and those that were emotional. He gave some examples of the consequences that occurred when the needs of those in relationships were mismatched with respect to the proportion of emotional and rational content. He had not finished what he wanted to say before one of the others suggested that the 'predator' was an emotional cripple in that its associations were free of emotive content. The psychologist agreed, but qualified the comment by adding that the problem affecting the current group of decision makers was that the predator was diluting the emotive component of information that was delivered to them. This particular group were relatively dependent upon emotive content to asses motivation and the capacity to deliver. He suggested that the evolving estrangement was because the decision makers were finding that they lacked a key cue.

Another of the engineer's, the one who had coined the name 'predator' for the system, looked up and spoke forcefully. She suggested that perhaps they had chosen the wrong site, and particularly the wrong decision making group for testing their system, because emotionally based decision making had no place in highly competitive market places. There was a long pause, before each of the others cautiously rejected this. The way ahead for the 'predator', so definite a short time ago, was far from clear.

Many elements of the sharing-centred approach to automation are present in this example (Fig. 13.1). Thus, alignment of purpose, trust and recognition of differences are well entrenched, both in the design of the machine, and in the machine interacting capabilities of the leadership group. There is even some sharing at the level of decision making. It should come as no surprise that in this situation the machine is given human attributes, and that the lack of an emotional component in its interactions becomes a problem. This problem has many precedents. For example, when cars were less reliable than they are today, their personification was common. It should not be surprising that machines that share cognitively are prone to being personalised and solutions are straightforward[14]. Again it is worth considering role definition.

Clarity in role definition While organisations can be prey to larger systems, and thus prey to conflicting influences (6.7.2), most have considerable freedom and capacity to define roles and to redraw them as circumstance demands. Hence, a highly evolved leadership group, as in this example, which understands that its role involves the creative defining and translating of the higher levels of purpose[15], has to fit this role in with other roles[16] which also make demands on creativity. In the example, limitations in the supply of creativity have been acknowledged, and the human role and the role of the machine are carefully tailored to bolster what is available. The human's role of being the creator of associations is limited by an inadequate capacity to do parallel processing, and this deficiency is buffered by the machine. The machine also enhances the pattern recognition role by funnelling the information to the individual in a way that is tailored to the person's needs. This clarity in role definition enhances the interaction with the environment and will enhance a leadership group's creativity.

Leadership groups possess key synthesised information about the internal organisational environment and the external world and each member of a leadership group has responsibilities for the integration of that information into the knowledge pool of the group. In this example, a machine assists in detecting associations in the internal and external environment, particularly those associations that are linked to the leadership group's interpretation of organisational purpose. The machine amplifies the capacity of each person to assimilate the new knowledge of others. Currently, it is challenging for each individual in such a group to assimilate their own new information, let alone that of fellow leaders. Currently, this new knowledge and environmental information has to be squashed, funnelled, and summarised to be communicated. In some situations this is sufficient. However, the existing approach can also neuter the potency of information, and even denature it. At those times when the need for an innovatory approach is high, more information is required, but with the same need for judgement and clarity. Limitations in human processing capacity must intervene. Thus, there is significant complementarity between human and machine in an information processing system that shares some of the associative load, within a context which is alterable by the human. The information processing capacity of machines, their speed, their ability to use rules without exhaustion, their capacity to be free of criteria shift, are all useful. When coupled with the sheer volume of information that leadership groups can face, and the inadequate means of coping with it, there is obvious potential for complementarity and large benefits from working together.

13.5 Application of the sharing-centred approach

The approach created in the last chapter allows current human-machine sharing deficiencies to be recognised easily, and in some instances provides immediate directions as to where solutions lie. This applies to both a specific human-machine interface, as well as to an organisational wide approach to the blending of humans and machines. A number of additional features, such as role clarity, procedures, rituals, and motivation have been considered in the examples in this chapter (13.2-13.4), and these must be taken into account when the sharing-centred approach is applied. The approach does not require a recipe, nor is it necessary that all features of human-machine sharing be considered.

13.5.1 Placing partnerships on the sharing model

Each of the human-machine partnerships described in this chapter can be positioned on the sharing scheme, as can any of the previous examples (Fig. 13.1). Once the partnerships have been placed, an overall direction for enhancing creativity and converting it into innovatory behaviour becomes more obvious. An organisational wide approach samples human-machine partnerships, determines their average span on the scheme, and directs development to the first level of sharing that is not adequately covered.

In carrying out this approach across an organisation or group, it might become obvious that only a few human-machine interfaces were adequately allowing the human and machine to share a common purpose. Currently, many human-machine interfaces are inadequate at sharing purpose and this has been discussed previously (12.2). Some general antidotes have been described (12.2.3). Too commonly the inability to share purpose reflects role uncertainties or the effects of externalities which can be intra or extra-organisational (*Example 9, 14, 17*). When intra-organisational purposes are poorly aligned or role uncertainties are present, many antidotes can be effective at the human-machine interface, as long as there is sufficient will and clarity. When extra-organisational factors are responsible, purpose misalignment at the human-machine interface can be very difficult to counter and salvage solutions (*Example 17*) become unavoidable.

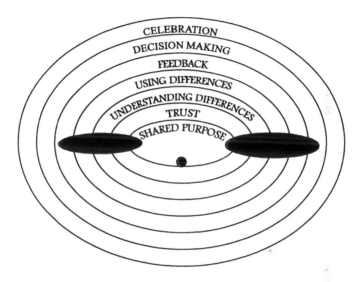

Figure 13.1. Human-machine partnerships can be located on the scheme for sharing-centred automation (See Fig. 12.1). The positions for the vignettes of future work places in this chapter are shown, *example 16* (left), *example 17* (middle) and *example 18* (right).

When the placement of a sample of human-machine interactions on the sharing model reveals that there is an issue of trust, antidotes are not as forthcoming, as has been pointed out previously (12.3.2). In situations where trust is insufficient (*Example 17*), it is possible to help humans and machines, but excessive trust is more difficult to modulate and awaits a better understanding of faith and complacency (12.3.3). When placement points to problems with even more evolved levels of sharing, solutions can be even more elusive. Identification of these problems in the context of an automation philosophy allows the correct development questions to be concocted.

13.5.2 Focussed development within a human machine partnership

Within any partnership, it is possible to look at local factors, many of which have been discussed previously. Some of these will be considered briefly.

Level of sharing Any local factor is likely to be influenced by the level of sharing between human and machine. For example, in the context of a human-machine relationship that is not well aligned for purpose, procedures are likely to have an external locus-of-control (11.4.2), whereas in developed relationships where feedback occurs, even in a rudimentary form, procedures are likely to have a neutral or internal locus-of-control. Creativity and its conversion into innovatory behaviour will be differentially affected, purely on the basis of the level of development of the relationship (Fig. 13.2). Thus, in tailoring the procedures, there is the need to take account of the level of sharing achieved and the level of sharing desired.

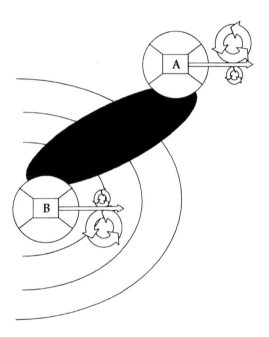

Figure 13.2 There are interactions between the degree of development of human-machine sharing and the capacity of organisational modulators to alter creativity (Fig. 5.5). Sharing at the level of recognition and using differences (position A rather than B) makes the locus-of-control more internal (bigger driving circle above the arrow, see Fig. 6.5) and the rituals more likely to promote innovatory behaviour.

Ritualising factors Rituals which reinforce an external locus-of-control, such as those associated with repetitive tasks (6.6.1), or the alignment of behaviours (6.6.3), are bound to affect human-machine interfaces as well, and any one of a number of approaches might be used to produce appropriate behaviours. Unfortunately, most behavioural descriptions ignore the human-machine interface, and most initiatives to modify behaviour ignore the amount of time people spend working with machines using 'inappropriate' behaviours.

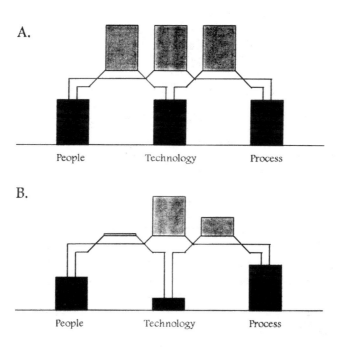

Figure 13.3 In (A) the optimal progress in key organisational change areas (black) and in the interaction areas (grey) is shown. In (B) is the usual progress made with change using the total quality management approach. Here, process has precedent over people, and technology is relatively ignored, while the interactions for human and machine are minimal.

Maturity of change management approach Most change management approaches make little attempt to help individuals cope with the sharing issues at the human-machine interface. Currently, change management approaches struggle to deal simultaneously with the building blocks of change, namely people, process and technology (Fig. 13.3). They become particularly unstuck in dealing with all the interactions between the blocks, namely those between people and technology, people and process, and process and technology. For example, total quality management makes little attempt to address sharing issues between people and technology (Fig. 13.3), while approaches that rely on values, belief or culture do not take on the building block issue of technology or any of its interactions. In these approaches, technology and its interactions remain a passive, external item which is not addressed. Even change management approaches that look at processes and their alteration, see technology as something that must be addressed synchronously with people and process, but they underplay the interaction between human and machine compared with their attention to the interactions between technology and process, and process and people. All these approaches require an underpinning of an automation philosophy and its translation.

13.6 From an automation philosophy to organisational competitiveness

Competitiveness is being affected by human-machine interactions. A diverse and multifaceted approach is required to make these interactions provide unique advantages. There are a number of immutable preconditions for sustained competitiveness in our technologically complex work environments, starting with values which put humans above all other factors. This state must translate into a purpose framework which has humans as ends in themselves, and with key roles in being the means to ends. Such values require translation in the philosophy of human-machine interaction. In this book, this philosophy is called the sharing-centred approach to automation, but this is not the unique solution, nor is it likely to be sufficient in its current form. It is an attempt to move to a human driven form of human-machine complementarity, both as an end and a means to an end. From this starting point there are a myriad of approaches, one using the framework of ritual, which allows a description and subsequent orchestration of the work environment in which an individual's creativity is to be expressed. There are other approaches which will prove to be equally worthy. What is essential for achieving competitiveness is the coupling of a behavioural pathway, as provided by a framework like rituals and their linkages to creativity, with an agenda for human machine interaction, as provided by the sharing-centred approach to automation.

Notes

1 See the F-22 story, in Warwick (1977), in particular pp. 11-12 of the supplement.
2 See Chen and Kim (1994/1995) for a summary of information retrieval research.
3 See note 6 in chapter 11 and note 25 in chapter 12 about mobile phones.
4 This example is modified from pp. 149-150 of Satchell (1993). Some points about the example follow:

    1.) Currently there are no vigilance management systems of this form in aircraft under normal operating conditions. An aircraft is fitted with a reveille system and add-on devices have been contemplated. Various systems have been used in the development of flightdecks and flightdeck procedures as well as for research into fluctuations in vigilance levels during normal commercial operations (Satchell, 1993).

    2.) The concept of specialist roles, one for take-off and landing, and one for cruise is not new.

    3.) The work practice of having a single person on a flightdeck is controversial and not currently acceptable. Given the current approaches to maintaining awareness, a single person, whose capacity to provide situation awareness is monitored, is likely to provide better awareness across many criteria than two unassisted individuals.

4.) No future large aircraft is contemplated with five engines. Current engine technology appears capable of providing sufficient thrust with the current type of aircraft engine configurations.

5   Personal observation suggests that it is more important for developing good sharing to have simultaneous initiatives in all elements, purpose, trust, differences and feedback, rather than to have near perfection in one, with the others unconsidered.

6   The detection of complacency will not be possible in the foreseeable future. Vigilance, complacency and trust are loosely interrelated, and the example suggests that vigilance measurement, coupled with response times, may help track complacency, although there is no evidence for this (9.2.1, 12.3..3).

7   The Boeing F22 cockpit has displays which continuously provide tactical situation awareness in a basic form. As a threat evolves, the level of information on the threat becomes increasingly detailed and sophisticated.

8   See the flight path predictor vector in the HSI map mode, pp. 65-66 (Weiner, 1993). Also comments on predictive systems on pp. 73-74.

9   Flightdeck crews that have good work practices with respect to maintaining their situation awareness, reduce the need to be reactive in later phases of a flight

10 This example is a concoction. It is technically feasible now. All the technological pieces in this example are currently available, and the choices made by this group of doctors and their practice manager are logical positions for a primary care provider group in a number of developed country health systems. Some points about the material in the example follow:

1.) Multifund practices in the UK employ ex-industry people who have retired or been retrenched.

2.) User-centred design in areas where cognitive activities are being aided is vital (Landauer, 1995).

3.) There are a multiplicity of players who would like presence in a doctor's practice. In one interface proposed for general practice there were 76 icons which provided access to consumers, doctor groups, suppliers, other providers, insurers etc, etc.

4.) The importance of the relationship continues through all forms of care, including that in tertiary treatment institutions. Even in primary care, with its time constraints and disorder, there is a central role for the relationship, both in triaging patients for the health system and for healing. For an excellent and brief description, see Stewart, Brown and McWhinney (1995).

11 See comments on clarity in role definition.

12 There are many aspects of referral medicine, specialist medicine and tertiary care where the technology in this example could be used, partly because their need for creativity is less. This has consequences. An individual coming into this part of the health system with an incorrect label can suffer, as creative engagement with the original issues is difficult. The tales of patients who have had to disengage from one slot in the health system and move to another are often fraught. Individuals who have conditions which sit astride health system areas are also significantly disadvantaged and the development of a new disorder while within the system for another disorder can result in significant morbidity.

13 This example is entirely fictitious. As far as the author knows there is no 'predator' system currently in use. However, the current capacity for artificial intelligence based systems to do many of the tasks envisaged in the example suggests that it is not too far fetched. Some points about the material in the example follow:

1.) The example is based on the assumption that a great deal of information coming into decision makers in organisations is inappropriately filtered or ignored.

2.) While obtaining benefit from data related to use of systems is straight forward, partnership data would be much more complex and would require the machine learning about the evolution of use for each individual and being able to put a current level of use in the context of prior use.

3.) Already rule-based software systems are used to help in decision making.

4.) The body tracking system is required to detect presence, which may not be associated with machine interaction. The absence of an individual in the absence of use must be distinguished from the absence of use in the presence of an individual. A partner must know if their partner is present. For example, in a motivated individual, pauses in use might indicate reflection, requiring different types of response from a machine partner.

14 Counselling

15 Definition of principle purpose and purpose as choice, See Kinston, 1995.

16 See Figure 6.4 and the design component of the table.

14 Conclusions

Humans have changed many aspects of the way they live with immense consequences on themselves and their environment. Technology has been a key part of all these changes and has always had profound repercussions on humans and human existence. When technology was used to amplify and replace human force, more time was made for humans to use their cognitive powers. When technology was used to relieve humans of doing repetitive tasks, further freedom was given. Technology is now being used to reduce cognitive loads though it is no longer clear that there are meaningful outlets for the further freedom that will result.

During these waves of technology induced change, the human design has not altered. Human cognitive capacity has not expanded, though changes to health have meant that more people retain their cognitive prowess for longer. With technology's increasing capacity to compete with human cognitive capabilities, the complete displacement of humans has loomed as an attractive alternative to some. Others have realised that competition between humans and machines is a self limiting exercise, for societies require that humans work, and machines will always be cognitively impaired compared with almost all types of humans. But too many have only a limited interested in humans, covering this with a veneer of people centredness, which has never sought or tapped into the unique contributions that humans will always have to offer.

The disinterest in humans stems from the fear of grappling with their humanness. This fear has driven technology-linked change into a cul-de-sac on its evolutionary path. For those that can maintain and develop their exploration of human uniqueness and mix this with technology designed to share cognitive activities there will be the most extraordinary benefits.

This book has focussed on one aspect of human uniqueness, namely human creativity and the current way this is corralled in organisations. It has demonstrated that increasingly, current approaches to automation are unthinking partners in the suppression of creativity and this is likely to get worse. As a way of guiding all of us out of the cul-de-sac, the book suggests that a new approach to automation, the sharing-centred approach, be used when humans and machines share tasks. This approach, coupled with the awareness of human potential, and an acceptance of the behavioural issues surrounding sharing between humans and machines will once again allow humanness the place it must have in our threatened environment.

Bibliography

Adams, M., Tenney, Y. and Pew, R. (1995), 'Situation awareness and the cognitive management of complex systems', *Human Factors*, vol. 37, pp. 85-104.

Adams, R., and Victor, M. (1993), Principles of Neurology (5th Edition), McGraw Hill, New York.

Alston, N. (Ed.)(1992), Airbus A320 Accident Le Mont St Odile, *Australian Airlines Aircrew Bulletin*, No. 411, pp. 3-7.

Alter, K. and Regal, D. (1992), *Definition of the 2005 flight deck environment*, NASA Contractor Report 4479, NASA.

Amabile, T. (1983), *The social psychology of creativity*, Springer-Verlag, New York.

Amabile, T., Conti, R., Coon, H., Lazenby, J. and Herron, M. (1996, 'Assessing the work environment for creativity', *Academy of Management Journal*, vol. 39, pp. 1154-1184.

Archer, D. ad Saarlas, M. (1996), *Introduction to aerospace propulsion*, Prentice Hall, New Jersey.

Arrow, K. (1962), 'The economic implications of learning by doing', *Review of Economic Studies*, vol. 29, pp. 155-173.

Australian Graduate School of Engineering Innovation (1995), Submission No. 43 to the Innovation Inquiry, House of Representatives Standing Committee on Industry, Science and Technology, The Parliament of the Commonwealth of Australia.

Barber, B. (1983), *The logic and limits of trust*, Rutgers University Press, New Bruswick.

Barkun, J., Wexler, M., Hinchey, E., Thibeault, D. and Meakins, J. (1995), 'Laparoscopic versus open inguinal herniorrhaphy: preliminary results of a randomized controlled trial', *Surgery*, vol. 118, pp. 703-709.

Barnard, W. and Wallace, T. (1994), *The innovation edge*, Oliver Wight Publications, Essex Junction.

Barrie, D. (1997), 'Dull, dirty and dangerous', *Flight International* 4578, vol. 151, pp. 58-65.

Becker, G. (1978), *The mad genius controversy: a study in the sociology of deviance*, Sage Publications, Beverly Hills.

Beer, M., Eisenstat, R. and Spector, B. (1990), 'Why change programs don't produce change', *Harvard Business Review*, November-December, pp. 158-166.

Benbasat, I and Lim, L. (1993), 'The effects of group, task, context, and technology variables on the usefulness of group support systems', *Small Group Research*, vol. 24, pp. 430-462.

Berggren, U, Zethraeus, N, Arvidsson, D., Haglund, U. and Jonsson, B. (1996), 'A cost-minimization analysis of laparoscopic cholecystectomy versus open cholecystectomy', *American Journal of Surgery*, vol. 172, pp. 305-310.

Billings, C. (1991), *Human-centered aircraft automation: a concept and guidelines*, NASA Technical Memorandum 103885, NASA.

Billings, C. (1996), *Human-centered aviation automation: principles and guidelines*, NASA Technical Memorandum 110381, NASA.

Billings, C. and Dekker, S. (1996), 'Advanced and novel automation concepts in the future system', in C. Billings, *Human-centered aviation automation: principles and guidelines*, Technical

Memorandum 110381, NASA, pp. 155-161.

Billings, C. and Reynard, W. (1984), 'Human factors in aircraft incidents: results of a 7-year study', *Aviation, Space and Environmental Medicine*, vol. 55, pp. 960-965.

Birmingham, H. and Taylor, F. (1954), 'A design philosophy for man-machine control systems', *Proceedings IRE New York*, vol. 42, pp. 1748-1758.

Bolman, L. (1991), 'Organizational culture and symbols', in *Reframing Organizations*, Josey-Bass, San Francisco, pp. 243-271.

Boston Consulting Group. (1991), *Review of findings, international new product development survey*, by The Boston Consulting Group, Product Development Consulting Inc., and the Management Roundtable.

Boston Consulting Group. (1992), *Product development practices and organizational capabilities survey*, Management Roundtable Update, Prepared by The Boston Consulting Group, Product Development Consulting Inc.

Bower, J. (1994), 'Communication between professionals and innovation management in NHS trusts', *Management Research News*, vol. 17, pp. 74-76.

Brown, J. (1995), *Charles Darwin voyaging*, Jonathan Cape, London.

Burke, T., Genn-Bash, A. and Haines, B. (1991), *Competition in theory and practice*, Routledge, London.

Burkart, R (1994), 'Reducing R&D cycle time', *Research Technology Management*, vol. 37, pp. 27-32.

Cabon, P., Mollard, R., Coblentz, J-P., Fouillot, C. and Molinier, G. (1991), 'Vigilance of aircrews during long-haul flights', in R. Jensen (ed.), *Proceedings of the Sixth International Symposium on Aviation Psychology*, pp. 799-804.

Carr, C. (1994), *The competitive power of constant creativity*, AMACOM, New York.

Casas, A. and Gadacz, T. (1996), 'Laparoscopic management of peptic ulcer disease', *Surgical Clinics of North America*, vol. 76, pp. 515-522.

Chen, H and Kim, J (1994/1995), 'A machine learning approach to document retrieval', *Journal of Management Information Systems*, vol. 11, pp. 7-41.

Clark, P. and Staunton, N. (1989), *Innovation in technology and organization*, Routledge, London.

Cohen, C. (1995), 'Striving for seamlessness: procedures manuals as a tool for organizational control', *Personnel Review*, vol. 24, pp. 50-57.

Connolly, T., Jessup, L. and Valacich, J. (1990), 'Effects of anonymity and evaluative tone on idea generation in computer-mediated groups', *Management Science*, vol. 36, pp. 689-703.

Cook, R. and Woods, D. (1996), 'Adapting to new technology in the operating room', *Human Factors*, vol. 38, pp. 593-613.

Costley, J., Johnson, D. and Lawson, D. (1989), 'A comparison of cockpit communication B737 - B757', in R. Jensen, (ed.), *Proceedings of the Fifth International Symposium on Aviation Psychology*, pp. 413-418.

Csikszentmihalyi, M. (1988), 'Society, culture, and person: a systems view of creativity', in R. Sternberg (ed.), *The nature of creativity*, Cambridge University Press, Cambridge, pp. 325-339.

Davies, D. (1979), *Handling the big jets*, CAA, London.

Degani, A., Mitchell, C. and Chappell, A. (1995), 'Use of the operator function model to represent mode transitions', *Eigth International Symposium on Aviation Psychology*, Ohio State University, Columbus.

Degani, A., Shafto, M. and Kirlik, A. (1995), 'Mode usage in automated cockpits: some initial observations', *Proceedings of the International Federation for Automatic Control (IFAC)*, Elsevier, Amsterdam.

Degani, A and Wiener, E. (1991), 'Philosophy, policies and procedures: the three p's of flight deck operations', in R. Jensen (ed.), *Proceedings of the Sixth International Symposium on Aviation Psychology*, pp. 184-191.

Degani, A and Wiener, E. (1994), *On the design of flight-deck procedures*, NASA Contractor Report 177642, NASA.

De Keyser, V. (1988) 'How can computer-based visual displays aid operators?' in E. Hollnagel, G. Mancini, and Woods, D. (eds), *Cognitive engineering in complex dynamic worlds*, Academic Press, London.

Deutsch, M. (1958), 'Trust and suspicion', *Journal of Conflict Resolution*, vol. 2, pp. 265-279.

Diehl, M. and Strebe, W. (1987), 'Productivity loss in brainstorming groups: toward the solution of a riddle', *Journal of Personality and Social Psychology* vol. 53, pp. 497-509.

Doyle, A and Pite, J. (1995), 'Power surge' *Flight International*, 4483, vol. 148, pp. 27-45.

Dreistadt, R. (1968), 'An analysis of the use of analogies and metaphors in science', *Journal of Psychology*, 68, pp. 97-116.

The Economist, 4 January, 1992, *Economic growth*, pp. 17-20

Eisenburg, J. (1986), *Doctors' decisions and the cost of medical care*, Health Administration Press Perspectives, Ann Arbor.

Endsley, M. (1995a), 'Toward a theory of situation awareness in dynamic systems', *Human Factors*, vol. 37, pp. 32-64.

Endsley, M. (1995b), 'Measurement of situation awareness in dynamic systems', *Human Factors, vol.* 37, pp. 65-84.

Endsley, M. and Kiris, E. (1995), 'The out-of-the-loop performance problem and the level of control in automation', *Human Factors*, vol. 37, pp. 381-394.

Endsley, M. and Smith, R. (1996), ' Attention distribution and decision making in tactical air combat', *Human Factors*, vol. 38, pp. 232-249.

Fadden, D. (1990), 'Aircraft automation challenges', in Abstracts of AIAA-NASA-FAA-HFSSymposium, *Challenges in aviation human factors*: The National Plan. Washingtin, DC.: American Institute of Aeronautics and Astronautics.

Farr, R. and Markova, I. (1995), 'Professional and lay representations of health, illness and handicap: a theoretical overview', in I. Markova and R. Farr (eds), *Representations of health, illness and handicap*, Harwood, Australia, pp. 93-110.

Federal Aviation Administration Human Factors Team (1996), *The interfaces between flightcrews and modern flight deck systems*, Federal Aviation Administration.

Feldman, D.H. (1988), 'Creativity: dreams, insights, and transformations', in R. Sternberg (ed.), *The nature of creativity*, Cambridge University Press, Cambridge, pp. 271-297.

Fitts, P. (1951), *Human engineering for an effective air navigation and traffic control system*, National Research Council, Washington.

Flach, J. (1995), 'Situation awareness: proceed with caution', *Human Factors*, vol. 37, pp. 149-157.

Flannery, T. (1994), *The future eaters*, Reed, Sydney.

Flight International, (1996), 'NTSB urges increase in inspection of JT8D fan-hubs', *Flight International*, 4535, vol. 150, p. 11.

Freeman, C. (1974), *The economics of industrial innovation*, Penguin, Harmondsworth.

Freeman, C. (1994), 'The economics of technical change', *Cambridge Journal of Economics*, vol. 18, pp. 463-514.

Gaba, D., Howard, S. and Small, S. (1995), 'Situation awareness in anesthesiology', *Human Factors*, vol. 37, pp. 20-31.

Gardner, H. (1988), 'Creative lives and creative works: a synthetic scientific approach', in R. Sternberg (ed.), *The nature of creativity*, Cambridge University Press, Cambridge, pp. 298-321.

Gardner, H. (1995), *Leading minds*, BasicBooks, New York.

Gerren, D. (1995), *Design, analysis, and control of a large transport aircraft utilizing selective engine thrust as a backup system for the primary flight control*, NASA Contractor Report 186035, NASA.

Ghiselin, B. (1952), *The creative process*, University of California Press, Berkeley.

Goffman, I. (1967), *Interaction ritual*, Penguin, England.

Grimes, R. (1995), *Marrying and burying*, Westview, Boulder.

Gruber, H. (1981), *Darwin on man: a psychological study of scientific creativity* (2nd ed.), University of Chicago Press, Chicago.

215

Gruber, H. and Davis, S. (1988), 'Inching our way up Mount Olympus: the evolving-systems approach to creative thinking', in R. Sternberg (ed.), *The nature of creativity*, Cambridge University Press, Cambridge, pp. 243-270.

Gryskiewicz, S. (1987), 'Predictable creativity', in S. Isaksen (ed.), *Frontiers of creativity research: beyond the basics*, Bearly Limited, Buffalo, pp. 305-313.

Guilford, J. (1950), 'Creativity', *American Psychologist*, vol. 5, pp. 444-454.

Hadamard, J. (1945), *The psychology of invention in the mathematical field*, Princeton University Press, Princeton.

Hale, D. (1996), 'Patterns of innovation in pharmaceutical research', *Scrip Magazine* July/August, pp. 54-56.

Hancock, P. and Parasuraman, R. (1992), 'Human factors and safety in the design of intelligent vehicle-highway systems (IVHS)', *Journal of Safety Research*, vol. 23, pp. 181-198.

Hartman, E., Tower, B. and Sebora, T. (1994), 'Innovation sources and their relationship to organizational innovation in small businesses', *Journal of Small Business Management*, vol. 32, pp. 36-47.

Hastings, M. (1987), *The Oxford book of military anecdotes*, Oxford University Press, Oxford.

Hayes, J. (1989), *The complete problem solver*, (2nd ed.), Lawrence Erlbaum Associates, New Jersey.

Hennessey, B.A. and Amabile, T.M. (1988), 'The conditions of creativity', in R. Sternberg (ed.), *The nature of creativity*, Cambridge University Press, Cambridge, pp. 11-38.

Helson, R., Roberts, B. and Agronick, G. (1995), 'Enduringness and changes in creative personality and the prediction of occupational creativity', *Journal of Personality and Social Psychology*, vol. 69, pp. 1173-1183.

Hewitt, F. (1995), 'Business process innovation in the mid-1990s', *Integrated-Manufacturing-Systems*, vol. 6, pp. 18-26.

Hollingsworth, R and Streeck, W. (1994), 'Countries and sectors', in R. Hollingsworth, P. Schmitter and W. Streeck (eds), *Governing capitalist economies*, Oxford University Press, New York, pp. 270-300.

Hollnagel, E. (1993), *Human reliability analysis*, Academic Press, London.

Hopfl, H. (1994), 'The paradoxical gravity of planned organizational change', *Journal of Organizational Change Management*, vol. 7, pp. 20-3:.

Hopper, T. and Joseph, N. (1995), 'The dissection of a dinosaur: Experiments in control at Toyota', *Management Accounting*, vol. 73, pp. 34-38.

Horwitz, P. (1979), 'Direct government funding of research and development: intended and unintended effects of industrial innovation', in C. Hill and J. Utterback (eds), *Technological innovation for a dynamic economy*, Pergamon, New York, pp. 255-291.

House of Representatives Standing Committee on Industry, Science and Technology Report (1995), *Innovation: a concept to market*, Australian Government Publishing Service, Canberra..

Howell, J. (1995), *Tools for facilitating team meetings*, Integrity Publishing, Seattle.

Huse, E. and Beer, M. (1971), 'Eclectic approach to organizational development', *Harvard Business Review*, September-October, pp. 103-112.

Industry Commission (1995), *Research and development*, Report No. 44, Australian Government Publishing Service, Canberra.

Isaksen, S. (1987), 'Introduction: an orientation to the frontiers of creativity research', in S. Isaksen (ed.), *Frontiers of creativity research: beyond the basics*, Bearly Limited, Buffalo, pp. 1-26.

James, W. (1890), *The principles of psychology*, Macmillan, London.

Jamison, K. (1989), 'Mood disorders and patterns of creativity in British writers and artists', *Psychiatry*, vol. 32, pp. 125-134.

Jane's All the World's Aircraft (1945-46, 1955-56, 1965-66, 1975-76, 1985-86, 1995-96), Jane's Yearbooks, London.

Johnson-Laird, P. (1988), 'Freedom and constraint in creativity', in R. Sternberg (ed.), *The nature of creativity*, Cambridge University Press, Cambridge, pp. 202-219.

Jordan, N. (1963), 'Allocation of functions between man and machines in automated systems', *Journal of Applied Psychology*, vol. 47, pp. 161-165.

Kaempf, G., Klein, G., Thordsen, M. and Wolf, S. (1996), 'Decision making in complex naval command-and-control environments', *Human Factors*, vol. 38, pp. 220-231.

Kamien, M. and Schwartz, N. (1982), *Market structure and innovation*, Cambridge University Press, Cambridge.

Kano, N. and Koura, K. (1991), 'Development of quality control seen through companies awarded the Deming prize', *Reports of statistical application research*, JUSE 37, No.1-2, pp. 79-105.

Kantowitz, B. and Sorkin, R. (1987), 'Allocation of functions', in G. Salvendy (ed.), *Handbook of human factors*, Wiley, New York, pp. 355-369.

Keane, M. (1991), 'Consciousness, analogy and creativity', *Behavioural and Brain Sciences*, vol. 14, p. 682.

Kelly, K. (1994), *Out of control*, Addison-Wesley.

Kennedy, C. and Thirlwall, A. (1973), 'Technical progress', in *Surveys of Applied Economics*, vol. 1, Royal Economic Society and Social Science Research Council, Macmillan, London, pp. 115-176.

Kessel, N. (1989), 'Genius and mental disorder: a history of ideas concerning their conjunction', in P. Murray (ed.), *Genius: the history of an idea*, Basil Blackwell, Oxford, pp.   .

Kingsley-Jones, M. (1996), 'Aging-airliner census 1996', *Flight International*, 4537, vol. 150, pp. 35-49.

Kingston, W. (1977), *Innovation*, Calder, London.

Kinston, W. (1995), *Working with values: software of the mind*, The Sigma Centre, London.

Kirton, M (ed.) (1994), *Adaptors and innovators*, Revised edition, Routledge, London.

Koestler, A. (1964), *The act of creation*, Arkana, London.

Krugman, P. (1994), 'Competitiveness: a dangerous obsession', *Foreign Affairs*, vol. 73, pp. 28-44.

Lamm, H. and Trommsdorff, G. (1973), 'Group versus individual performance on tasks requiring ideational proficiency (brainstorming): a review', *European Journal of Social Psychology*, vol. 3, pp. 361-388.

Landauer, T. (1995), *The trouble with computers*, MIT Press, Cambridge.

Langley, P. and Jones, R. (1988), 'A computational model of scientific insight', in R. Sternberg (ed.), *The nature of creativity*, Cambridge University Press, Cambridge, pp. 177-201.

Learmount, D. (1992), 'Human factors', *Flight International*, 4238, vol. 139, pp. 30-33.

Lewis, L. and Seibold, D. (1993), 'Innovation modification during intraorganizational adoption', *Academy of Management Review*, vol. 18, pp. 322-354.

Liscomb, F. (1975), *The British submarine*, Conway Maritime Press, Greenwich.

Logsdon, E., Infield, S., Lozito, S., McGann, A., Mackintosh, M. and Possolo, A. (1995), 'Cockpit data link technology and flight crew communication procedures', *8th International Symposium on Aviation Psychology*, Ohio State University, Columbus, Ohio.

Long, C. and Vickers, M (1995), 'Is it process management and, with, or instead of TQM?, *Journal for Quality and Participation*, vol. 18, pp. 70-74.

Ludwig, A. (1994), 'Mental illness and creative activity in female writers', *American Journal of Psychiatry*, vol. 151, pp. 1650-1656.

Mackie, R. and Wylie, C. (1991), 'Countermeasures to loss of alertness in truck drivers. Theoretical and practical considerations', in M. Vallet (ed.), *Le maintien de la Vigilance dans les Transports*, L'Institut National de Recherche sur les Transports et leur Securite: Caen, pp. 104-110.

Mackworth, N. (1950), 'Researches on the measurement of human performance', *Medical Research Council Special Report Series*, vol. 268, His Majesty's Stationary Office, London.

Markt, C. and Johnson, M. (1993), 'Transitional objects, pre-sleep rituals, and psychopathology', *Child Psychiatry & Human Development*, vol. 23, pp. 161-173.

Marr, D. (1991), *Patrick White a life*, Random House, Australia.

Maschio, T. (1992), 'To remember the faces of the dead: mourning and the full sadness of memory in Southwestern New Britain', *Ethos*, vol. 20, pp. 387-420.

Meyer, J. and Rowan, B. (1992), 'Institutionalized organisations: formal structure as myth and ceremony', in J. Meyer and W. Scott (eds), *Organizational environments ritual and rationality*, Sage, Newbury Park, pp. 21-44,.

Meyer, J. and Scott, R (1992), 'Centralization and the legitimacy problems of local government', in J. Meyer and W. Scott (eds), *Organizational environments ritual and rationality* , Sage, Newbury Park, pp. 199-215.

Mink, O., Mink, B. and Owen, K. (1987), *Groups at work*, Educational Technical Publishers, New Jersey.

Moll van Charante, E., Cook, R., Woods, D., Yue , L. and Howle, M. (1992), 'Human-computer interaction in context: physician interaction with automated intravenous controllers in the heart room', in *Proceedings of the Fifth Symposium on Analysis, Design, and Evaluation of Man-Machine Systems*, The Hague, Netherlands, pp. 263-274.

Mooney, R. (1963), 'A conceptual model for integrating four approaches to the identification of creative talent', in C. Taylor and F. Barron (eds), *Scientific creativity: its recognition and development*, Wiley, New York, pp. 331-340.

Morgan, M. (1993), *Creating workforce innovation*, Business and Professional Publishing, Chatswood.

Mowery, D and Oxley, J. (1995), 'Inward technology transfer and competitiveness: the role of national innovation systems', *Cambridge Journal of Economics*, vol. 19, pp. 67-93.

Moxon, J. (1997), 'Airbus intensifies research efforts into human factors', *Flight International* 4577, vol. 151, p. 26.

Muir, B. (1994), 'Trust in automation: Part I. Theoretical issues in the study of trust and human intervention in automated systems', *Ergonomics*, vol. 37, pp. 1905-1922.

Muir, B. And Moray, N. (1996), 'Trust in automation. Part II. Experimental studies of trust and human intervention in a process control simulation', *Ergonomics*, vol. 39, pp. 429-460.

Mullen, B., Johnson, C. and Salas, E. (1991), 'Productivity loss in brainstorming groups: a meta-analytic integration', *Basic and Applied Psychology*, vol. 12, pp. 3-23.

Nagasundaram, M. and Bostrom, R. (1995), 'The structuring of creative processes using GSS: a framework for research', *Journal of Management Information Systems*, vol. 11, pp. 87-114.

Nelson, R. (1993), 'A retrospective', in R. Nelson, (ed.), *National innovation systems*, Oxford University Press, New York.

Norman, S., Billings, C., Nagel, D., Palmer, E. Wiener, E. and Woods, D. (1988), 'Aircraft automation philosophy: a source document', in NASA/Industry/FAA workshop, *Flight Deck Automation: Promises and Realities*, National Aeronautics and Space administration, Ames Research Center, California.

Norman, D. (1990), 'The "problem" with automation: Inappropriate feedback and interaction, not "over -automation", *Philosophical Transactions of the Royal Society of London*, B327.

Norris, G. (1996), 'Dedicated test', *Flight International*, 4513, vol. 149, pp. 28-30.

Odagiri, H. (1992), *Growth through competition, competition through growth*, Clarendon, Oxford.

Obradovich, J. and Woods, D. (1996), 'Users as designers: how people cope with poor HCI design in computer-based medical devices', *Human Factors*, vol. 38, pp. 574-592.

Ohlsson, S. (1984), 'Restructuring revisited: II. An information processing theory of restructuring and insight', *Scandinavian Journal of Psychology*, vol. 25, pp. 117-129.

OECD (1992), *Technology and the economy, the key relationships*, Technology/Economy Programme, OECD, Paris.

Orasanu, J. (1995), 'Situation awareness: its role in flight crew decision making', *8th International Symposium on Aviation Psychology*, Ohio State University, Columbus, Ohio.

Orlando, R. and Russell, J. (1996), 'Managing gallbladder disease in a cost-effective manner', *Surgical Clinics of North America*, vol. 76, pp. 117-128.

Osborn, A. (1953), *Applied imagination*, Charles Scribner's, New York.

Palmer, E and Degani, A. (1991), 'Electronic checklists: evaluation of two levels of automation', in R. Jensen (ed.), *Proceedings of the Sixth International Symposium on Aviation Psychology*, pp. 178-

183.

Palmer, E., Hutchins, E., Ritter, R. and vanCleemput, I. (1993), *Altitude deviations: breakdowns of an error tolerant system*, NASA Technical Memorandum DOT/FAA/RD-92/7.

Palmer, M., Rogers, W., Press, H., Latorella, K. and Abbott, T. (1995), *A crew-centred flight deck design philosophy for high-speed civil transport (HSCT) aircraft*, NASA Technical Memorandum TM-198171, Hampton, NASA Langley Research Centre.

Parasuraman, R., Bahri, T., Deaton, J., Morrison, J. and Barbes, M. (1990), *Theory and design of adaptive automation in aviation systems*, Progress report for Naval Air Development Centre, Contract N62269-90-0022-5931.

Parasuraman, R., Molloy, R. And Singh, I. (1993), 'Performance consequences of automation-induced "complacency"', *International Journal of Aviation Psychology*, vol. 3, pp. 1-23.

Parasuraman, R., Mouloua, M. and Molloy, R. (1996), 'Effects of adaptive task allocation on monitoring of automated systems', *Human Factors*, vol. 38, pp. 665-679.

Parasuraman, R., Mouloua, M., Molloy, R. and Hilburn, B. (1993), 'Adaptive function allocation reduces performance costs of static automation', *Proceedings of the 7th International Symposium on Aviation Psychology*, Columbus, Ohio.

Parkes, O. (1970), *British battleships*, Seeley Service, London.

Pavitt, K. (1986), 'Chips' and 'Trajectories': how does the semiconductor influence the sources and directions of technical change?', in R. MacLeod (ed.), *Technology and the human prospect*, Frances Pinter, London. pp. 31-54.

Paye, J-C (1995), 'Technology, employment and structural change', *OECD-Observer*, vol. 194, pp. 4-5.

Perkins, D. (1981), *The mind's best work*, Harvard University Press, Cambridge.

Peter, J., Cassel, W., Ehrig, B., Faust, M., Fuchs, E., Langanke, P., Meinzer, K. And Pfaff, U. (1990), 'Occupational performance of a paced secondary task under conditions of sensory deprivation. II. The influence of professional training', *European Journal of Applied Physiology*, vol. 60, pp. 315-320.

Phelan, P. (1996), 'Fast data', *Flight International*, 4542, vol. 150, pp. 29-30.

Pinelli, T, Barclay, R. and Kennedy, J. (1995), *NASA/DoD aerospace knowledge diffusion research project. Report 34. How early career-stage US aerospace engineers and scientists produce and use information*, NASA, Langley Research Center.

Porter, M.E. (1990), *The comparative advantage of nations*, Macmillan, London.

Post, F. (1994), 'Creativity and psychopathology', *British Journal of Psychiatry*, vol. 165, pp. 22-34.

Previc, F., Yauch, D., DeVilbiss, C., Ercoline, W. and Sipes, W. (1995), 'Commentary - in defense of traditional views of spatial disorientation and loss of situation awareness: a reply to Navathe and Singh's "An operational definition of spatial disorientation", *Aviation, Space and Environmental Medicine*, vol. 66, pp. 1103-1106.

Quinn, D. (1992), *Ishmael*, Bantam/Turner, New York.

Reason, J. (1987), Collective planning and its failures, in J. Rasmussen, K. Duncan and J. Leplat (eds), *New technology and human error*, John Wiley & Sons, Chichester, pp. 121-128.

Reason, J. (1990), *Human error*, Cambridge University Press, Cambridge.

Rempel, J., Holmes, J. and Zanna, M. (1985), 'Trust in close relationships', *Journal of Personality and Social Psychology*, vol. 49, pp. 95-112.

Riley, V. (1989), 'A general model of mixed-initiative human-machine systems', in *Proceedings of the Human Factors Society 33rd Annual Meeting*, Human Factors Society, Santa Monica, pp. 124-128.

Romer, P. (1990), 'Endogenous technological change', *Journal of Political Economy*, vol. 98 (No. 5, Part 2), pp. s71-s102.

Ross, M and Ross, C. (1983), 'Mothers, infants and the psychoanalytic study of ritual', *Signs: Journal of Women in Culture and Society*, vol 9, pp. 26-39.

Roth, E., Bennett, K. and Woods, D. (1988), 'Human interaction with an "intelligent" machine, in E. Hollnagel, G. Mancini and D. Woods (eds), *Cognitive Engineering in Complex Dynamic Worlds*,

Academic Press, London, pp. 23-69.

Rothwell, R. (1994), 'Towards the fifth-generation innovation process', *International marketing Review*, 11, pp. 7-31.

Rouse, W. (1977), 'Human-computer interaction in multitask situations', *IEEE Transactions on systems, man, and cybernetics*, SMC-7, pp. 384-392.

Sarter, N. (1994), *Strong, silent and 'out-of-the-loop': properties of advanced (cockpit) automation and their impact on human-automation interaction*, Dissertation for Ph.D., Graduate School of the Ohio State University.

Sarter, N. and Woods, D. (1992), 'Pilot interaction with cockpit automation: operational experiences with the flight management system', *International Journal of Aviation Psychology*, vol. 2, pp. 303-321.

Sarter, N. and Woods, D. (1995), 'How in the world did we ever get into that mode? Mode error and awareness in supervisory control', *Human Factors*, vol. 37, pp. 5-19.

Satchell, P. (1993), *Cockpit monitoring and alerting systems*, Ashgate, Aldershot.

Scherer, F. (1980), *Industrial market structure and economic performance*, (2nd ed.), Rand McNally, Chicago.

Schumpeter, J. (1950), *Capitalism, socialism and democracy*, George Allen and Unwin, London.

Scott, R (1992), 'Health care organisations in the 1980s: the convergence of public and professional control systems', in J. Meyer and W. Scott (eds), *Organizational environments ritual and rationality*, Sage, Newbury Park, pp. 99-127.

Scott, S. (1994), 'Cultural values and the championing process', *Entrepreneurship: theory and practice*, vol. 18, pp. 25-41.

Scott, S. and Bruce, R. (1994), 'Determinants of innovative behaviour: a path model of individual innovation in the workplace', *Academy of Management Journal*, vol. 37, pp. 580-607.

Selye, H. (1956), *The stress of life*, McGraw-Hill, New York.

Shelden, M. (1992), *Orwell*, Minerva, London.

Shorter Oxford English Dictionary (3rd ed.) (1973), Clarendon, Oxford.

Simon, H. (1977), 'Models of discovery', in R. Cohen and M. Wartofsky (eds), *Boston studies in the philosophy of science*, (Vol. 54), Riedel, Dordrecht.

Simonton, D. (1984), *Genius, creativity, and leadership: Historiometric inquiries*, Harvard University Press, Cambridge.

Simonton, D. (1988), 'Creativity, leadership, and chance', in R. Sternberg (ed.), *The nature of creativity*, Cambridge University Press, Cambridge, pp. 386-426.

Singh, I, Molloy, R. and Parasuraman, R. (1993) 'Automation-induced "complacency": development of the complacency-potential rating scale', *International Journals of Aviation Psychology*, vol. 3, pp. 111-121.

Smith, D and Tegano, D. (1992), 'Relationship of scores on two personality measures: creativity and self-image', *Psychological Reports*, vol. 71, pp. 43-49.

Smith, K. and Hancock, P. (1995), 'Situation awareness is adaptive, externally directed consciousness', *Human Factors*, vol. 37, pp. 137-148.

Solow, R.. (1957) 'Technical change and the aggregate production function', *Review of economics and statistics*, vol. 39, pp. 312-320.

Spearmen, C. (1930), *Creative mind*, Cambridge University Press, Cambridge.

Spender, J. and Kessler, E. (1995), 'Managing the uncertainties of innovation: extending Thompson (1967)', *Human Relations*, vol. 48, pp. 35-56.

Stein , M. (1953), 'Creativity and culture', *Journal of Psychology*, vol. 36, pp. 311-322.

Steiner, C. (1995), 'A philosophy for innovation: the role of unconventional individuals in innovation success', *Journal of Production and Innovation Management*, vol. 12, pp. 431-440.

Sternberg, R. (1988), 'A three-facet model of creativity', in R. Sternberg (ed.), *The nature of creativity*, Cambridge University Press, Cambridge, pp. 99-121.

Sternberg, R. and Lubart, T. (1991), 'An investment theory of creativity and its development', *Human*

Development, vol. 34, pp. 1-31.

Stewart, G. (1950), 'Can productive thinking be taught?', *Journal of Higher Education*, vol. 21, pp. 411-414.

Stewart, M., Brown, J, and McWhinney, I. (1995), 'The fifth component. Enhancing the patient-doctor relationship' in M. Stewart, J. Brown, W. Weston, I. McWhinney, C. McWilliam and T. Freeman (eds), *Patient-centered medicine*, Sage Publications, Thousand Oaks, pp. 89-101.

Tardif, T. and Sternberg, R. (1988), 'What do we know about creativity', in R. Sternberg (ed.), *The nature of creativity*, Cambridge University Press, Cambridge, pp. 429-440.

Taylor, C.(1988), 'Various approaches to and definitions of creativity', in R. Sternberg, (ed.), *The nature of creativity*, Cambridge University Press, Cambridge, pp. 99-121.

Taylor, R. (1990), 'Trust and awareness in human-electronic crew teamwork', in *Proceedings of the Conference on the Human-Electronic Crew: Is the Team Maturing?*, Ingolstadt, Germany, pp. 99-103.

Teece, D. (1992), 'Competition, cooperation and innovation', *Journal of Economic Behaviour and Organizations*, vol. 18, pp. 1-25.

Tenny, Y., Adams, M., Pew, R., Huggins, A., and Rogers, W. (1992), *A principled approach to the measurement of situation awareness in commercial aviation*, NASA Contractor Report 4451, NASA, Langley.

Tenny, Y., Rogers, W. and Pew, R. (1995), *Pilot opinions on high level flight deck automation issues: toward the development of a design philosophy*, NASA Contractor Report 4669, NASA, Langley.

Torrance, E.P. (1988), 'The nature of creativity as manifest in its testing', in R. Sternberg (ed.), *The nature of creativity*, Cambridge University Press, Cambridge, pp. 43-75.

Utterback, J. (1979), 'The dynamics of product and process innovation in industry', in C. Hill and J. Utterback (eds), *Technological innovation for a dynamic economy*, Pergamon, New York, pp. 40-65.

Utterback, J. (1994), *Mastering the dynamics of innovation*, Harvard Business School Press, Boston.

VanGundy, A. (1987), 'Organizational creativity and innovation', in S. Isaksen (ed.), *Frontiers of creativity research*, Bearly Limited, Buffalo, pp. 358-379.

Vasillopulos, C. (1988), 'Heroism, self-abnegation and the liberal organization', *Journal of Business Ethics*, vol. 7, pp. 585-591.

Wain, J. (1994), *Samuel Johnson*, Papermac, London.

Waldersee, R., Simmons, R. and Eagleson, G. (1995), *Pluralistic leadership in service change programs: some preliminary findings*, Centre for Corporate Change, Australian Graduate School of Management, Paper No. 47.

Walker, P. (1971), *Early aviation at Farnborough*, MacDonald, London.

Wallas, G. (1926), *The art of thought*, Cape, London.

Warwick, G. (1997), 'The F-22 story', *Flight International*, 4569, vol. 150, pp. 1-35 (Supplement).

Wiener, E. (1989), *Human factors of advanced technology ("glass cockpit") transport aircraft*, NASA Contractor Report 177528, NASA, Ames Research Center.

Wiener, E. (1993), *Intervention strategies for the management of human error*, NASA Contractor Report 4547, NASA, Ames Research Center.

Wiener, E., Chidester, T., Kanki, B., Palmer, E., Curry, R. and Gregorich, S. (1991), *The impact of cockpit automation on crew coordination and communication: 1. Overview, LOFT evaluations, error severity and questionnaire data*, NASA Contractor Report 177587, NASA, Ames Research Center.

Wiener, E. and Curry, R. (1980), 'Flight-deck automation: promises and problems', *Ergonomics*, vol. 23, pp. 995-1011.

Weisberg, R. (1988), 'Problem solving and creativity', in R. Sternberg (ed.), *The nature of creativity*, Cambridge University Press, Cambridge, pp. 148-176.

Wickens, C. (1987), ' Information processing, decision-making, and cognition', in G. Salvendy (ed.), *Handbook of Human Factors*, New York, Wiley, pp. 72-107.

Wolfe, R. (1995), 'Human resource management innovations: determinants of their adoption and implementation', *Human Resource Management*, vol. 34, pp. 313-327.

Woodman, R., Sawyer, J. and Griffin, R. (1993), 'Toward a theory of organizational creativity', *Academy of Management Review*, vol. 18, pp. 293-321.

Woods, D. (1988), 'Commentary: cognitive engineering in complex and dynamic worlds', in E. Hollnagel, G. Mancini, and D. Woods (eds), *Cognitive engineering in complex dynamic worlds*, Academic Press, London, pp. 115-129.

Woods, D., O'Brien, J. and Hanes, L. (1987), 'Human factors challenges in process control: the case of nuclear power plants', in G. Salvendy (Ed.), *Handbook of Human Factors*, New York, Wiley, pp. 1724-1770.

Woods, D. and Sarter, N. (1995), 'Learning from accidents: the need to look behind human error', *Proceedings of FAA workshop on Flight Crew Human Factors*, pp. A109-110.

Zhuang, L (1995), 'Bridging the gap between technology and business strategy: A pilot study on the innovation process', *Management Decision*, vol. 33, pp. 13-21.

Index

223